THE AMUSEMENT PARK GUIDE

"The *Amusement Park Guide* is the definitive source for information on North America's funspots—a must-have guidebook for anyone who visits amusement parks and attractions."
—*At the Park* magazine

"If your vacation plans include a visit to one or more amusement parks, don't leave home without *The Amusement Park Guide*."
—*Park World* magazine

"Whether you are a carousel or coaster enthusiast, or just out for family fun, *The Amusement Park Guide* is loaded with tips, hints, facts, and trivia that will take you through the labyrinth of North America's greatest amusement parks. . . . I had no idea there were so many. . . . It is sure to help you get the most out of your amusement park outings. . . . What a great book."

—William Manns,
    author of *Painted Ponies, American Carousel Art*

"If you're planning to visit a park, *The Amusement Park Guide* is a great way to find out what you're getting into."
—*The Inside Track* magazine

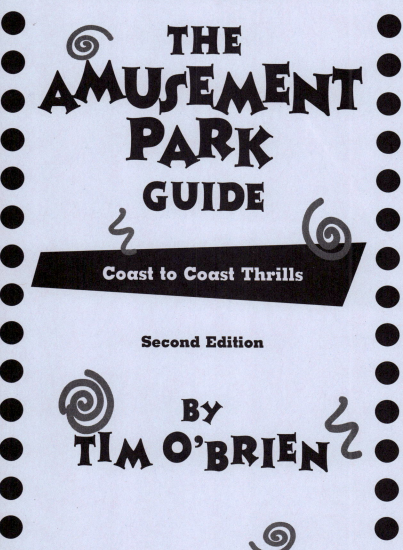

THE AMUSEMENT PARK GUIDE

Coast to Coast Thrills

Second Edition

BY TIM O'BRIEN

A Voyager Book

The Globe Pequot Press

Old Saybrook, Connecticut

Interior photo credits: P. xiii: courtesy of Paramount Kings Island;
pp. xv, 178: courtesy of Frontier City; pp. 1, 35: © 1996 Busch
Entertainment Corp.; pp. 8, 132: courtesy of Raging Waters; p. 16:
courtesy of Paramount's Great America; p. 39: © 1995 Cypress
Gardens; p. 43: © 1996 Sea World; p. 49: © 1993 Wild Waters; p. 54:
© 1994 Wild Waters; pp. 58, 65: courtesy of Six Flags Over
Georgia; p. 157: courtesy of Paramount's Carrowinds; p. 74, 162,
165, 175: by Dan Feicht, courtesy of Cedar Point; p. 171: © 1996
Paramount Parks Inc.; p. 193: © 1996 Sesame Place; p. 207: cour-
tesy of Tim O'Brien; p. 215: courtesy Schlitterbahn Waterpark &
Resort; p. 216: © 1996 Sea World, Inc.; p. 228: © 1994 Bush Gardens,
Williamsburg, Va.; p. 237 courtesy of the Wisconsin Dells Visitor &
Convention Bureau.

Cover photo credits: Front, top: "Viper," Six Flags Over Georgia;
bottom: "Escape from Pompeii™, reproduced with permission of
Busch Gardens Williamsburg, © Busch Entertainment Corp.;
spine: © New Elitch Gardens, photo by Jason Barry Winter; bot-
tom, from top: "Master Blaster®", Schitterbahn Waterpark Slides;
"Land of the Dragons," © Busch Entertainment Corp.; "Montu," ©
Busch Entertainment Corp.; "Nets N' Climbs," ©1996 Sesame
Place.

Cover and text design by Maryann Dubé

This book makes reference to various Disney copyrighted characters,
trademarks, and registered marks owned by The Walt Disney Company
and Disney Enterprises, Inc.

Library of Congress Cataloging-in-Publication Data
O'Brien, Tim.
    The amusement park guide : coast to coast thrills / by Tim O'Brien.—
2nd ed.
        p. cm.
    "A voyager book."
    Includes index.
    ISBN 0-7627-0048-3
    1. Amusement parks—United States—Directories. 2. Amusement
    parks—Canada—Directories. I. Title.
GV1853.2.025 1997
                                                        96-37013
                                                        CIP

Manufactured in the United States of America
Second Edition/First Printing

This text is printed on recycled paper.

To my daughters Molly and Carrie, who
unselfishly volunteered to help me
research the amusement parks and
waterparks of North America.

ACKNOWLEDGMENTS

There are a lot of terrific people running the amusement parks and waterparks of America and Canada, and I met a good many of them while researching the parks of North America! During the compilation of information for this second edition, I talked with hundreds of people, and they were all willing to share valuable information with me during their busy summer season. I talked with a good many friends, and I met a good many new ones during the months of updating and adding to this guide, originally published in 1991. Thanks to everyone at the parks for so much help and additional insight into the industry!

Of the hundreds who helped put this edition together, James Futrell, a park historian and a parkie at heart, deserves special mention. He combined his knowledge, his love for amusement parks, and much of his summer park-time in helping me with research. Thanks Jim, good job! Bill Manns, a carousel historian and author of *Painted Ponies, American Carousel Art*, kindly provided the list of the top park carousels I've listed.

CONTENTS

INTRODUCTION

I don't know about you, but when I enter an amusement park, every one of my senses starts working overtime. The color, the excitement, the smells, and the sounds all join together to give me a feeling of total escape from the cares of the world.

I eat foods I normally wouldn't eat, I do silly things and play games, and if I'm lucky enough to win a prize, I feel like a youngster again as I carry that teddy bear along the midway.

Growing up in a resort area that had an amusement park, I was "hooked" at a very young age on the trappings of merriment that such establishments provide. Little could I guess that years later when I was a grown-up with a wife and children of my own, I would visit the world's finest amusement parks, ride the rides, eat the food, and allow my senses to rejoice again . . . and get paid while doing so.

Well, that's what I now do as Southeast Editor of *Amusement Business*, a trade publication that covers the mass-entertainment industries, including amusement parks. Even on assignment, with a camera and notepad in hand, I still experience the thrill of being in a park.

It's great being a journalist who chronicles an industry in which the main purpose is to create an environment where people have fun. And amusement parks of all sizes are discovering new ways to help people of all ages do just that. As a result, amusement parks are more popular today than they've ever been. During the past few years, more than 250 million people have flipped the turnstiles of America's parks each year. Major league baseball's published gate attendance, including play-offs and the World Series, comes in at around 60 million yearly. Who says baseball is America's favorite pastime?

A Very Brief History of America's Amusement Parks

Most people today take for granted the sophisticated rides, shows, and attractions found in modern parks. With all the excitement a park has to offer, few people take the time to consider how the park or the rides came to be. Actually, the amusement park phenomenon has an interesting, albeit humble beginning.

During the nineteenth century, beach clubs were popular along the shores of New York. These clubs were gathering places to drink beer, play games, and socialize. By 1850, the Coney Island area of Brooklyn was becoming a popular resort area, and thousands made their way to the beaches every weekend during the summer. There was a plethora of entertainment pavilions at which those city folks who didn't want to swim could drink, socialize, and watch musical productions.

The first real "ride" didn't make it to the beach area until 1877, when a 300-foot-tall observatory from the Philadelphia Centennial Exposition was moved there and renamed the Iron Tower. Then in 1884, LaMarcus Thompson built a Switchback Railway ride, the forerunner of the roller coaster, in Coney Island. Others soon copied and improved on Thompson's railway idea. But it wasn't long until he was eager to enhance the concept even more. Two years later, in 1886, Thompson built a "real" roller coaster, and the success of that ride soon brought a steady stream of other amusement rides—and bigger crowds—to the beach.

While this activity was taking place in New York, folks in other parts of the country were enjoying their weekends and holidays at entertainment facilities built near their homes. Picnic parks with swimming pools and sports fields were springing up throughout America. As the crowds grew, so did the need for other activities.

Restaurants and dance halls were added for the adults, and pony rides were added for the kids. As mechanical rides became available, they were added, and before long, hundreds of amusement parks were in operation.

Many of those early parks were originally developed by a trolley or steamship company. They were built at the end of the line, or in a remote area served by the company, to help build weekend and holiday use of the transit system. These "trolley parks," as they were often called, were tremendously successful and prospered into the 1930s. Most survived the Great Depression, but by this time the automobile was increasing the scope of leisuretime opportunities available to the public. The smaller parks started losing their weekend guests, who could now drive to a larger park, or to the beach 50 or 60 miles away.

Although many of the small parks closed, most of the strong, clean, well-run family operations continued to prosper. But by the early 1950s, only a small percentage of those early parks were still in operation, and many experts were writing death notices for the American amusement park. The parks couldn't compete, many thought, with motion pictures and television.

Along Came Walt

Then, in 1955, Walt Disney combined color, fantasy, and excitement with food, rides, and shows, and put that com-

"The Helix," Paramont Kings Island, Ohio

bination into a safe, clean family environment. He called it Disneyland—and the theme park industry as we know it today was born.

The almost-immediate success of Disneyland paved the way for more corporate investments in the park industry, and soon other large, multimillion-dollar theme parks started showing up all over the country. These megaparks breathed new life into the entire industry. As a result, many of the smaller trolley parks were able to take advantage of America's new attitude toward amusement parks and began to grow and prosper once again.

Although the large destination parks in the country today get most of the attention, the backbone of the industry is still the small, family-run park. On the whole, these parks are professional, well-run attractions but are unknown to most outside a small marketing area.

There are more of these small "traditional" parks, as they are called, than larger theme parks. Most often, though, they don't have themes and don't have many of the multimillion-dollar rides that are so abundant today. What they do have, however, is history, quaintness, and nostalgia. They are well-preserved examples of true Americana and provide visitors with great opportunities for low-key fun.

The Rides, Parks, and Other Things

Roller coasters are still the most popular ride in amusement parks, and the coaster resurgence of the late 1980s and early 1990s has left us with some mighty big, fast, and expensive thrill machines in the parks across America.

Right behind roller coasters in popularity are the water-oriented rides found in so many parks today. More log

THE AMUSEMENT PARK GUIDE

flumes, raging rapids, and spill-water raft rides are being added each year. Usually equipped with a warning sign that proclaims YOU WILL GET WET, PROBABLY SOAKED, these rides offer a way to cool off during a hot summer's day at the park.

In addition to regular rides that run in or over the water, several parks have been adding regular waterpark elements to their lineup of attractions. Patrons must wear swimsuits to participate, and the parks have built bathhouses and locker rooms to accommodate the water lovers.

A more recent category of water rides is the wet/dry slide. Although such rides resemble waterpark flumes and slides, people in street clothes can ride them in small, raft-type boats. Instead of having its riders splash down into a deep pool, these rides have long run-outs at the bottom so that the raft ends up on dry land after skimming across a shallow pool of water.

Some parks charge extra for using the waterpark elements, whereas others include such use in the general admission price.

Parks are Changing with the Times

A major concern of park owners and officials today is the declining number of youth in the marketplace and the so-called graying of America. As a result, park officials have been reevaluating their priorities and making their parks a more comfortable place for older people to visit.

Asphalt has been ripped up and replaced with brick paths, flower beds, and shaded areas graced by an ample supply of park benches. There are also more air-conditioned, table-service restaurants in parks today than there have ever been, and the quality of food has improved dramatically during the past few years. Many parks even provide a "healthy choice" menu.

Moreover, the entertainment package is also being seen as a way of giving adults a reason to rediscover amusement parks: Everything from indoor, Broadway-style revues to circus acts to world-class ice-skating shows is being produced and is usually included in the park admission fee.

Purpose of This Book

This book is intended to show off the parks of North America and to call attention to some of the great entertainment treasures hidden within our continent. Sure, you've probably heard of many of them, but unless you live in Minot, North Dakota, I'll bet you've never heard of Lucy's Amusement Park. And I'd wager that few people outside Little Rock, Arkansas, have ever heard of that city's War Memorial Amusement Park or Burns Park Funland.

You'll be amazed and delighted by what's out there.

HOW TO USE THIS BOOK

In an effort to be as thorough as possible and to paint a realistic picture of amusement and theme parks, I've listed not only the larger, better-known facilities but also the small, family-owned parks offering just a few rides. Thus, you will find two types of listings in this book, major and minor.

The Minor Listings

The minor listings are for those parks that I feel are special enough to be included but that don't necessarily have as much to offer as the major parks. Some of these parks have only three or four rides, but because of their setting, theme, attractions, or activities, I felt they should be included.

As you will discover, some of the neatest parks in the country have little more to offer than a few good rides and a great deal of atmosphere.

Many of the waterparks listed in this book are located within amusement parks. If the waterpark is included in

Rowdy Ranch, Frontier City, Oklahoma

THE AMUSEMENT PARK GUIDE

the admission price of the amusement park, its listing is included within that park's major listing. If a small water-park with only a few attractions is located within an amusement park, but still charges an extra fee, it is listed in that amusement park's listing, because of its size.

If, however, an amusement park owns a major waterpark and either charges an additional price for its use, or if it is located away from the amusement park, the waterpark will have a separate listing, in alphabetical order, within that state.

Most of the amusement park–owned waterparks listed in this volume, which are not included in the admission price of the amusement park, offer money-saving combination tickets that are good at both the waterpark and the amusement park.

The Major Listings

Most of the major listings are self-evident, but for a better overview, here are a few additional comments:

✳ If a park is not a year-round facility, most are usually open on a weekend-only basis prior to Memorial Day and after Labor Day. I have listed the first and last days of seasonal operation; unless the listing specifies otherwise, assume the park is open only on weekends in the spring and fall.

✳ You will encounter three common types of admission policies. At pay-one-price parks, you'll pay one price at the gate; after that, almost every ride, show, and attraction is included.

Parks that charge general admission require you to pay one fee, usually less than $5.00, and then pay extra for rides and attractions. Quite often, general admission permits you to enjoy most of the live shows and productions; usually, a pay-one-price ride ticket is available once you get into the park, or you can play on a pay-as-you-go basis.

Parks that allow free admission charge nothing to get in; you pay for anything you want to do as you go. Again, pay-one-price ride tickets are often available.

✳ Probably in no other business existent today do open hours fluctuate as much as in the amusement park business. In listing these hours, I've tried to be as exact as possible; nevertheless, to list some parks' hours would take an entire paragraph. So, if you plan to visit a park either early or late in the day, be sure to call first. Also, although the hours and admission fees listed in this guide were confirmed at press time, it's generally a good idea to call for the most current information before traveling.

TIM'S TIPS ON HOW TO MAKE YOUR AMUSEMENT PARK TRIP MORE FUN

Your trip to an amusement park ought to be fun for every member of your family, even if you have a bunch of kids in tow. Sure, you're probably there in the first place because the kids wanted to come. But with a little planning and common sense, the outing can be fun for everyone. Here are a few tips on how to make your trip to an amusement park fun, memorable, and maybe even relaxing.

1. Be kind to your feet. Wear comfortable sneakers. Although the park may look small, you'll probably circle it at least twice—plus, you'll be standing in lines.

2. Pick up a guidebook and entertainment schedule when you buy your ticket. It's wise to plan your day around the specific times of the shows you don't want to miss. Make a list of must-do's and plan your route so that you won't be doing a lot of time-consuming and tiring backtracking.

3. If you have kids old enough to go off on their own, give them a marked map or a sheet of paper with a meeting place and time well specified. In the excitement of the day, kids have a way of forgetting specific directions.

4. When entering the park, point out the facility's uniformed workers to your children. Tell them to report to one of those workers or to a police officer if they become lost or need help.

5. Make sure you're dressed for the day. Take along a rain parka or a folded-up trash bag to use in case of a sudden shower. It's also wise to take along sweaters or jackets and leave them in the car, just in case. A change of clothing is advisable as well, especially if you enjoy riding the wet rides.

6. Beat the lunch rush by eating before noon or after 2:30 P.M. Although parks have sufficient food-service staff and outlets most of the time, it seems everyone wants to eat during prime "lunch" hours. Don't waste your time in food lines. If you schedule your eating for non-prime times, you'll be able to ride the rides while everyone else stands in food lines.

7. Although most parks don't allow food to be brought onto the grounds, it still makes sense to take along an apple or two to tide you over until eating time. This guideline is especially important if you have children.

8. Don't eat a lot of high-sugar-content foods while you're in the park. Most parks today offer good alternatives in the way of food and drink. You don't need anyone in your group to be on a "sugar high" in addition to all the excitement of the park.

9. Plan to eat before a show, and not before that big ride on the roller coaster. Let your stomach rest awhile after eating or drinking.

10. If the day is hot and sunny, be sure to wear a hat, apply sunscreen, and drink lots of fluid. If you start feeling ill, report immediately to the park's first-aid station.

11. If you have medication that needs refrigeration, most first-aid stations should be able to keep it for you. If not, ask at the office. All parks with any sort of food service have large coolers.

12. Even if you don't have children with you, consider renting a stroller to hold your camera equipment, souvenirs, and so on. A camera bag gets awfully heavy by midafternoon.

13. Souvenirs are enjoyable, but don't buy them before you're ready to leave. Hauling around some breakable item or a large balloon or teddy bear all day isn't too much fun. Tell the children that each can pick out one thing to buy before leaving but not before then.

14. Most of the larger parks have rental lockers. If you want to take along a lot of stuff but don't want to leave it in your car, rent a locker.

15. Take your children to the bathroom *before* getting in a long waiting line for a ride. In addition, make sure the kids understand what the ride does and how it works *before* waiting in line—it's frustrating to finally reach the front of a line, only to have the little one get scared and refuse to ride.

16. Never force children to ride if they don't want to; doing so could turn them off to amusement rides for the rest of their lives. If your child does get on a ride, but you think he or she may chicken out once it begins, alert the ride operator. It is possible to signal the operator to stop the ride so as to allow your child to get off. And don't be shy—the operators are used to this situation.

17. In-park entertainment is very popular, and there is usually standing room only at most of the shows. Get there early and pick out a good (and shady) seat for yourself.

18. Your visit is not a marathon—plan a rest break during the hot afternoon. If you've rented a motel room nearby, go back and take a swim or a nap and then come back around 5:00 P.M., when most people are leaving for the day. If you have kids with you, not only will this kind of break help them physically, but they'll feel they've been to the park twice.

19. If you do leave the park, make sure that you have your parking receipt with you and that you won't have to pay to park again. Be sure, too, to get your hand stamped for readmittance. (And if your plans call for swimming while away from the park, try to protect the stamp.)

20. At larger parks, make sure you remember where you park your car. In the excitement of the day, it's all too easy to jump out of the car and head to the park without paying attention to your exact location. After a long day in the park, it's no fun to spend an hour hunting for your car.

21. Many larger parks sell their tickets off-premises at hotels, rental-car agencies, and the like. If you can buy your ticket before you reach the park, you'll eliminate one line right away.

22. When riding rides, make a mental note of the number of the car you're in. If after getting off the ride you realize that something fell out of your pocket or that you left your purse, you can tell the operator exactly where that item should be.

23. If you're lucky enough to win a lot of stuffed animals, you may have a hard time carrying all of them. Most of the plush toys found in parks have small loops attached. You can easily carry these toys by looping them over your belt.

24. Rules are usually made for safety reasons, so for your own safety, follow them. There are good reasons for not standing up on the roller coaster and for keeping your arms and hands inside the flume log. Nothing can ruin a day quicker than an unexpected injury, especially if it could have been prevented by using common sense. Don't lock your brain in the car.

25. Try to avoid visiting a park on the opening day of the season. Everyone has been waiting for that day, and most parks are packed. Moreover, lines tend to be slow at both food stands and rides while the new employees grow comfortable with their responsibilities.

HAPPY TRAILS!

Tim's Terrifying Top Ten Roller Coasters

1. **The Beast,** Kings Island, Kings Island, Ohio
2. **Magnum XL 200,** Cedar Point, Sandusky, Ohio
3. **The Viper,** Six Flags Great America, Gurnee, Illinois
4. **The Raptor,** Cedar Point, Sandusky, Ohio
5. **The Cyclone,** Astroland, Brooklyn, New York/Coney Island
6. **Big Bad Wolf,** Busch Gardens, Williamsburg, Virginia
7. **Phoenix,** Knoebels Amusement Resort, Elysburg, Pennsylvania
8. **Giant Dipper,** Santa Cruz Beach Boardwalk, Santa Cruz, California
9. **Georgia Cyclone,** Six Flags Over Georgia, Atlanta, Georgia
10. **The Rattler,** Six Flags Fiesta Texas, San Antonio, Texas

Tim's Top Five Non-Roller-Coaster Rides

1. Slidewinder, Dollywood, Pigeon Forge, Tennessee
A fast, scary ride down a mountainside through a water trough in a 6-passenger, foam-rubber boat. Next to the Beast roller coaster, this is the most exciting ride in the whole world!

2. Derby Downs, Cedar Point, Sandusky, Ohio
A large, fast carousel whose horses move back and forth and actually race one another as the ride spins. One of only two such rides left in the country, this one was built in 1925; the other one can be found at Rye Playland, Rye, New York.

3. Pirates of the Caribbean, Disneyland, Anaheim, California/Walt Disney World, Lake Buena Vista, Florida
A dark boat ride through the loud, crazy, and often-scary life of the pirate. It's nicely paced, nice and cool, and marked by a great theme song.

4. Kongfrontation, Universal Studios Florida, Orlando, Florida
You board an aerial tram, and no sooner have you left

The Amusement Park Guide

the station, than you find out King Kong is loose and your life is in danger. He misses you the first time, but the second time, look out—he gets so close you can smell his banana breath.

5. Skooters, Knoebels Amusement Resort, Elysburg, Pennsylvania

There are two ways you can identify a quality bumper-car operation: First, you smell the graphite when you get within 20 feet of the place. Second, the cars must be the classic Lusse Skooter cars, in near-perfect condition. Knoebels passes the test on both counts.

Top Antique Wooden Carousels Located in U.S. Amusement Parks

1. Hersheypark, Hershey, Pennsylvania, circa-1919 Philadelphia Toboggan Company, no. 47. This is an extraordinary, four-row machine containing elaborate artistic carvings by John Zalar, one of the most noted artists in the field.

2. Riverside Park, Agawam, Massachusetts, created in 1909 by the Coney Island carver Marcus Illions. This ride has the finest and most flamboyant horses ever created that still operate on a carousel. The machine also features several menagerie (nonhorse) animals, including rare Illions carvings of a lion, a tiger, and a deer.

3. Dollywood, Pigeon Forge, Tennessee, 1903 Gustav Dentzel Philadelphia-style carousel, with original factory paint. It features some of the rarest Dentzel animals, including a rooster and a dog, and operates with an antique band organ and a brass-ring dispenser.

4. Six Flags Over Georgia, Atlanta, circa-1908 Philadelphia Toboggan Company, no. 17. This is the largest antique merry-go-round in the country, with five rows.

5. AstroWorld, Houston, Texas, circa-1915 Dentzel, with the outer row carved by Daniel Muller, one of the premier carousel artists.

6. Cedar Point, Sandusky, Ohio, has three antique carousels, two by Dentzel and one by Muller. The one in Frontiertown has a Muller "ghost horse" and is the only haunted merry-go-round in the country.

7. Elitch Gardens, Denver, Colorado, circa-1920 Philadelphia Toboggan Company, no. 51, has four rows containing beautiful, floral-decorated chariot horses and a monogrammed, armored-style lead horse carved by John Zalar.

8. Playland, Rye, New York, has the finest surviving

XXII

carvings by the Coney Island artist Charles Carmel. This circa-1928 ride features armored horses, and the horses on the outside row are laden with cherubs and eagles. It was designated a National Historic Landmark in 1987.

9. Disneyland, Anaheim, California, has a hybrid machine with horses by Dentzel, Carmel, Stein and Goldstein, and Muller, on a Dentzel frame. It has some extremely fine horses not found anywhere else.

10. Oaks Amusement Park, Portland, Oregon, has a Spillman Engineering carousel built in 1921. It boasts a wonderful assortment of menagerie animals, including one of the rarest, a kangaroo.

These listings, arranged in no particular order, courtesy William Manns, a carousel historian.

Top 10 North American Amusement/Theme Parks By Attendance

(For 1996, all numbers are estimates)

1. Disneyland, Anaheim, California, 15,000,000
2. The Magic Kingdom at Walt Disney World, Lake Buena Vista, Florida, 13,803,000
3. EPCOT at Walt Disney World, 11,235,000
4. Disney-MGM Studios at Walt Disney World, 9,975,000
5. Universal Studios Florida, Orlando, 8,400,000
6. Universal Studios Hollywood, Universal City, California, 5,400,000
7. Sea World of Florida, Orlando, 5,100,000
8. Busch Gardens Tampa, 4,170,000
9. Six Flags Great Adventure, Jackson, New Jersey, 4,000,000
10. Sea World of California, San Diego, 3,890,000

Courtesy Amusement Business

Tim's Top 10 North American Waterparks

(For 1996, all figures are estimates)

1. Wet'n Wild, Orlando, Florida, 1,380,000
2. Typhoon Lagoon at Walt Disney World, Lake Buena Vista, Florida., 1,250,000
3. Blizzard Beach at Walt Disney World, 1,100,000
4. Schlitterbahn, New Braunfels, Texas, 775,000
5. Raging Waters, San Dimas, California, 752,000

THE AMUSEMENT PARK GUIDE

6. **Six Flags** Wet'n Wild, Arlington, Texas, 700,000
7. **White Water,** Marietta, Georgia, 600,000
8. **Water Country USA,** Williamsburg, Virginia, 540,000
9. **Wild Rivers,** Irvine, California, 535,000
10. **Wet'n Wild,** Las Vegas, Nevada, 500,000

Courtesy *Amusement Business*

Ten of the Most Notable Theme/Amusement Parks

1. **Busch Gardens,** Williamsburg, Virginia—Acres and acres of beautifully mature trees, colorful flowers, and intricate Old World theming, combined nicely with high-tech rides and attractions make it unique. Great shopping for quality gift items from Europe.

2. **Cedar Point,** Sandusky, Ohio—More rides and more roller coasters than any other amusement park on the planet. One of the oldest continuously operated parks in the United States. Plenty of mature trees, classic rides, and turn-of-the-century architecture.

3. **Disneyland,** Anaheim, California—The original Disney park, opened July 17, 1955. It has the intimacy and the beauty that fulfilled Walt's dream. Trees are mature and the flowering bushes are beautiful. The Matterhorn is the world's first steel roller coaster.

4. **Holiday World,** Santa Claus, Indiana—Formerly known as Santa Claus Land, the 50-plus-year-old family-owned park is widely considered as America's first theme park. The clean, beautifully kept park features three wooded, themed areas celebrating three holidays: Christmas, July 4th, and Halloween. The Raven is the only Edgar Allan Poe–themed roller coaster in the world.

5. **Kennywood,** West Mifflin, Pennsylvania—A superb family picnic park loaded with Pittsburgh tradition, classic rides, and warm and fuzzy nostalgia! One of the only two American parks listed as a National Historic Landmark.

6. **Knoebels Amusement Resort,** Elysburg, Pennsylvania—A traditional park at its finest, with free admission, plenty of classic rides, and beautiful surroundings. It has the best bumper cars in the world, and possibly the best pizza you'll ever eat!

7. **Playland Park,** Rye, New York—On the shores of Long Island Sound, this 1920s-era park is the other American park (see Kennywood Park listing above) that is listed as a National Historic Landmark. It has a large beach area, plenty of colorful neon; tall, mature trees; and plenty of classic rides.

8. **Six Flags Fiesta Texas,** San Antonio—Located with-

in an abandoned stone quarry, the 100-foot-tall limestone cliffs surrounding most of the park provide a stunning backdrop to some of the most intricate theming you'll find in any park on the planet!

9. Universal Studios Florida, Orlando—The entire park was built as a working film studio. All buildings, restaurants, and retail shops are used regularly as props in Universal films. That's realism! All but a few of the rides are located in huge, themed buildings.

10. Walt Disney World, Lake Buena Vista, Florida—The largest resort complex in the world. Among other things, the 48-square-mile "world" includes three of the world's top six theme parks: Magic Kingdom, EPCOT, and the Disney-MGM Studio Theme Park. Blizzard Beach and Typhoon Lagoon, two of the world's top three waterparks, are also located here. All this, plus plenty of Disney magic, color, and hospitality.

North America's Oldest Operating Roller Coasters

(in operation at the same location)

1. Jack Rabbit, Clementon (New Jersey) Amusement Park, 1919

2. Jack Rabbit, Seabreeze Park, Rochester, New York, 1920

3. Jack Rabbit, Kennywood, West Mifflin, Pennsylvania, 1921

4. Roller Coaster, Lagoon Park, Farmington, Utah, 1921

5. Zippin Pippin, Libertyland, Memphis, Tennessee, 1923

(Opened at another location and moved here in 1923.)

> *Courtesy: Jim Futrell, National Amusement Park*
> *Historical Assocation*

North America's Oldest Amusement Parks

(Continuously operated)

1. Lake Compounce, Bristol, Connecticut, 1846

2. Cedar Point, Sandusky, Ohio, 1870

3. Idlewild Park, Ligonier, Pennsylvania, 1878

4. Seabreeze Park, Rochester, New York, 1879

5. Dorney Park, Allentown, Pennsylvania, 1884

> *Courtesy: Jim Futrell, National Amusement Park*
> *Historical Association*

THE PARKS

The Amusement Park Guide

ALABAMA

Waterville USA
906 Gulf Shores Parkway
Gulf Shores, AL (334) 948–2106

Once you enter the 14-acre complex you'll realize there's a lot more here than what the name implies. Sure, there's plenty of cool, clear water, but you'll also find 2 miniature golf courses, a go-kart track, an indoor laser tag arena, a large games arcade, a Trampoline Thing, and 5 kiddie rides.

The waterpark has 3 body slides, 2 tube slides, 2 speed slides, a wave pool, a lazy river, and a children's activity pool with slides and crawls.

Open year-round, 10:00 A.M. to midnight. Waterpark open daily 10:00 A.M. to 6:00 P.M., Memorial Day through Labor Day. All activities on a pay-as-you-play basis, pay-one-price at the waterpark, under $16.

(The park has a wooden roller coaster, The Cannonball Run, built in 1995, but it was not open during the last half of the 1996 season. The owners hope to have it up and running, starting again in Spring 1997.)

ALASKA

Alaskaland
Airport Way and Peger Road
Fairbanks, AK (907) 452–4244

Founded in 1967 to celebrate the hundredth anniversary of the purchase of Alaska from Russia, this 44-acre historical theme park has a playground, a native village, a mining valley, an art gallery, and a miniature golf course. It also has 2 family rides, including the Crooked Creek and Whiskey Island Railroad train ride around the park, and an antique carousel.

Two live shows take place daily: a spoof on the state's history, and a Broadway-style production, *Riversong*. The park is home to the famous Alaska Salmon Bake, served daily.

Open daily from Memorial Day to Labor Day, 11:00 A.M. to 9:00 P.M. Call for admission prices.

ARIZONA

Castles & Coasters
9445 Metro Parkway East
Phoenix, AZ (602) 997-7576

There's a lot more stuff than golf here. In fact, the state's only major permanent roller coaster is located in this 7-acre complex, across from the huge Metrocenter regional mall.

In addition to the looping steel coaster are a log flume, a Sea Dragon and several kiddie rides, 4 miniature golf courses, bumper boats, and a Lil' Indy go-kart track.

The park is marked by a mammoth stucco castle with big blue fiberglass domes, housing the arcade games and a few other smaller attractions.

Open 365 days a year. Golf opens at 10 A.M., rides open at noon. Rides priced individually, or an all-day ride and golf pass may be purchased for $18–$25.

 Roller coasters: Desert Storm, 2-loop (S); Patriot, junior, (S).

Enchanted Island
In Encanto Park
1202 W. Encanto Boulevard
Phoenix, AZ (602) 254-2020

Nestled in the heart of a large city park sits this top-notch fun park for young families. Occupying a 6-acre island, the amusement park is on the former site of the Encanto Kiddieland, which dated back to 1933. When that popular park closed in 1987, the city completely renovated the facility then reopened it as Enchanted Island in 1991.

Today, the park has 10 rides, including 8 for the little ones. Among the popular attractions are a carousel and a train. Also featured is a playland with 8 action stations, games, and a snack bar. Off the island, the city park offers canoe rides, paddle boats, hiking trails, and a golf course.

Open year-round, and hours differ greatly with the seasons and day of week. During the summer months, opening hours tend to be later, due to the heat. Admission is free, with rides on a pay-as-you-play basis, or an all-day wristband, under $10. Individual tickets cost 50 cents, with each ride taking from 1–3 tickets.

THE AMUSEMENT PARK GUIDE

Old Tucson Studios
201 South Kinney Road
Tucson, AZ (602) 883–0100

Howdy, partner—welcome to the real West. This intriguing desert facility was created in 1939 as the set for the film *Arizona*, and at that time was the largest film location ever built outside Hollywood; in fact, it was called Hollywood in the Desert. The park is Hollywood's version of what the Old West looked like, including Southwestern adobe sets and an Old West Frontier Street. Filming still takes place here, and the enterprise has more than 300 film, TV, and commercial credits.

In addition to any film action taking place, you'll find numerous shows and 4 mechanical family rides.

 Extras: Petting Corral and a horse-drawn stagecoach ride are available, free. Pan for gold, or enter a cave and search for geodes, extra fee. One part of the town features an 1880s-era circus Big Top with circus acts, and another honors the cultures and the traditions of Native Americans.

 Special events: Western Music Festival, November; intercollegiate rodeo competition, February, March, and November.

 Season: Year-round.

 Operating hours: 10:00 A.M. to 7:00 P.M. Closed Thanksgiving and Christmas only.

 Admission policy: Pay-one-price, under $15. Free parking.

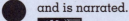 **Top rides:** Iron Door Mine Ride, a ride-through fun house; A-Car, antique autos; a carousel; a narrow-gauge train ride that circles the facility and is narrated.

 Plan to stay: 4½ hours.

 Best way to avoid crowds: Come midweek. Peak season here is between Thanksgiving and Easter.

 Directions: Directions: Take the Speedway Boulevard exit off I–10. Go west 12 miles. When Speedway dead-ends, take a left; the park is about ¼ mile on the left.

ARKANSAS

Burns Park Funland
Funland Drive
North Little Rock, AR (501) 753-7307

Located in the heart of Burns Park, a 1,562-acre city park, Funland bills itself as the place to have "good old-fashioned fun."

With 14 rides, including 8 for kids, Funland is a shaded oasis set apart from the rest of the park activities.

 Extras: Miniature golf, extra charge.

 Special events: Easter Egg Hunt, Easter Sunday; Summerfest, an arts-and-crafts festival on Labor Day weekend.

 Season: March through mid-October.

 Operating hours: 11:00 A.M. to 5:00 P.M. on weekdays; 11:00 A.M. to 6:00 P.M. on weekends.

 Admission policy: Free gate; rides on a pay-as-you-go basis. Free parking.

 Top rides: A mile-long train ride; Spook House, a dark ride; kiddie jets.

 Plan to stay: 2 hours.

 Directions: Take the Burns Park exit off I-40; follow signs into the park and then to Funland.

 # TIM'S TRIVIA

Based on averages, if you rode every ride in America's amusement parks and watched every show, you'd spend twice as much time watching as riding

The Amusement Park Guide

War Memorial Amusement Park
Jonesborough Drive
Little Rock, AR (501) 663–7083

Lying deep in War Memorial City Park, this good old-fashioned amusement park rests next to the Little Rock Zoo. The 15 acres are filled with stately trees, plenty of colorful landscaping, and 17 rides.

 Special events: Special celebrations and activities on the three major holidays during the summer.

 Season: Easter through October.

 Operating hours: 10:00 A.M. to 6:00 P.M., Saturday and Sunday only.

 Admission policy: Free gate admission; rides on a pay-as-you-go basis. Pay-one-price also available, under $5. Free parking.

 Top rides: Bumper cars; Tilt-A-Whirl; Scrambler; Star Jet.

 Plan to stay: 1 hour.

 Best way to avoid crowds: Usually not a problem here, but come early on weekends.

 Directions: Take the Fair Park exit off I–630; then follow the signs to the park and the zoo.

TIM'S TRIVIA

Three major amusement parks opened during our nation's 1976 bicentennial: Libertyland, Memphis, Tennessee; Paramount's Great America, Santa Clara, California; and Six Flags Great America, Gurnee, Illinois.

CALIFORNIA

Adventure City
10120 South Beach Boulevard
Stanton, CA (714) 236-9300

Talk about unique! Located in the Hobby City complex, a collection of unique hobby, craft, and collectible shops, Adventure City is a miniature version of an American City.

Kids can pilot a barnstormer or take to the skies in the Balloon Race at the airport, pilot an emergency vehicle on the 911 Ride, see the city from the Crazy Bus, or take the train around town. There are 8 rides in all, including the Kid's Coaster and the Carousel. Other attractions include face painting, live shows, and a petting zoo.

The park is located down the street from Knott's Berry Farm and is open year-round, daily in the summer, and weekends and select days in winter and spring. Hours vary, so call first. Choose from three admission options—general admission, an admission that includes 3 rides, or unlimited rides. The latter option is less than $10.

Balboa Fun Zone
600 East Bay Avenue
Newport Beach, CA (714) 673-0408

Located on the Balboa Peninsula, this is one of the last coastal amusement parks in California. The park makes good use of its waterfront location, offering whale watching cruises, parasailing, water bikes and sightseeing cruises, along with its 5 traditional amusement park rides, including a Ferris wheel on the waterfront and the Scary Dark Ride.

There are a variety of shops and restaurants, and with the nearby beach and pier, there's enough here to make a day of it. Dating back to 1936, the park was completely rebuilt by its current owners in 1986. Free admission, all attractions on a pay-as-you-go basis. Hours vary, so call first.

THE AMUSEMENT PARK GUIDE

Belmont Park
3190 Mission Boulevard
San Diego, CA (619) 488-1549

The Giant Dipper wooden roller coaster lives! Following 14 years of legal battles and fund-raising efforts, this circa-1925 National Historic Landmark has been restored to its splendor and is open to the public.

Belmont Park, of which the coaster was once the major draw, was closed down in 1976. Now, as the only ride from that park still existing in its original location, the coaster is the focal point of an upscale shopping village. The owners have added a beautiful replica of an antique carousel to accompany the coaster classic, as well as bumper cars, Tilt-A-Whirl, and 5 kiddie rides.

Roller coaster: Giant Dipper (W)
Also on the grounds is a roller-coaster museum, and The Plunge, Belmont Park's original indoor swimming pool, is still in operation.

Open daily during the peak summer months at 11:00 A.M. with closing at either 10:00 or 11:00 P.M. In winter, operations are cut back. Pay-as-you-play policy.

"Shotgun Slides," Raging Waters, California

Castle Amusement Park
3500 Polk Street
Riverside, CA (909) 785–4140

Castle Park was founded by Bud Hurlbut in 1976 to show-case his large collection of rides. He previously had the rides concession at nearby Knott's Berry Farm, and when that enterprise decided to operate its own rides, Hurlbut built his own facility.

The 25 acres are divided into three sections and feature a large castle as the centerpiece. The castle itself is an arcade, offering more than 400 games, and to the right of the castle are 32 rides, including 16 for kids. Behind everything are four 18-hole championship miniature golf courses, widely regarded as four of the best such courses in the country, and 2 go-kart tracks.

 Extras: Hurlbut has designed and built more than 50 "little trains" for parks throughout the world; 2 are set up here.

 Season: Year-round.

 Operating hours: Rides open at 6:00 P.M. during the week and at noon on weekends and close at 11:00 P.M. or midnight. Golf courses are open 10:00 A.M. to 10:00 P.M. daily. Rides are closed on Mondays during the summer and open only on weekends and holidays in winter.

 Admission policy: Free admission to the park. Rides are on a pay-as-you-go basis. Pay-one-price only available during special promotions. Parking charge when rides are open.

 Top rides: Haunted Mansion, a dark ride through the rooms of a haunted mansion; Falling Star; Sea Dragon; The Log Ride, a flume ride; antique cars; a circa-1905 Dentzel carousel.

 Roller coaster: Tornado (S)

 Plan to stay: 4 to 6 hours if you plan to play arcade games and/or golf.

 Directions: Located at 3500 Polk Street, off Riverside Expressway between the La Sierra and Tyler Street exits.

Disneyland
1313 Harbor Boulevard
Anaheim, CA (714) 781-4445
http://www.disney.com/disneyland

A plaque at the entrance to Disneyland tells it all: HERE YOU LEAVE TODAY AND ENTER THE WORLD OF YESTERDAY, TOMORROW, AND FANTASY. This creation of Walt Disney was the world's first ride park to offer major themes, and it set the standards for all the other theme parks.

Divided into seven lands and Main Street U.S.A., the park is clean and friendly and has all the charm you'd expect to find at Disneyland. Most of the 38 rides can be ridden as a family, and many are longtime favorites that never grow old, no matter how often you ride them.

TIM'S TRIVIA

The fantasy castle at California's Disneyland is Sleeping Beauty's Castle, whereas that at Florida's Walt Disney World is Cinderella's castle. Walt Disney wanted something bigger for his Florida park.

There's Disney magic in the air. There's also a whole cast of familiar characters walking around the park, including Mickey Mouse, Pluto, Donald Duck, Minnie Mouse, and Roger Rabbit. They'll hug you and give you an autograph, but you'll never hear them utter a word—they want to preserve that cartoon magic.

Mickey's Toontown is a fun, scaled-down village, where you'll find the homes of Mickey, Minnie, and Donald Duck. Various other kiddie rides, shows, and activities are located there as well.

Extras: The Haunted Mansion, a walk- and ride-through adventure, is absolutely the best haunted house in the world. The Disney Gallery, displaying more than 35 years of rare Disneyland art, is housed in the structure that was originally built as an apartment for Roy and Walt Disney. Both these attractions are free with admission. And, for great souvenirs, Disneyland has its own paper currency, featuring Disney characters on $1, $5, and $10 bills. The Disney parks are the only ones in the world that feature Orville Redenbacher popcorn, and it's delicious! The parkwide live entertainment lineup includes a full array of stage shows, most of which are based on current Disney films. Though Disney characters can be found throughout the park, the best way to see Mickey is to visit Town Square, his usual hangout.

 Special events: Main Street Christmas parade, Thanksgiving through New Year's Day; Main Street parade, summer months.

 Season: Year-round.

 Operating hours: During peak summer hours, 9:00 A.M. to midnight or 1:00 A.M. During winter months, 10:00 A.M. to 6:00 or 10:00 P.M.

 Admission policy: Pay-one-price, under $37. Two- and 3-day passes also available, at some saving. Parking charge.

 Top rides: Indiana Jones Adventure, a jeep ride through the jungle; Splash Mountain, a log-flume ride with a *Song of the South* theme; Star Tours, a ride simulation through the galaxies; Dumbo the Flying Elephant, a landmark that you *have to ride*; Pirates of the Caribbean, an indoor boat ride with frisky pirates watching you from all angles; Jungle Cruise, a boat ride down a tropical river.

 Roller coasters: Space Mountain, indoor (S); Big Thunder Mountain Railway, mine train (S); Matterhorn Bobsleds, indoor (S); Gadget's Go-Coaster, kiddie (S).

 Plan to stay: Unless you're there during an extremely slow period, plan to stay at least 1½ days, or 2 days if you want to see everything.

 Best way to avoid crowds: Come in the winter months during midmorning or midafternoon. Crowds surge when the park opens and right after lunch; they also tend to rush to the major rides first.

 Directions: Take the Harbor Boulevard exit off I–5 (Santa Ana Freeway) and go south on Harbor. The park is right next to the interstate.

Escondido Family Fun Center
830 Dan Way
Escondido, CA (619) 741-1326

If you can find your way out of the challenging, ½-acre Giant Maze here, you might want to try one of the three 18-hole miniature golf courses—or the batting cages, go-karts, bumper boats, or pillow bounce. Or you might want to visit the Kid's County Fair attractions and ride the train, a mini-roller coaster, planes, pirate ships, swings, or a Ferris wheel.

Free admission and you pay-as-you-play or you can purchase an all-day pass. Hours and days of operation vary; call first.

Frasier's Frontier
14011 Ridgehill Road
El Cajon, CA (619) 390-3440

There's something for everyone here! Located mostly under the canopy of oak and palm trees, this 16-acre park has 12 rides and a whole lot more to provide a fun, low-key adventure for the family.

The ride lineup includes a Tilt-A-Whirl, Octopus, Ferris wheel, and the Little Dipper children's roller coaster and there's a water slide, go-karts, 2 swimming pools, 2 play structures, and plenty of picnic areas. Birthday parties take place under a Conestoga wagon–shaped shade structure.

Open daily 10:00 A.M. to 6:00 P.M., March through October, pay-one-price admission is cheaper for adults than it is for the kids! Since there is much more here for the little ones to enjoy, adults pay under $6, while kids pay under $8. Located 1 mile off I-8, 21 miles east of San Diego.

Funderland
In William Land Park
1465 Sutterville Road
Sacramento, CA (916) 456-0115

Thousands of families have enjoyed this cozy traditional park since its founding in 1948. It's located in a spacious city park, across the river from the Sacramento Zoo and adjacent to Fairytale Town, a storybook village.

Outside the gate is a large picnic area, and nearby is a pony-ride concession. Rides include a carousel, train, boats, planes, tea cups, Oscar the fish, and Fort Sutter children's play area. In all there are 10 rides. A snack bar offers a full line of snack items, including popcorn, pink popcorn, ice cream, soft drinks, and candy.

Open daily from 10:00 A.M. to 6:00 P.M. during the summer and only on weekends from February through May and from Labor Day through November. Free admission, with rides on a pay-as-you-go basis; pay-one-price available only on weekends.

Funderwoods
In Micke Grove County Park
11793 Micke Grove Road
Lodi, CA (209) 369-5437

Surrounded by picnic groves, this small traditional family park lies in the middle of a county-owned park, directly next to the Micke Grove Zoo.

A Tilt-A-Whirl, a carousel, and a small steel family roller coaster are among the 11 rides the park has to offer. A compact snack bar serves such fare as nachos, candy, ice cream, and popcorn, as well as a park specialty, pink popcorn.

Open daily from 11:00 A.M. to 6:00 P.M. during the summer and only on weekends from February through May and from September through November. Admission to the amusement park is free, with rides priced on a pay-as-you-go basis; pay-one-price available only on weekdays. The county charges a parking fee for all who enter the county park.

Golf N' Stuff
10555 East Firestone Boulevard
Norwalk, CA (310) 864–7706

In addition to 4 beautifully landscaped miniature golf courses, this small family park has bumper cars, bumper boats, Model-T cars, Lil' Indy race cars, and 2 large arcades.

There is no admission charge; all activities are on a pay-as-you-go basis. Call for hours.

Knott's Berry Farm
8039 Beach Boulevard
Buena Park, CA (714) 220–5200

http://www.knotts.com

This is probably the only amusement park in the world that began as a chicken restaurant. Mrs. Knott's Chicken Dinner Restaurant was (and still is) a popular eatery, and during the 1940s the Knott family added a few attractions to keep people busy while they waited for a table.

Today the 150-acre park, divided into six areas with a theme, features 43 rides: Ghost Town is the original area, and the 6-acre Camp Snoopy, reminiscent of the California High Sierra, centers on Snoopy and all the Peanuts gang.

Extras: The Mystery Lodge is a multimedia, multisensory experience. Gold panning is available in Ghost Town for an extra charge, and a free museum dedicated to the Big Foot creature is set up across from the entrance to Big Foot Rapids.

Special events: The park becomes "Knott's Scary Farm" each Halloween season; "Knott's Merry Farm," Thanksgiving through Christmas.

Season: Year-round.

Operating hours: 9:00 A.M. to midnight or 1:00 A.M. during peak season and 10:00 A.M. to 6:00 P.M. during winter months.

Admission policy Pay-one-price, under $32; a saving of 50 percent can be had after 4:00 P.M. Parking charge.

Top rides: Kingdom of the Dinosaurs, an indoor ride through the days of the dinosaurs; Timber Mountain Log Ride, one of the first flume rides in the country; Big Foot Rapids, a raging-rapids ride; Calico Mine Ride, a narrated ride through a gold mine; Stage-coach, involving a ride around the park in a vintage stagecoach during which your party is attacked by bad guys; a 1902 Dentzel carousel; full-size steam train; and the Hammerhead, a Roto-Shake.

 Roller coasters: Windjammer, twin racing (S); Jaguar!, family (S); Boomerang (S); Montezooma's Revenge, shuttle loop (S); Timberline Twister, junior (S).

 Plan to stay: 8 hours.

 Best way to avoid crowds: Come during off-season or on a weekday morning during season.

 Directions: Located 30 minutes south of downtown Los Angeles. Take the Beach Boulevard exit off I–5 and go 5 miles to Knott's.

Oasis Water Park
1500 Gene Autry Trail
Palm Springs, CA (619) 327–0499

You don't have to add much to create a tropical atmosphere when you build a waterpark in Palm Springs. Hundreds of native palm trees and colorful plants inhabit this facility, which has 16 water attractions, including the popular slow-drifting White Water River.

The 27,000-square-foot The Wave provides plenty of wave action, and Creature Fantasy is a great little children's play area. There are 8 adult slides and 5 toddler slides. Most of the slides and rides come off the man-made mountain in the center of the park. A rock-wall climbing area requires an extra fee, as does the year-round on-premise health club.

Open daily mid-March through Labor Day, weekends in September and October. Admission, under $20.

Pacific Park
On Santa Monica Pier
Santa Monica, CA (310) 260–8747

Located on two acres at the end of the famous Santa Monica Pier, this is the only major pier park on the West Coast and it is spectacular. There are 11 rides, midway games, and food locations within the park itself.

On the pier outside the park are myriad eateries and the historic Looff Hippodrome building, which has housed a hand-carved carousel since 1916. The current, circa 1922 Philadelphia Toboggan Company carousel, was brought to this location in 1947 and was restored in 1981.

The focal point of the park is the Giant Gondola Ferris wheel at the very end of the pier. It has a great lighting package on it and is especially beautiful at night, and visible for miles. Additional rides include a motion-based simulator, a Pharoah's Fury, a Rock and Roll, bumper cars, and 5 kiddie rides. Free admission with rides on a pay-as-you-go basis.

 Roller coasters: The Westcoaster, family (S)

Open year-round, with summer opening hours at 10:00 A.M. and closing at 10:00 P.M. Sunday through Thursday, and midnight on Friday and Saturday. Winter operating hours depend on weather. There is limited parking on the pier, with additional parking in city lots along the beach.

"The Grizzly," Paramount's Great America, California

Paramount's Great America
2401 Agnew Road
Santa Clara, CA (408) 988–1776

Beautifully landscaped and offering a great variety of rides, this 100-acre park rests in the middle of famed Silicon Valley. The park, founded in 1976, has a patriotic theme and features 31 rides, including 6 for kids.

The Carousel Plaza, just inside the front gate, is one of the most beautiful entrances to any park in the country. The double-decked Carousel Columbia (listed in *Guinness* as the tallest one in the world) rests peacefully beside a small lake filled with ducks.

Such Hanna-Barbera characters as Yogi Bear and Huckleberry Hound can be seen throughout the park, and the slimy, messy fun of the Nickelodeon kid's cable channel comes alive in the 3-acre Splat City.

 Extras: Redwood Amphitheater, providing concerts all summer long by big-name entertainers, extra charge in addition to park admission. The Pictorium IMAX theater, one of the largest of its kind in the world, shows exciting, huge-screen movies for an extra charge.

 Special events: Spring Celebration, Christian music day, May; fireworks and special events on Memorial Day, July 4, and Labor Day; Joy Celebration, Christian Music Day, September.

 Season: Mid-March through October.

 Operating hours: Opens at 10:00 A.M. daily and closes at varying times during the season.

 Admission policy: Pay-one-price, under $30. Parking charge.

 Top rides: Drop Zone, a 224-foot-tall free-fall drop; Days of Thunder, a simulated motion-based race car adventure; Rip Roaring Rapids, a raging-rapids ride; Skyhawk, a participatory flight ride; Rue Le Dodge, bumper cars; Whitewater Falls, a spill-water raft ride; a 1918 Philadelphia Toboggan Company carousel.

 Roller coasters: Tidal Wave, shuttle loop (S); The Demon, corkscrew/loop (S); The Grizzly (W); The Green Slime Mine Car kiddy coaster (S); Vortex, stand-up (S); Top Gun, inverted (S).

The Amusement Park Guide

Plan to stay: 7 hours.

Best way to avoid crowds: Arrive at opening hours on weekdays or Sunday morning.

Directions: Located 5 miles north of downtown San Jose. Take the Great America Parkway exit off Highway 101; then go east to the park.

Pharaoh's Lost Kingdom
1101 California Street
Redlands, CA (909) 335–7275

You'll find 20 acres full of all kinds of fun here. The owner explains it: "We're a waterpark and a theme park. We're more than a family fun center, and we're not a full-blown amusement park."

Translated: This Egyptian-themed hybrid of a fun spot is a guaranteed fun time! You walk under a large sphinx to enter the tall, gold, glass pyramid in the middle of the park. Inside you'll find a huge, 300-game arcade, a laser tag arena, a soft-play participatory play area for the little ones, an educational area for displays and traveling exhibits, and a restaurant.

Outside, there are 14 rides, including 5 for the kiddies. Among the offerings is a train ride, Tilt-A-Whirl, Ferris wheel, carousel, and a family roller coaster. Other action includes a Skycoaster, bumper boats, 4 miniature golf courses, 3 go-kart tracks, and 10 midway games.

The waterpark has a 5-slide tower, a lazy river, a children's activity pool, an adult activity pool, and a Wave Rider surfing machine. A sand beach, volleyball courts, and an amphitheater with live entertainment round out the offerings.

Admission is free, with rides and activities on a pay-as-you-go basis. An unlimited-use ticket is available, under $30. Unlimited use of either park by itself is under $15. Open daily, 9:00 A.M. to midnight, year-round.

Pixieland Park
In Willow Pass Park
2740 East Olivera Road
Concord, CA (415) 689-8841

You don't have to be a pixie to enjoy this inviting little family fun park nestled in the pleasant surroundings of a large community park. The gently rolling terrain and tree-lined walkways add to the attractiveness of this traditional park for the entire family.

A colorful family carousel, spinning tea cups, airplanes, a Flying Dragon roller coaster, and a train ride around a small pond are among the 7 rides. A small snack bar serves typical amusement park fare, and a great many picnic areas are available.

The rides are open daily from 10:30 A.M. to 6:00 P.M. during the summer and only on weekends from February through May and from September through November. There's no admission charge, and rides are on a pay-as-you-play basis. A pay-one-price ticket is available only on weekdays.

Raging Waters
Off Tully Road
In Lake Cunningham Regional Park
San Jose, CA (408) 654-5450

The largest waterpark in the Bay area, the 23-acre Raging Waters is owned by Paramount Parks and is the sister park to nearby Paramount's Great America.

Anchored by the park's landmark attraction, the 7-story Serpentines water slide, the park offers nearly 20 water rides and attractions for the entire family. An 80-degree water temperature is constantly maintained in all attractions.

Buccaneer Bay wave pool simulates true tidal movements, from small swells to whitecaps, creating an active playground for action-lovers. For those preferring a more tranquil setting, the Endless River lazy river provides a gentle current on which to float. Pirate's Cove is an interactive family water play area, with a 40-foot mast topped by a water-spilling pirate's skull.

The park is open daily 10:00 A.M. to 7:00 P.M. from mid-June through August, and on two weekends in May and two weekends in September, from 10:00 A.M. to 6:00 P.M. Unlike most major waterparks, there are no fees to use inner tubes here. Admission is under $20, and there is a city-charged parking fee in Lake Cunningham Regional Park.

The Amusement Park Guide

Raging Waters
111 Raging Waters Drive
San Dimas, CA (909) 592–8181

Situated within a 50-acre parklike setting of tropically wooded rolling hills, this is one of the top five most popular, by visitor count, waterparks in the country. Remembering the offerings here is easy. "We have 50 acres, 50 million gallons of water, and 50-plus rides, attractions, and pools," says the owner.

In all, there are 51 slides (many attractions have more than one slide); Typhoon Lagoon wave pool; the Dark Hole two-person tube ride in the dark; Raging Rivers, the world's longest man-made river slide, with several pools along the route; Thunder Rapids six-person raft ride; Amazon Adventure lazy river; and the Drop Out, a body slide that drops you 78 feet straight down in 4 seconds.

Additionally, the Vortex is a themed, enclosed slide with lights, fog, and sound effects, and the Volcano Fantasy children's attraction features steam, smoke, sound, and slides. Splash Island Adventure is a large interactive family play area.

There are 2 sand volleyball courts, and a sandy beach, where a disc jockey plays music for "sand dancing" each evening. And don't be surprised by a large, funny-looking frog walking around. That's Freddy, the park's mascot.

Open mid-April through October, 10:00 A.M. to 9:00 P.M. during the peak season. Admission, under $25.

Rotary Kids Country
890 West Belmont
Fresno, CA (209) 486–2124

This classic little fun zone has been entertaining Fresno residents since 1955. Located in the large, city-owned Roeding Park, Rotary Kids Country consists of Storyland, a magic garden where fairy tales are brought to life, and Playland, a ride park featuring 10 rides, with half of them being for the wee ones.

The miniature railroad, Starfighter, and kiddie roller coaster are among the more popular rides. Paddle boats and motor boats can be rented at the boathouse. A concession stand and gift shop are also available, and live entertainment is presented during the summer at the Pinocchio Theater.

The facility is operated by the local Rotary Club, and all profits are used for cultural and recreational activities. Free admission, with rides on a pay-as-you-play basis. The most costly ride in the park is 70 cents. Open daily during the summer, hours vary, so call ahead.

Santa Cruz Beach Boardwalk
400 Beach Street
Santa Cruz, CA (408) 423-5590
http://www.beachboardwalk.com

History lives on in the West Coast's largest remaining major seaside amusement park. In fact, this park is so special that the entire facility is on the State Historic Landmark list, and 2 of the rides are on the National Historic Landmark list. Visiting the park, especially at night, is nostalgic—the smells, lights, and music coming from the park's ballroom could easily be those from a long-gone decade. Lined up neatly along the mile-long boardwalk, the 28 rides, including 8 kiddie rides, present a colorful backdrop to the sandy beach.

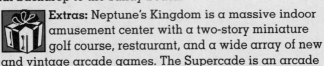 **Extras:** Neptune's Kingdom is a massive indoor amusement center with a two-story miniature golf course, restaurant, and a wide array of new and vintage arcade games. The Supercade is an arcade filled with high-tech games, including virtual reality and laser tag. Classic rock-and-roll bands play on the beach every Friday night in July and August. The water off the mile-long beach is a great (albeit cold) place to swim and surf. And the fresh and tasty Marini's famous saltwater taffy is still being made daily.

 Special events: Clam Chowder Cook-Off and Festival, February; sports and adventure expo, spring; craft and gifts fair, November.

 Season: Year-round; during winter months, weekends only.

 Operating hours: 11:00 A.M. to 6:00, 9:00, or 11:00 P.M., depending on season, crowds, and weather.

 Admission policy: Free admission to boardwalk; rides on a per-ride basis. Pay-one-price also available. Prices are rolled back every Monday and Tuesday from late June through August for "1907 Nights." Parking charged in lots or at meters.

 Top rides: A circa-1911 Looff carousel, one of the few that still give riders an opportunity to grab for the brass ring; Logger's Revenge, a log flume; Wave Jammer, a beach-theme spinning ride.

 Roller coasters: Giant Dipper (W); Hurricane (S).

THE AMUSEMENT PARK GUIDE

 Plan to stay: 6 hours.

 Best way to avoid crowds: Come midweek during the day.

 Directions: Take Highway 17 or Highway 1 into Santa Cruz; then follow the numerous signs to the boardwalk.

Santa's Village
Highway 18
Skyforest, CA (909) 336–3661

Tucked away among the tall firs and pine trees in the San Bernardino National Forest, this colorful, 15-acre fun park with an alpine theme continues to please entire families. "We're a magical blend of fun, forest, and fantasy," says the owner. Santa is always here, along with his elves and reindeer. The buildings, all variations of log cabins, are quite interesting from an architectural standpoint.

In addition to the 13 mechanical rides are rides on live burros and ponies, as well as a pumpkin-coach ride, drawn by two ponies.

 Extras: Alice's Mirror Maze, a petting zoo, and a 6-foot-tall frozen North Pole, with an elf sitting on top.

 Special events: Mountain Residents Week, mid-July.

 Season: Open daily in summer months and in mid-November through mid-December. The rest of the year, weekends only. Closed March through May.

 Operating hours: 10:00 A.M. to 5:00 P.M.

 Admission policy: Pay-one-price, under $10.

 Top rides: A circa-1922 Allan Herschell carousel; a Ferris wheel; antique cars; Bobsled, a small steel coaster; Bee-Ride, a monorail; a Christmas tree ride, in which kids ride in ornaments as they revolve around the tree.

Plan to stay: 3 hours.

 Best way to avoid crowds: Come during the early part of the week. The largest crowds are here during November and December.

 Directions: Take the Mountain Resorts Freeway (Highway 30) to the Waterman Avenue exit. Turn north on Waterman (Highway 18). The park is about 2 miles past the Lake Arrowhead turnoff. Located 20 miles from San Bernardino.

Sea World of California
1720 South Shores Road
San Diego, CA (619) 226–3901
http://www.4adventure.com

Marine studies and animal shows have not been the same since Sea World came onto the scene with its professional staff of animal experts. This is the original Sea World park, and it has the prettiest views of them all. Founded in 1964, the 150-acre park is located on Mission Bay.

The Sea World parks, although not true amusement parks, are educational gems. Best of all, you learn about marine life and marine conservation while you're having fun.

 Extras: The Back Stage Tour is a 90-minute guided tour of behind-the-scenes action, extra charge. Penguin Encounter, an Antarctic habitat, contains more than 300 penguins, and 4 aquariums hold a large collection of fresh- and saltwater fish. Wild Arctic, an opportunity to visit a scientific base camp where you can go face to face with walruses and polar bears.

 Special events: Summer Nights, a summer-long celebration of special shows, laser-light productions, and fireworks.

 Season: Year-round.

 Operating hours: 9:00 A.M. to 9:00 P.M. or later in summer, and 9:00 A.M. to dusk in winter.

 Admission policy: Pay-one-price, under $32. Parking fee.

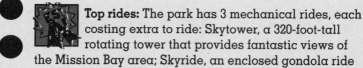

Top rides: The park has 3 mechanical rides, each costing extra to ride: Skytower, a 320-foot-tall rotating tower that provides fantastic views of the Mission Bay area; Skyride, an enclosed gondola ride across Mission Bay and back. In addition, Mission: Bermuda Triangle is a motion-based simulator ride that takes guests on a journey below the sea. Shamu's Happy Harbor features more than 20 interactive water and play elements for the kids.

Plan to stay: 8 hours.

Best way to avoid crowds: Come during off-season, or come midweek during peak summer months. Because the killer whale show is extremely popular, get to Shamu Stadium early and plan the rest of your stay around this show.

Directions: Take the Sea World Drive exit off I–5 and follow signs west to the park.

Six Flags Hurricane Harbor
26101 Magic Mountain Parkway
Valencia, CA (805) 255–4111
http://www.sixflags.com

The legend says it was Captain Red Eye the Pirate whom we can thank for this wonderful, wet, and exciting oasis right here in Southern California. Hurricane Harbor is a park of the Six Flags California complex and is adjacent to Magic Mountain.

The tropical-themed waterpark offers more than 20 different activities, including the Forgotten Sea wave pool; River Cruise lazy river; 10 slides, including the park's showcase attraction, Taboo Tower; and Shipwreck Shores, with dozens of different interaction activities for the entire family. There are a beach shop, an arcade, and several eateries.

Admission to Hurricane Harbor is under $20, with a 2-day combination ticket available to both parks, under $50. Entrance to the waterpark is to the right of the ticket booths for the theme park, off Six Flags Plaza.

Six Flags Magic Mountain
26101 Magic Mountain Parkway
Valencia, CA (805) 255–4111
http://www.sixflags.com

Don't forget your sneakers if you're coming to this 111-acre park in the Santa Clarita Valley—you'll be doing a great deal of walking. A fantastic arsenal of thrill rides, plenty of exciting shows, and colorful landscaping will dominate your attention here.

There are 44 rides, including 13 for the kids in the 6-acre High Sierra Territory and Bugs Bunny World area. The major rides are almost hidden from one another by the heavy woods and steep terrain throughout, whereas the kiddie rides are located near the entrance on relatively flat land. Like the rest of the Six Flags parks, the Looney Tunes cartoon characters are the official residents and can be found just about everywhere.

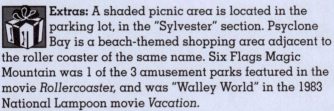 **Extras:** A shaded picnic area is located in the parking lot, in the "Sylvester" section. Psyclone Bay is a beach-themed shopping area adjacent to the roller coaster of the same name. Six Flags Magic Mountain was 1 of the 3 amusement parks featured in the movie *Rollercoaster*, and was "Walley World" in the 1983 National Lampoon movie *Vacation*.

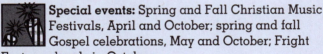 **Special events:** Spring and Fall Christian Music Festivals, April and October; spring and fall Gospel celebrations, May and October; Fright Fest, weekends in October.

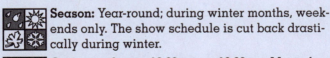 **Season:** Year-round; during winter months, weekends only. The show schedule is cut back drastically during winter.

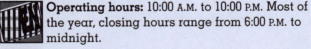 **Operating hours:** 10:00 A.M. to 10:00 P.M. Most of the year, closing hours range from 6:00 P.M. to midnight.

Admission policy: Pay-one-price, under $35. Parking charge.

Top rides: Superman the Escape, a 100 mph, 415-foot-tall freefall thrill ride; Grand Carousel, a circa-1912 Philadelphia Toboggan Company carousel; Sandblaster, bumper cars; Log Jammer, a log flume; Tidal Wave, shoot-the-chute; Roaring Rapids, raging-rapids ride; Jet Stream, a log-flume-type boat ride.

THE AMUSEMENT PARK GUIDE

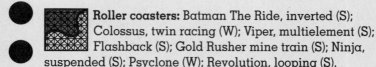

 Roller coasters: Batman The Ride, inverted (S); Colossus, twin racing (W); Viper, multielement (S); Flashback (S); Gold Rusher mine train (S); Ninja, suspended (S); Psyclone (W); Revolution, looping (S).

Plan to stay: 8 hours.

 Best way to avoid crowds: Get to the top of Samurai Summit either by walking or by taking a tram, monorail, or gondola ride. Then go up in the 38-story-tall Sky Tower. You'll be able to see every inch of the park and see the lay of the land and where the crowds are bottlenecked. Take along a map and plot your day around the show schedules. The crowds are fewer during the week and during off-season weekends.

Directions: Take the Magic Mountain Parkway exit off I–5 in Valencia. Go west a couple of minutes and you'll be at the park. Located 30 miles north of Hollywood.

Tahoe Amusement Park
2401 Lake Tahoe Boulevard
South Lake Tahoe, CA (916) 541–1300

The soil beneath your feet around here isn't your basic dirt; it's decomposed granite. The 10 rides are set in a large, peaceful grove of tall pine trees, and even on a hot day it's pleasant in the park.

The park was founded in 1969. Its most popular rides are the Giant Slide, Tilt-A-Whirl, and Paratrooper. It also has a go-kart slick track.

Open Easter to mid-October, hours vary, so call first. Admission is free, with rides on a pay-as-you-go basis.

 TIM'S TRIVIA

Santa Claus' lap is available all summer long at six parks: Holiday World, Santa Claus, Indiana; Santa's Land, Cherokee, North Carolina; Three Worlds of Santa's Village, Dundee, Illinois; Santa's Village, Skyforest, California; Santa's Workshop, North Pole, Colorado, and Santa's Village, Jefferson, New Hampshire.

Universal Studios Hollywood
100 Universal City Plaza
Universal City, CA (818) 508–9600
http://www.mca.com/unicity/

Action is one thing you'll get plenty of here. You'll float through the terrifying world of *Jurassic Park*, feel the heat from *Backdraft*, and ride to the Green Planet with E.T. You'll also go face to face with King Kong, see the seas part, watch Jaws attack a fisherman, be stranded in a subway during an earthquake, and be caught in the middle of a flash flood—and all this can be experienced during your first 45 minutes in the park.

The working studio here has been in operation since 1925; the public tour segment opened in 1964. Once primarily a tram tour through the back lots, the facility has become more visitor-friendly and now allows visitors to proceed at their own pace, rather than being kept prisoner in the tram for 2 hours.

You'll enter at the top of the hill in the Entertainment Center, where you'll find a multitude of live action shows, active movie sets, and fine restaurants and shops. To visit the new Studio Plaza in the lower lot, adjacent to the sound stages, follow the signs to the Starway Escalator and ride it down a 200-foot vertical drop. There you'll find more shops, attractions, and the boarding area for the action-packed tram ride.

 Extras: The Lucy Tribute is an exhibition and museum honoring the late Lucille Ball. You'll see a large collection of memorabilia, a composite film of her career, and much more; don't miss it. Fievel's Playland, a participatory play area based on the movie *An American Tail*, lets the little ones experience life from a mouse-eye perspective, slide down a 15-foot banana peel, and find their way out of an 11-foot-tall hunk of Swiss cheese.

 Season: Year-round.

 Operating hours: Open daily, except Thanksgiving and Christmas. Peak-season hours: 7:00 A.M. to 11:00 P.M. Restaurants and shops stay open longer. Hours are shortened during off-season months.

 Admission policy: Pay-one-price, under $37. Parking charge.

Top rides: Jurassic Park, The Ride, a dark boat ride past dinosaurs and over the world's steepest water drop; E.T.—The Ride, join the alien on

THE AMUSEMENT PARK GUIDE

bicycle for a trip to the Green Planet; Back Draft, experience an explosion up close; Back to the Future, a simulator ride with Doc Brown; the 45-minute tram ride is action packed, and will take you through the top attractions, including Earthquake—The Big One, Jaws, King Kong, the flash flood, and the collapsing bridge.

 Plan to stay: 8 hours.

 Best way to avoid crowds: Come early in the day during the week and during nonholiday times.

 Directions: Take the Universal Center or Lankershim Boulevard exit off the Hollywood Freeway (Highway 101). The studio is located between Hollywood and the San Fernando Valley.

COLORADO

Elitch Gardens
Island Kingdom
Elitch Circle
Denver, CO (303) 595–4386

After 104 years of providing thrills and entertainment in its original location in Northeast Denver, Elitch Gardens moved here to its new location in 1995 in order to have more room to expand and build its offerings. Premier Parks purchased the establishment in late 1996 and have promised to make the new facility a Denver landmark.

It will take the flowers, trees, and the overall landscaping quite a bit of time to even come close to rivaling the beauty of the original park, but with an area of 80,000 square feet dedicated to new (and transplanted) plantings, the owners have put a strong effort into re-creating many of the famous garden areas of the old park.

Many of the favorite old rides were moved, and many new spectacular rides and attractions were added, including the Total Tower, a 300-foot-tall observation ride and the huge Twister II wooden roller coaster. There are 46 rides, including a kiddieland that features 22 kiddie and family rides.

Extras: The Caribbean-themed waterpark has a large slide complex, wave pool, adventure river, and a large water play area.

Season: May through Labor Day.

 Operating hours: Opens at 10:00 A.M. daily. Closes at 10:00 P.M., weekdays, 11:00 P.M. Friday and Saturday.

 Admission policy: Pay-one-price, under $22.

 Top rides: Shipwreck Falls, Shoot-the-Chute; Tower of Doom, 220-foot tall free fall; Disaster Canyon, rapids ride; Top Spin; Tea Cups; Big Wheel, a 100-foot wheel offering a great view of downtown Denver; Sea Dragon; Mine Shaft, rotor.

 Roller coasters: Mind Eraser, inverted (S); Twister II (W); Sidewinder, shuttle loop (S).

 Plan to stay: 5 hours.

 Best way to avoid crowds: Be there at opening during midweek.

 Directions: Speer Boulevard South (Exit 212A) off I–25.

Fun Junction
2878 North Avenue
Grand Junction, CO (970) 243–1522

There's much to do here in beautiful western Colorado, and visiting this small but nice amusement park is a popular summertime outing for many local families. There are 18 rides, including bumper cars; a Ferris wheel; Wild Mouse, a compact steel coaster; flying scooters; and a kiddie roller coaster. Also here are paddle boats, go-karts, bumper boats, miniature golf, castle-bounce, puppet shows, and a large games arcade.

Open daily at 6:30 P.M. and on weekends at 1:00 P.M.; the season starts in May and runs through September. Call for admission prices.

The Amusement Park Guide

Funtastic Nathan's
Indoors at the Cinderella City Mall
701 West Hampden Avenue
Englewood, CO (303) 761–8701

Physical activity is the name of the game here. In addition to the ball crawls, net and rope climbs, and a giant slide, there are 4 mechanical kiddie rides. Plus you'll find a giant rocking chair, a giant horse, and giant teddy bear to climb on. And a little-tyke activity room amuses those under age 3.

Admission is pay-one-price, under $7, with adults getting in free. Tuesday and Wednesday are half-price days. Food service consists of a nostalgic candy shop. Hours are basically the same as the mall's.

Hyland Hills Water World
1800 West 89th Avenue
Denver, CO (303) 428–7488

Crystal-clear warm (heated) water and some of the best waterpark ride theming in the world await as you enter this 65-acre facility, built on a hillside in the Denver suburb of Federal Heights. With 33 different attractions, including 3 river rides and 2 wave pools, the park is a regional favorite in this part of the state.

The Lost River of the Pharaohs and the Voyage to the Center are two family river-raft rides that take you through highly themed indoor thrill experiences, something like you'd find at a major theme park. High-tech robotics and intricate scenery and effects make both rides unique for a waterpark!

The Raging Colorado is the park's first river-raft ride. The Wave is a double Flow Rider surfing experience, The Screamin' Mimi is one of the most popular slides, Calypso Cove is the family interactive play area, and Wally World provides water activities for the wee ones.

A gondola skylift helps transport guests to the top of the hill and at the same time provides a great view of the nearby airport. Many of the rides and slides follow the hilly terrain, so you won't find as many tall towers here as you'd expect in a park with this many offerings.

Open 10:00 A.M. to 6:00 P.M. daily, Memorial Day through Labor Day. There are plenty of shaded picnic areas, and you're allowed to bring in your own food. Admission is under $20.

Lakeside Park
4601 Sheridan Boulevard
Denver, CO (303) 477-1621

Nostalgia buffs will love this intriguing park, founded in 1908. Everywhere you look, there is Art Deco architecture and neon lighting. Where neon doesn't light something, thousands of light bulbs do, and this place is a delight at night.

Through the years, the owner has been successful in blending contemporary rides and attractions while preserving as much of the classic elements of the park as possible. There are 38 rides, including 16 for kids, set off in their own kiddieland.

 Special events: Dime Day is July 4, and Nickel Days are over Labor Day weekend—all rides are 5 cents or 10 cents.

 Season: May through Labor Day.

 Operating hours: Kiddie Playland, 1:00 to 10:00 P.M.; major rides, 6:00 to 11:00 P.M. All rides open at noon on weekends, with closing times depending on crowds and weather.

 Admission policy: General admission, with rides and attractions on a pay-as-you-play basis. Pay-one-price also available, under $12. Free parking.

 Top rides: Dragon, a kiddie roller coaster; Steam Train, a trip around the lake in the train that ran at the 1904 World's Fair; a circa-1908 Parker carousel; bumper boats.

 Roller coasters: Cyclone (W); Wild Chipmunk (S); Dragon, kiddie (S).

 Plan to stay: 5 hours.

 Best way to avoid crowds: Mondays are the slowest days.

 Directions: Take the Sheridan Boulevard exit off I-70 and go south for 2 blocks. The park is on the right.

The Amusement Park Guide

Santa's Workshop
Highway 24
North Pole, CO (719) 684-9432

If you didn't do so before, you'll believe in the big bearded guy after visiting this park—his magic is everywhere.

Located on 27 acres at the foot of Pike's Peak, the park has 24 rides, including 16 for children. The park's layout is unusual: It's located on a hillside and has five distinct levels of activities. In the middle of the Alpine theme park is a duck pond, and next to that is the North Pole, a tall pole that stays frozen all year and provides a great place to cool down on a hot summer's day.

 Extras: A petting zoo, complete with reindeer, is included in the gate admission. And, of course, Santa and Mrs. Claus are here every day to meet people.

 Season: Mid-May through Christmas.

 Operating hours: 9:00 A.M. to 6:00 P.M.

 Admission policy: Pay-one-price, under $15. Free parking.

 Top rides: Peppermint Slide, a giant slide inside a tall stack of candy canes, with Santa on top; a circa-1920 Herschell–Spillman carousel, with reindeer and horses; Christmas Tree Ride, enabling kids to ride ornaments; antique cars; Candy Cane Coaster, a small steel, kiddie roller coaster.

 Plan to stay: 3 hours.

 Best way to avoid crowds: Come either on fall weekends or midday during peak season.

 Directions: Take Exit 141 off I–25 and go west on Highway 24. Located 10 miles west of Colorado Springs.

CONNECTICUT

Lake Compounce
822 Lake Avenue
Bristol, CT (860) 683–3631

After all these years, the oldest continuously operated amusement park in the country is more beautiful than ever, and its future is brighter than it has been for more than a decade.

Kennywood Entertainment Company, which owns Kennywood Park and Idlewild Park, in Pennsylvania, bought this park out of bankruptcy court in 1996 and has big plans to build it back to a viable source of enjoyment for people throughout the Northeast.

 TIM'S TRIVIA

The oldest continuously operated amusement park in America is Lake Compounce in Bristol, Connecticut. It started out as a picnic and swimming park in 1846.

They expect to be able to reopen the park on Memorial Day weekend, 1997, with 20 major rides and 10 kiddie rides in operation. Among the rides that will reopen will be the Wildcat, a circa-1927 wooden roller coaster, which was completely rebuilt in 1986. Another classic to reopen will be a one-of-a-kind carousel, assembled in 1911 from older carousel pieces dating to 1896 and restored in 1986.

Other rides will include bumper cars, a Great Wheel, a Boomerang roller coaster, a river rapids ride, a log flume, and "several new major family rides still to be purchased," said the owners. Surrounded by wooded hills, the 70-acre complex has a 28-acre lake and is nicely landscaped throughout. The facility opened in 1846 as a picnic and swimming park.

THE AMUSEMENT PARK GUIDE

Quassy Amusement Park
Route 64 at Lake Quassapaug
Middlebury, CT (203) 758–2913

If you're looking for a quaint, traditional family amusement park, you've found it here. This 22-acre lakefront complex features 26 rides, including 15 for children, and a large arcade for video and other games.

Quassy is known as a picnic park; for more than 80 years, the locals have been coming here with family and friends for the entertainment and the nice sandy beach.

 Extras: Swimming beach, miniature golf, and boat rides, extra charge. Free petting zoo.

 Special events: Fireworks, July 4.

 Season: Late-April through Labor Day.

 Operating hours: Rides open at 11:00 A.M. or noon and close at 8:00 or 10:00 P.M.

 Admission policy: Free admission, with rides and attractions on a pay-as-you-play basis. Pay-one-price also available, under $11 for all day, and $5 after 5:00 P.M. Every Friday night from 5:00 to 10:00 P.M., all rides, hot dogs, colas, snow cones, and cotton candy are 25 cents each. Parking charge.

 Top rides: Train ride around park; reproduction of antique carousel; Flying Bobs; bumper cars; Chaos.

 Roller coaster: Monster Mouse (S).

 Plan to stay: 2 hours.

 Best way to avoid crowds: The crowds are lightest during midweek.

 Directions: Take Exit 17 (Route 64) off I–84. Go west about 4 miles; the park is on the right.

DELAWARE

Funland
6 Delaware Avenue
Rehoboth Beach, DE (302) 227-2785

This little boardwalk park is one of the least expensive amusement parks in the United States. It's amazing what you get for your money here. What's more, Funland has friendly folks running the place, a nice selection of family rides, and a splendid view of the Atlantic Ocean.

You won't have to walk much, either. With 18 rides on 1¼ acres, the park keeps everything pretty close to everything else. Among the notable rides is the great, 2-story Haunted Mansion, one of the best dark rides in the country. Other rides include Sea Dragon, Paratrooper, bumper cars, and a carousel.

The park itself has no food service, but as is true of most other East Coast boardwalk parks, a bevy of additional attractions and food outlets can be found within a few blocks. The arcade opens daily at 10:00 A.M., and the rides open at 1:00 P.M.; the Haunted Mansion opens at 6:30 P.M. Closing time varies, depending on crowds and the weather.

Open from mid-May through September. Admission is free, with rides and attractions on a pay-as-you-play basis.

"Montu," Busch Gardens Tampa Bay, Florida

FLORIDA

Adventure Island
McKinley at Bougainvillea Avenues
Tampa, FL (813) 987–5600
http://www.4adventure.com

As the largest themed waterpark on Florida's West Coast, this is truly a tropical paradise! The 36-acre park features dozens of water activities, sand volleyball courts, an outdoor cafe, and dedicated sunbathing areas.

Among the activities are 15 water slides, with such descriptive names as Runaway Rapids, Water Moccasin, Gulf Scream, and the Tampa Typhoon. Key West Rapids is a 5-story-tall tube slide featuring many surprises, including geysers, spurts, and showers. Fabian's Funport is a children's play area with an activity pool, a miniwave pool, and various other slides and activities. The Endless Surf is the wave pool, and the Rambling Bayou is a lazy river.

The park is owned by Busch Entertainment Corporation, and is located adjacent to Busch Gardens. Open April through October, 10:00 A.M. to 5:00 P.M. Hours are extended during the summer peak periods. Admission is under $22 for the waterpark, and a 2-day combo pass with Busch Gardens sells for under $47.

Adventure Landing
Shipwreck Island
1944 Beach Boulevard
Jacksonville, FL (904) 246–4386

The family entertainment center features go-karts, miniature golf, batting cages, laser tag, a large games arcade and is priced on a pay-as-you-play basis. Shipwreck Island, the waterpark, has 11 slides, a lazy river, and The Rage uphill water coaster and has a one-price admission of under $15.

A special, after-4:00 P.M. ticket is available, under $10. A nice thing about this little oasis along the Intercoastal Waterway is that you can play in the water for a while, then go over to the other attractions and pick and choose, and pay for only what you want to do. If you do, make sure you get your hand stamped so you can come back into the waterpark.

The family fun center is open year-round at 10:00 A.M., with various closing times. The waterpark is open mid-March through October, from 9:00 A.M. to 8:00 P.M.

Busch Gardens
3000 Busch Boulevard
Tampa, FL (813) 987–5082

http://www.4adventure.com

Here's your chance to visit Africa during your Florida vacation. When you walk through the front gates, you'll feel like you're entering turn-of-the-century Africa. Complete with areas representing Morocco, the Serengeti Plain, and other regions, the park combines its tropical landscape with Florida's humid climate to create a realistic effect.

Along with its 25 rides, the 335-acre park also features a zoological garden that ranks among the top ones in the country. And, some of the Budweiser Clydesdales call the park their home.

Egypt, a 7-acre area provides guests with a tour through a replica of King Tut's tomb during its excavation in the 1920s. There's Edge of Africa, a 15-acre walk-through area with numerous naturalistic habitats. Shopping bazaars and authentic artisans are also present.

 Extras: Included in park admission is a monorail, skyride, and steamtrain ride through the 60-acre Serengeti Plains, where more than 500 large African animals live. There's also a petting zoo.

 Season: Year-round.

 Operating hours: 9:30 A.M. to 6:00 P.M. Extended closing times during peak summer season.

 Admission policy: Pay-one-price, under $38. Parking charge.

 Top rides: Questor, a motion-based simulator ride; Ubanga-Banga Bumper Cars; Land of the Dragons, a children's play area with several kiddie rides; Tanganyiki Tidal Wave, a spill-water raft ride; Congo River Rapids, a raging-rapids ride; Stanley Falls, a log flume.

 Roller coasters: Kumba, multi-element (S); Montu, inverted (S); Python, corkscrew (S); Scorpion, looping (S).

 Plan to stay: 8 hours.

The Amusement Park Guide

 Best way to avoid crowds: Come during the fall, when the crowds are most scarce, or midafternoon during the peak season.

 Directions: Located at the corner of Busch Boulevard and 40th Street, 8 miles northeast of downtown Tampa. Take Exit 33 (Busch Boulevard) off I–75 and go east 2 miles to the park. Or take Exit 54 (Fowler Avenue) off I–75 and go east 2 miles to the park. Or take Exit 54 (Fowler Avenue) off I–75, go west 2 miles, and follow the signs.

Cypress Gardens
State Road 540
Winter Haven, FL (800) 237–4826

Historically speaking, this may be the most significant theme park in the country, next to Disneyland. Nestled along the banks of Lake Eloise, the 233-acre botanical garden and show park is steeped in history and tradition. The facility's gardens, water-ski shows, and lovely Southern Belles have been a draw since 1936. Of all Florida's attractions, this one has the most colorful, mature, and lush surroundings. If you're looking for beauty and solitude after visiting the other attractions in central Florida, stop here to regain your sanity.

 Extras: Cypress Junction is the site of an elaborate model railroad, containing 1,200 feet of track, free with park admission. Narrated tours of Lake Eloise on a pontoon boat are available for an extra charge. And the beautiful young ladies you see standing around in those charming dresses are the world-famous Southern Belles. Moscow on Ice, ice show.

 Special events: Gospel Sing-out, end of October; Mustang Car Show, end of October; Chrysanthemum Festival, November; Halloween Festival; Poinsettia Festival, late-November through New Years Day.

 Season: Year-round.

Operating hours: 9:30 A.M. to 5:30 P.M., longer hours during summer.

 Admission policy: Pay-one-price, under $30. Free parking.

 Top rides: Carousel Cove feature 7 kiddie rides and a Grand Carousel that the entire family can ride. The Island in the Sky is a rotating platform that is raised by a counterbalance to a height of 153 feet.

 Plan to stay: 6 hours.

 Best way to avoid crowds: Come during the park's off-season: July and August. Otherwise, come around noon on any day.

 Directions: Located about 45 minutes south of Walt Disney World, a few miles off Route 27 on State Road 540, near Winter Haven.

Cypress Gardens, Florida

THE AMUSEMENT PARK GUIDE

Fun 'N Wheels
3711 West Vine Street
Kissimmee, FL (407) 870-2222

Unlike many family fun centers, this one actually does cater to the entire family. Everywhere you look, you'll see parents enjoying the activities with their children. Those activities include a Ferris wheel, carousel, adult and kiddie bumper boats, adult and kiddie go-karts, bumper cars, participatory play area, and a moon walk.

There is no charge to get in, and rides are on a pay-as-you-go basis. Open daily 10:00 A.M. to midnight.

 TIM'S TRIVIA

The world's largest breeding program for the endangered Asian elephant is located at Busch Gardens, Tampa, Florida.

Fun 'N Wheels
6739 Sand Lake Road
Orlando, FL (407) 351-5651

Although laid out a bit differently, this fun center is similar to its sister park in Kissimmee. Admission fees and hours of operation are also the same.

Fun World at Flea World
Highway 17-92
Sanford, FL (407) 330-1792

Adjacent to Flea World, "America's Largest Flea Market," this fun little family park offers 21 rides, including 9 for the kiddies and young children. In addition, there are 3 go-kart tracks, a motion-based simulator capsule, 9 batting cages, miniature golf, and a huge video arcade/game room with 350 games. Plus you can go shopping if you get tired of riding!

Among the rides are a vintage carousel, Tilt-A-Whirl, bumper cars, Himalaya, Loop-O-Plane, Round-Up, and a giant slide. At the Fun World Pavilion stage, animal acts, magic shows, and family circus–style shows are scheduled year-round, free to visitors.

Admission to Fun World (and Flea World, featuring more than 1,700 dealers) is free, with rides on a pay-as-you-play basis. Unlimited rides for the 9 kiddie rides in Kids World are available for under $7; unlimited rides for all rides in park, under $14.

Open every Friday and Saturday, 10:00 A.M. to midnight, and Sunday, 10:00 A.M. to 10:00 P.M. Open year-round, free parking.

Miracle Strip Amusement Park
12000 West Highway 98A
Panama City, FL (904) 234–5810/
(800) 538–7395

Across the street from the beautiful white-sand beaches of the Gulf of Mexico, this park is a traditional, well-maintained, family-oriented attraction offering a good mix of rides, games, and excitement.

Along with its 27 rides, the park offers a wide selection of things to do. Three of the rides are inside unique structures and feature music, light shows, and air-conditioning. Though the park itself has no theme, many of the individual rides do. One such ride is Dante's Inferno, housed in a giant, devil-shaped building that you enter by walking across the devil's tongue. Another ride is set inside a huge igloo.

Make sure you're in the park after dark—its colorful lights, including neon lining all the ticket booths, are spectacular. Many of the original buildings, dating to 1963, when the park was constructed, are still in use today.

 Extras: A large midway games area plus arcade is a popular stopping place. The Old House is an excellent walk-through haunted house, and Route 63 consists of small, 1960s-era electric cars in a turnpike setting. Both are free with pay-one-price admission.

 Special events: High School band festival, three weekends during May.

 Season: Mid-March through Labor Day.

 Operating hours: Open every night until 11:30 P.M. Opens at 6:00 P.M. on weekdays, 1:00 P.M. on Saturdays, and 5:00 P.M. on Sundays.

 Admission policy: General admission plus rides. Pay-one-price also available, under $15. A 2-day combo, pay-one-price unlimited-use ticket for this park and its sister park, Shipwreck Island, located across the street, is available, under $26. Free parking.

 Top rides: A log flume; Haunted Castle, a dark ride; The Dungeon, an enclosed Tilt-A-Whirl; a Ferris wheel that offers a great view of the park; Shockwave, a 360-degree swinging ship.

 Roller coaster: Starliner (W).

 Plan to stay: 3½ hours.

 Best ways to avoid crowds: Avoid Saturdays. Best times to visit are weekday nights or anytime during the last two weeks in August, when the resort community begins to thin out.

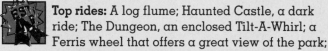 **Directions:** Take Route 231 south from I–10. Turn right on Highway 98 and go 10 miles. The park is on the right.

Old Town
5770 West Irlo Bronson Highway
(Route 192)
Kissimmee, FL (407) 396–4888

Take a walk back in history when you enter Old Town, a re-creation of a Florida community at the turn of the century. More than 75 shops, 6 restaurants, and nearly a dozen amusement rides and attractions are open 365 days a year.

The classic "oldies" music from the 1950s and 1960s is broadcast on Old Town's own AM radio station, WOTS, and can be heard throughout the complex. To add to that nostalgic flavor, between 200 and 600 classic cars show up each Saturday for Cruise Night. Remember when cruising was in? Remember the music? Remember the fun?

Among the rides, you'll find bumper cars, a Mixer, a Wave Swinger, Scrambler, Ferris wheel, family roller coaster, bumper cars, go-karts, and the Human Slingshot, a reverse bungee. A first-class haunted house, laser tag, and a gyro are also in operation.

Free admission, with everything on a pay-as-you-go basis. Rides and attractions are open at noon, with closing at midnight, or, as the owner says, "until everyone goes home."

Sea World of Florida
7007 Sea World Drive
Orlando, FL (407) 351–3600
http://www.4adventure.com

Shamu and baby makes two. This marine park has gone down in history books as the facility where the first killer whale was born and thrived in captivity.

Similar to the other Sea World parks in Ohio, Texas, and California, this 135-acre park features a variety of marine animals in themed productions and exhibits.

In addition to award-winning marine animal exhibits and shows, there is Shamu's Happy Harbor, a 3-acre play area for kids. The Wild Arctic exhibit features a motion-based simulator ride.

 Extras: The Penguin Encounter lets you see a variety of penguins in an environment you'll find nowhere else except at the other Sea Worlds and the Antarctic. Mermaids, Myths & Monsters, a colorful show on the lagoon each night.

 Special events: Key West at Sea World is a themed area featuring three marine habitats and Key West architecture, a summer-long, nightly celebration that combines fireworks, lasers, and laser animation on a water-screen.

 Season: Year-round.

Sea World of Florida

The Amusement Park Guide

 Operating hours: 9:00 A.M. to 7:00 P.M. Extended hours during the peak summer season and on holidays.

 Admission policy: Pay-one-price, under $42. Parking fee.

 Top rides: Wild Arctic, ride simulator; a 400-foot-tall sky tower that rises over the lake in the center of the park, extra charge.

 Plan to stay: 8 hours.

 Best way to avoid crowds: Come during off-season, in late afternoon; few of the locals visit the park from May through Labor Day or on holidays. During the season, come early and take in the major shows first; then wander through the exhibits at your own pace.

 Directions: Located at the intersection of I–4 and the Bee Line Expressway, 10 minutes from downtown Orlando.

Shipwreck Island
12000 West Highway 98A
Panama City, FL (904) 234–2282

The fact that this nicely themed waterpark lies across the highway from some of the most beautiful white-sand beaches on the Gulf Coast doesn't deter the crowds from enjoying all this great family park has to offer. As a sister park to the adjacent Miracle Strip Amusement Park, it opens mid-April and runs through Labor Day weekend.

Open 10:30 A.M. to 5:30 P.M. daily, the park offers 12 slides and flumes, including the Tree Top Drop, a 3-story-high speed slide; Ocean Motion, the wave pool; Skull Island, adult activity pool; Tadpole Hole, children's area; lazy river; food service; and beach shop.

Admission is separate from the amusement park, but a 2-day combination pass that allows 2 days of unlimited use of both parks is available, under $26. The days do not have to be consecutive.

Universal Studios Florida
1000 Universal Studios Plaza
Orlando, FL (407) 363–8000
http://www.usf.com/

Here's your chance to come face to face with King Kong and feel the bite of Jaws. The newest of the major-studio theme parks, Universal is also the most sophisticated in its rides and attractions. Opened in 1990, the 444-acre park is a working film studio with everything having been built for use in the filmmaking process.

You can walk among the movie sets, whose facades range from the streets of New York City to the architecture and lagoons of Amity Harbor to the San Francisco wharf area. Although new, these streets and buildings look like they've been there for years.

The rides and attractions are located in various theme areas of the facility. All but one are located indoors, with most of the waiting lines for the attractions being shaded or in air-conditioned areas. The rides are all original and are state-of-the-art computer-driven operations. The park's slogan—"You'll ride the movies"—is accurate, as each ride puts the guest into a familiar movie setting. Meanwhile, the shows and attractions put you in the movies by making the audience part of the presentation.

All things considered, this operation is the most advanced and sophisticated amusement park in the world.

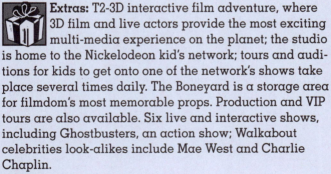 **Extras:** T2-3D interactive film adventure, where 3D film and live actors provide the most exciting multi-media experience on the planet; the studio is home to the Nickelodeon kid's network; tours and auditions for kids to get onto one of the network's shows take place several times daily. The Boneyard is a storage area for filmdom's most memorable props. Production and VIP tours are also available. Six live and interactive shows, including Ghostbusters, an action show; Walkabout celebrities look-alikes include Mae West and Charlie Chaplin.

 Season: Year-round.

 Operating hours: 9:00 A.M. to 10:00 P.M.

 Admission policy: Pay-one-price, under $45. Parking charge.

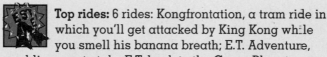

THE AMUSEMENT PARK GUIDE

Top rides: 6 rides: Kongfrontation, a tram ride in which you'll get attacked by King Kong while you smell his banana breath; E.T. Adventure, enabling you to take E.T. back to the Green Planet on a flying bicycle; Earthquake—The Big One, letting you experience an earthquake while riding a subway car; FUNtastic World of Hanna-Barbera, a ride simulator taking you on a space mission to rescue Elroy Jetson; Jaws, in which you're attacked by a huge shark while cruising the lagoon on a pontoon boat; Back to the Future, where you ride with Doc Brown to another time on one of the world's most advanced motion-based simulator rides.

Plan to stay: 1 long day or 2 slower-paced days.

Best way to avoid crowds: Most shows and attractions have preshows that help cut the anticipated waits. Don't be fooled by the short lines you see outside: Most of the lines here are inside air-conditioned buildings. Midmornings are least crowded.

Directions: Main entrance is ½ mile north of I–4, off Exit 30B (Kirkman Road/Highway 435). Another entrance is off Turkey Lane Road: Take Exit 29 (Sand Lake) off I–4 and turn right onto Turkey Lane Road within ½ mile of the interstate.

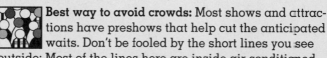

TIM'S TRIVIA

Employees in the Magic Kingdom at Walt Disney World, near Orlando, Florida, walk to their workstations via a series of underground tunnels. That's why you never see a person wearing a Tomorrowland uniform, for example, in Adventureland. Supplies are delivered to each area in the same manner.

Walt Disney World Resort
Routes 4 and 192
Lake Buena Vista, FL (407) 824–4321
http://www.disney.com/DisneyWorld/

The "Wonderful World of Disney" has never looked, sounded, or tasted better than it does today. Constantly adding rides, shows, and attractions, this place always has something new and magical going on. Covering 48 square miles, Walt Disney World is much more than an amusement park—it's the world's largest and most whimsical family resort complex. And the image of Mickey Mouse is everywhere: From the water tower (known as the Earful Tower) to the topiary to the bars of soap in the rest rooms, the mighty mouse makes his presence known.

There's something special about a company whose executives wear Mickey Mouse watches and ties. If there's a heaven on earth, no doubt this is it.

Located 20 miles southwest of Orlando, the resort has three separate theme parks that welcome more than 30 million guests a year: the Magic Kingdom, Epcot, and Disney-MGM Studios. In addition, the complex has myriad smaller attractions, including Typhoon Lagoon, Blizzard Beach, and River Country, all 3 waterparks.

Keeping in mind that entire volumes have been published about the complex, I have presented the basics and a few highlights about each of the 3 parks, and the 2 largest waterparks. That information is followed by general data pertaining to all the parks.

The Magic Kingdom

Carved out of the swamp in 1971, this park is the one most people associate with Walt Disney World. With 50 rides and attractions, the Magic Kingdom holds the hallmark Disney rides and is the top choice if you're looking for activities the whole family will enjoy. The 100-acre site is divided into 7 lands: Liberty Square, Frontierland, Adventureland, Main Street, USA, Fantasyland, New Tomorrowland, and the newest area, Mickey's Toontown Fair.

Shows and attractions: Stake your claim along Main Street in plenty of time to have a front-row view of the daily parade that starts near the front gate and winds through Frontierland; a special electrical parade is presented in summers and during holiday periods. Another must-see is the Country Bear Jamboree, offering animatronics at its best. Check the daily schedule for times and additional Disney-quality shows.

THE AMUSEMENT PARK GUIDE

Rides: A few of the landmark rides you must experience are Pirates of the Caribbean, a boat ride through a pirate's world; Haunted Mansion, the best of its kind worldwide; Big Thunder Mountain Railroad, a mine train roller coaster; Jungle Cruise, a ride on a boat that gets attacked by (animatronic) alligators and snakes; Space Mountain, an indoor roller coaster with a space theme; Dumbo, the flying elephant; Splash Mountain, a *Song of the South*-themed flume ride; and Alien Encounter, where you'll witness an experiment gone awry.

Epcot

The 300-acre Experimental Prototype Community of Tomorrow (EPCOT) represents a lifelong dream of Walt Disney that became a reality in 1982. It's divided into two sections: World Showcase, focusing on the culture, food, and products of eleven foreign nations, and Future World, highlighting man's past and future relationship with communication, the environment, energy, and transportation.

Shows and rides: It's hard to categorize the attractions at Epcot. In World Showcase, each of the eleven countries offers a variety of attractions, rides, food, and shopping experiences within its own pavilion. Norway, for example, features a fine restaurant, a large shopping area, a film depicting the nation's history, and a magnificent Viking boat ride, called Maelstrom, taking visitors through Nordic times. Other countries present similar experiences.

In Future World, attractions are much the same, except that the pavilions are sponsored by large corporations rather than countries and center on specific themes, such as communications, energy, and health. Spaceship Earth, the large sphere that has become an Epcot landmark, houses a fantastic dark ride that provides a look at our planet. A boat ride through The Land pavilion highlights experimental farming techniques; a restaurant in that pavilion also serves some of the best food in Epcot. And the Wonders of Life exhibit is the best the park has to offer. It combines shows, food, interactive educational exhibits, and a simulated ride through the body, called Body Wars.

Epcot closes each night with a magnificent show on the lagoon. Called IllumiNations, it's a laser, fireworks, fountain, and musical extravaganza. The General Motors Pavilion is now The Test Track, featuring a "behind-the-scenes ride" through the world of automobile testing. Honey, I Shrunk the Audience is the best 3-D interactive film in the world!

Disney–MGM Studios

The newest of the 3 parks, this one opened in 1989 and contains an operating movie production studio along with the rest of the attractions. Here's where you'll find the Muppets. Make sure you stop by the Prime Time Cafe, a fifties-style diner where you'll eat at chrome and Formica tables you may well remember from your childhood days. At most tables is a TV set showing reruns of the classics. You're the guest of "Mom" here, and if you misbehave or don't eat your veggies, you may well be ridiculed by the personnel. Prime Time is a show and a great place to eat all wrapped up in one. Try their peanut butter and jelly

"Wild Waves," Wild Waters at Silver Springs, Florida

milk shakes—there's nothing in this world better!

The indoor Sci-Fi Dine-In Restaurant has booths shaped like classic cars, all pointing to a drive-in screen where movies are shown. Servers, on roller skates, deliver food and beverages.

Shows and attractions: Most of the shows have a Hollywood or movie production theme. The Indiana Jones Epic Stunt Spectacular is one of the best stunt thrillers in production anywhere, and the Magic of Disney Animation studio and tour present a fascinating lesson in the art form that started it all for Walt Disney.

Several other movie-related shows are offered; many more are on the drawing boards. Check the daily show schedule for up-to-date information.

Rides: The Twilight Zone Tower of Terror offers guests a trip through an abandoned hotel, with a 13-story free fall. Don't miss Star Tours, the celebrated simulated journey through space. Although the Body Wars ride in Epcot uses the same technology, the journey in Star Tours is quite different. The Muppet 3-D Movie presents the characters at their orneriest best. The Great Movie Ride is a live-narration journey through the history of film; here you'll see good guys beat the gangsters both on the screen and in your car. And the Backstage Studio Tour tram ride takes you past several very familiar houses on the back lot and through Catastrophe Canyon, where you'll experience floods, fires, and explosions, all within a couple of minutes.

Blizzard Beach

A waterpark in Florida with a Northern snow-ski-resort theme? It sounds quite zany, but the creative folk at the Walt Disney stables can do just about anything and make it work! This 66-acre park has the atmosphere and excitement of a major ski resort but is totally tropical in reality.

Mt. Gushmore is the tall, snow-capped mountain in the middle of the park, where most of the slides start their downward journey. At the 120-foot-high summit, you'll find the amazing Summit Plummet, a 55-mph speed-slide plunge virtually straight down. Slush Gusher is another speed slide that takes you through a snow-banked mountain gully.

Teamboat Springs is a family raft ride down a series of rushing water falls, and Toboggan Racer is an 8-lane slide over short hops down the snowy slope of the mountain. Runoff Rapids is a tube run, and Melt-Away Bay is a 1-acre pool at the foot of the mountain constantly fed by a "melting snow" waterfall.

Tike's Peak contains kid-size versions of the adult rides, and Cross Country Creek is a lazy river that winds through an ice cave. You can walk to the top of the mountain, or take a whimsical chairlift ride. The Lottawatta Lodge, built to resemble a North American ski lodge with Caribbean accents, is a counter-service restaurant with dining areas overlooking Mt. Gushmore.

Typhoon Lagoon

This tropical shipwreck-themed park set a new standard for waterparks when it opened in 1989 and is still one of the most visited waterparks in the world. The crystal-clear water attractions on the 56 acres here have lush colorful landscaping and beautiful stonework as an enchanting background, adding a very realistic tropical island feel to the entire park.

Mt. Mayday is the centerpiece here, complete with the wrecked ship that aired that distress signal, just a little too late. Coming off the mountain are Humunga Kowabunga, a set of two speedslides; 3 body slides; and 3 white-water rafting adventures, including the family raft run known as Gangplank Falls.

The wave pool is the Typhoon Lagoon, and Castaway Creek is the lazy river that takes you through a misty rain forest and over a hidden grotto. Ketchakiddee Creek is an interactive, children's play area, and the Shark Reef is a 362,000-gallon salt water-coral reef diving environment, full of colorful fish, where you may snorkel.

The Leaning Palms Burger & Brew and Typhoon Tilly's Galley & Grog are the two main restaurants, with each offering a varied menu including sandwiches, seafood salads, and beer.

Viable Information for All Disney Attractions

 Food Service: In total, the complex has more than 175 locations where food can be purchased, ranging from counter service to buffeterias to full-menu, table-service restaurants. Beer, wine, and spirits are available at all table-service restaurants except those in the Magic Kingdom.

If you have kids with you, try to catch one of the character meals. There are 6 different breakfast and 2 lunch locations where Disney characters, including Mickey and Minnie, walk around and visit diners at their tables—a nice way to give your kids a little one-on-one time with their favorite character.

THE AMUSEMENT PARK GUIDE

Reservations are needed for the character meals, as well as for the 4 nightly dinner shows. Most of the other larger restaurants also require lunch or dinner reservations. If you're staying at one of the Disney hotels, you can call an in-park number. If you're staying off-property, find the guest relations building as you enter any of the parks; its staff can make them for you.

 Extras: Within the Walt Disney World complex are 5 other notable Disney attractions: Disney BoardWalk, a 1920s-era boardwalk featuring restaurants, clubs, and shopping; Pleasure Island, a 6-acre, 7-nightclub theme park for adults; River Country, a water-themed playground with swimming, slides, and other activities; Discovery Island, a zoological park containing more than 90 animal species; and Disney Village Marketplace, a shopping area whose 19 shops offer the latest in goods ranging from European designs to Mickey Mouse socks.

 Plan to stay: A family of four will want to spend at least a day in each of the theme parks. During the peak summer and holiday seasons, even more time is needed to see everything.

 Season: Everything is open every day of every year.

 Operating hours: During the peak season, the gates open at the three parks no later than 8:00 A.M. and close anywhere from 9:00 to 11:00 P.M.

 Admission policy: Pay-one-price, under $45. Four- and 5-day passports are available at a good saving and are honored at all three parks. The passports have no expiration date and don't have to be used on consecutive days; thus, you can use them anytime you choose. Parking charge.

 Best way to avoid crowds: Sundays, Thursdays, and Fridays are usually the least crowded days. In general, January, May, October, and November are the least busy times.

The best way to get around is to obtain a map and plan your visit. Arrive early, take a break during the heat of the midafternoon sun, and then come back and stay until the park closes.

Expect lines for everything; be grateful for a short wait, but don't be surprised by a long one.

Wet'n Wild
6200 International Drive
Orlando, FL (407) 351–1800

http://web.wetnwild.com

This is the world's first waterpark, founded by George Millay, the "Father of the Waterpark Industry." He first created the Sea World parks, sold them, and established Wet'n Wild here in Orlando in 1977. The rest is history, and by the way, George, thanks!

Today, as the oldest waterpark in the world, this one is still among the most visited of them all, with more than a million thrill seekers coming through the gates each year.

From more than 60 feet in the air, The Fuji Flyer sends 4-passenger toboggans down a 450-foot long trough of steep-banked curves. The scary, but popular Der Stuka free-fall slide drops you down a 250-foot slide, and the Bomb Bay is the ultimate free-fall slide. You don't know when the floor will drop out, sending you down a 76-foot-high, nearly vertical slide. The Blue Niagara and the Mach 5 also provide sliding fun.

The Bubba Tub is a 6-story, triple-dip family tube ride. The Surge is a 5-passenger tube ride down five stories through 600 feet of twisting, turning, banked curves, and on the Black Hole, 2-person rafts are pushed rapidly down 500 feet of dark tunnels by a 1,000-gallon-per-minute blast of water.

The Children's Playground is a unique play area for the kids. It includes miniature versions of the park's most popular adult rides and has kid-size tables, chairs, and a concession stand with a sunken floor so the kids are on eye level with the server. The Surf Lagoon provides 4-foot-high waves, and the Knee Ski is a cable-operated ski tow, which enables riders to be pulled around the lake on a half-mile course.

The Congo River Golf is an 18-hole miniature golf course, free with admission, but a tee-time must be reserved. Picnics are allowed; no alcohol can be brought in. It is open year-round, with the water being heated in cooler months. Open between 9:00 and 10:00 A.M., closing between 5:00 and 11:00 P.M., depending on season. Call first for specifics.

Admission is under $26. A special 5-day, money-saving pass allows unlimited visits to this park, Universal Studios Florida, and Sea World of Florida. Special hotel rates are also part of the package.

The Amusement Park Guide

Wild Waters
5656 East Silver Springs Boulevard
Silver Springs, FL (904) 236–2121

Tucked in beside its sister attraction, Silver Springs, this 10-acre family waterpark features slides, rides, and water attractions for all ages and thrill levels.

Among the attractions for the braver family members are the Thunderbolt free-fall speed slide and the Tornado, an enclosed flume with a 40-foot drop on the way down to the splash pool below. The Silver Bullet is a 220-foot-long racing flume, and the Hurricane is a 400-foot-long twin flume in which passengers receive an 80-gallon "turbocharge" blast half way through.

The water in the Wave Pool ranges in depth from 3 inches to 8 feet, with waves on for 10 minutes, off for 10. Over in the Tad Pool wading area, little tots get to play in shallow water as their older brothers and sisters play in an interactive area known as the Water Bonanza.

There's a miniature golf course, 4 eateries, and a beach shop. Open March through Labor Day, 10:00 A.M. to 5:00 P.M., with longer hours during the peak summer season. Admission is under $20. A combination pass may be purchased for the waterpark and Silver Springs.

"Tornado Touchdown," Wild Waters, Florida

GEORGIA

Alpine Amusement Park
Edelweiss Drive
Helen, GA (706) 878–2306

Situated in the foothills of the Great Smoky Mountains, Helen is a Bavarian-themed community with strict building and operating codes to ensure that virtually everything has at least a bit of a German feel and look to it.

Although employees here at the park don't dress in costume and the rides are not themed, the Bavarian influence is definitely here. There are 9 rides here and the largest go-kart facility in Northern Georgia. There's a Ferris wheel, bumper boats, 5 kiddie rides, batting cages, miniature golf, an arcade, and food concessions.

Open daily during summer and on weekends through the fall and spring seasons, weather permitting. The park is closed December through February. Rides open at noon, with the park closing at 10:00 or 11:00 P.M. Admission is free, rides on a pay-as-you-go basis.

American Adventures
250 North Cobb Parkway
Marietta, GA (770) 424–9283

To encourage family interaction and enjoyment, parents pay only $3 to ride with their children at this unique family entertainment center. With a turn-of-the-century ambience, the park offers Victorian-style rides and architecture, and a nostalgic setting.

The 15 family rides include a balloon ride, a buffalo-themed roller coaster, and a train. Hidden Harbor is a state-of-the-art, 18-hole miniature golf course providing animated characters, music, and audio presentations; an animatronic character talks you through the last hole. Indoors, the one-of-a-kind Foam Factory is a participatory play unit for children 7 to 15 years of age. The adjacent White Water waterpark is run by the same owners.

Year-round, the park opens at 11:00 A.M. and closes at 9:00 P.M., Sunday through Friday. Saturdays, 10:00 A.M. to 10:00 P.M. Admission is under $15 for kids, $3 for adults.

The Amusement Park Guide

Lake Winnepesaukah
Lakeview Drive
Rossville, GA (706) 866–5681

Established in 1925 on 110 acres, this is one of the Southeast's most beautiful traditional parks. With 33 rides, including 14 for kids, the park is built around three sides of a lake, just 4 miles from the Tennessee border, near Chattanooga.

It offers plenty of old-time charm and a great deal of lakeside shade and benches for relaxing.

 Extras: Miniature golf and paddleboats are available for an additional charge. Top-name entertainers perform most Sunday afternoons in Jukebox Junction, no additional charge.

 Season:: Mid-April through September.

 Operating hours: Opens at 10:00 A.M. on Thursday and Saturday, and noon on Friday and Sunday. Closed Monday (except holiday Mondays), Tuesday, and Wednesday.

 Admission policy: Small gate admission charged, with rides and attractions on a pay-as-you-go basis. Pay-one-price also available, under $15. Admission includes access to the park and to all entertainment. Free parking.

 Top rides: Himalaya; Pirate Ship, a swinging ride; Boat Shoot, a circa-1926, tunnel-of-love type spillwater attraction; Matterhorn; an aerial ride taking you over the lake and back; a circa-1916 Philadelphia Toboggan Company carousel in superb shape; Pipeline Plunge, a raft ride down a 72-foot water slide.

 Roller coaster: The Cannon Ball (W).

Plan to stay: 4 hours.

Best way to avoid crowds: Be there when the park opens and get to the far side of park, where the coaster is located. Enjoy that side of the park first, and then the area near the exit. Because there is only one path from one side of the lake to another, getting around through the crowds can be time-consuming.

Directions: Take the Route 41 exit off I–75. Take Ringold Road 2 miles to McBrien Road, turn left, and the park is about 2 miles at the end of McBrien Road on Lakeview Drive.

Six Flags Over Georgia
I–20 and Six Flags Parkway
Atlanta, GA (770) 948–9290
http://www.sixflags.com

All the Six Flags parks are known for their wide selection of rides, games, and attractions, but this one, founded in 1967, has also earned a reputation as one of the prettiest. Its 331 hilly acres have matured nicely and offer guests lots of shade and landscaping beauty to enjoy.

The park is especially pretty at night, when colorful neon and various other lighting packages illuminate the rides. There are 32 rides, with 7 of them being for kids and located in Bugs Bunny World. Other areas with specific themes are the Confederate, Cotton States, Georgia, Lick Skillet, Gotham City, British, French, U.S., and Spanish sections.

 Extras: The Riverview Carousel dates back to 1908 and has been ridden by President Warren Harding and Al Capone at its former location in Chicago's Riverview Park. The Southern Star Amphitheater features top-name entertainers throughout the summer, with some concerts requiring an additional fee.

 Special events: Spring Break Out, early April; Atlanta Fest, Southeast's largest Christian Music festival, mid-June; Fright Fest, weekends in October.

 Season: Mid-March through October. Reopens after Thanksgiving until the beginning of January.

 Operating hours: Opens 10:00 A.M. Closing varies throughout season.

 Admission policy: Pay-one-price, under $35. Second-day ticket for use anytime during the season also available for an additional $3. Parking charge.

 Top rides: Thunder River, a raging-rapids ride; The Great Gasp, a 20-story-tall parachute drop; Ragin' Rivers, a series of 4 wet/dry rides, including 2 speed slides and 2 tube slides. Six Flags Air Racer, 90-foot-tall airplane ride; Monster Plantation, boat ride

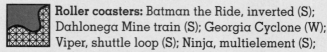

The Amusement Park Guide

through a flooded antebellum mansion; Splashwater Falls, shoot-the-chute; Log Jamboree, log flume.

 Roller coasters: Batman the Ride, inverted (S); Dahlonega Mine train (S); Georgia Cyclone (W); Viper, shuttle loop (S); Ninja, multielement (S); Great American Scream Machine (W); Mindbender, 2-loop (S).

 Plan to stay: 8 hours.

 **Best way to avoid crowds:** Come early in the week, and see everything in one area the first time you visit it. Doubling back at a park this size is very time-consuming.

Directions: 12 miles west of Atlanta on I–20. Take Exit 7B (I–20 West) off Outerbelt I–285 and go about 2 miles to Exit 13. The park is 1 block south on Six Flags Road.

"Thunder River," Six Flags Over Georgia

Summer Waves
On Jekyll Island
Jekyll Island, GA (912) 635-3636

There's a lot to do on the state-owned island with the nickname of "Georgia's Coastal Family Playground." Located 6 miles off the Georgia coast, the island was the site of an exclusive summer resort where America's wealthiest families came to play from 1886–1942. Today, 33 of the original buildings still stand and can be seen in the historic district.

Summer Waves, an 11-acre waterpark, is a major draw to the island and is quite a popular attraction in this part of the state. Rides include Pirates Passage, a 5-story-tall, totally enclosed tube ride; the Force Three tube and body slides; the Slow Motion Ocean lazy river; and the Frantic Atlantic wave pool. There's also a large children's water activity pool.

Hungry? There's a McDonald's at Summer Waves!

In addition to the waterpark, you'll find 10 miles of beaches, the state's largest public golf resort, tennis courts, miniature golf, and 20 miles of scenic bicycling paths.

Open daily at 10:00 A.M. and closes at 7:00 P.M. during the week, 8:00 P.M. weekends. Admission, under $13, includes the use of tubes and mats.

 TIM'S TRIVIA

During an average season of 163 operating days, guests at Six Flags Over Georgia in Atlanta consume 200,000 pounds of hamburger, 100,000 pounds of cheese, 250,000 pizzas, 200,000 giant pretzels, and 5,000,000 soft drinks.

THE AMUSEMENT PARK GUIDE

Tybee Island Amusement Park
16th Street and Butler Avenue
Tybee Island, GA (912) 786–8806

Just 50 yards from the beach, this park is a must-see if you're in the area. It's a small, family-owned and -operated facility in the center of the business district. The locals have supported this park since its opening in 1965 and are very proud of it. A small roller coaster and a Ferris wheel are the most popular of the 13 rides.

Open daily during the summer, the park has free admission, with rides on a pay-as-you-go basis.

White Water
250 North Cobb Parkway
Marietta, GA (770) 424–9283

Waterpark fans consistently rank this beautiful facility among the best three waterparks in the world, year after year. Its location on a heavily wooded hillside makes it a scenic visit as well as a cool and refreshing one. Owned by the same folk who own the adjacent American Adventure park and Silver Dollar City and White Water in Branson, Missouri, everything here is top notch and well kept.

There are a total of 45 rides, slides, and water activities, including the Little Hooch lazy river; the Atlanta Ocean wave pool; the Tree House, a 4-story-tall interactive play area for the kids; and the Bahama Bobslide, a 6-person raft ride.

Open May through September, 10:00 A.M. to 8:00 P.M. Admission is under $22, with a special Nightwater pass available after 4:00 P.M., Monday through Friday, under $14. Special family nights are held during the season, with all adults needing children with them in order to get in. Special rates apply.

IDAHO

Silverwood Theme Park
North 26225 Highway 95
Athol, ID (208) 683-3400

Although there are quite a few parks that you can visit by boat, this may very well be the only amusement park in the country that you can visit by flying your own plane to it. Originally solely an airstrip, the facility now has 24 rides and some beautiful turn-of-the-century Victorian (reproduced) architecture.

TIM'S TRIVIA

Silverwood Theme Park, in Athol, Idaho, was an airstrip before being converted to an amusement park. Now glider rides are available from that airstrip for about $65 apiece.

Upon entering the park, visitors walk down Victorian Main Street, where they are greeted with shops, eateries, and a colorful carousel. They then can go to Kid's Korner, Country Carnival, or Northwest Adventure areas of the park.

 Special events: May through September.

 Operating hours: 11:00 A.M. to 6:00, 8:00, or 10:00 P.M., depending on season.

 Admission policy: Pay-one-price, under $22. Parking fee.

 Top rides: Ferris wheel; bumper boats; antique cars; a narrow-gauge steam train, taking you out into the wilderness, where you'll be robbed; carousel; Thunder Canyon, rapids ride; Roaring Creek, log flume.

 Roller coasters: The Corkscrew (S); The Grizzly (W).

THE AMUSEMENT PARK GUIDE

 Plan to stay: 6 hours.

 Best way to avoid crowds: Come during the week and avoid the holidays.

 Directions: 15 miles north of I–90 and Coeur d'Alene, on Highway 95. Located 40 miles northeast of Spokane, Washington.

ILLINOIS

Blackberry Historical Farm
Barnes Road
Aurora, IL (630) 892–1550

You'll take a step back into time when you enter the front gates of this 54-acre complex, whose theme is Midwest village life during 1840 to 1910. Numerous costumed guides and other old-time touches make this an educational as well as entertaining place to visit.

There are 4 rides, including a train and a carousel; in addition, there are pony and wagon rides, as well as a free petting zoo. Special events are scheduled most Sundays.

Pay-one-price, under $10. Open May to mid-October, 10:00 A.M. to 4:30 P.M.

Kiddieland
8400 West North Avenue
Melrose Park, IL (708) 343–8000

A colorful neon sign, with two neon kids hanging from it, greets visitors to this 17-acre park in suburban Chicago. Though founded in 1929 as a kiddie park, the facility has grown beyond that scope and now bills itself as a family park. This is one of the best maintained parks in the country!

As you enter the park, you'll pass a beautifully restored, circa-1925 Philadelphia Toboggan Company carousel on your left and, to your right, a wonderful little German carousel. The park offers 25 rides, including 13 for kids, along with a delightful play area called Volcano Playcenter.

 Extras: A large forest preserve, located across the street, offers picnic areas and barbecue pits.

Special events: Large fireworks display every July 4.

 Season: April through October.

 Operating hours: Hours and days of operation vary greatly. During peak summer, daily, 10:30 A.M. to 10:00 P.M.

 Admission policy: Pay-one-price, under $12.50. Free parking.

 Top rides: Pipeline, water-coaster slide; Log Jammer, flume ride; Race-A-Bouts, antique cars; Ferris wheel; bumper cars; Galleon, a swinging pirate ship; Tilt-A-Whirl.

 Roller coaster: Little Dipper, junior (W).

 Plan to stay: 3 hours.

 Best way to avoid crowds: The area's day-camp groups come at opening and leave at 2:30 P.M. From that time to 7:00 P.M. is usually the slowest time of the day.

 Directions: Located between the Eisenhower and Kennedy expressways, 15 miles from downtown Chicago. Take I–294 to the Eisenhower Expressway and go east to First Avenue. Go north on First until you reach the park, at the corner of North and First avenues.

Knight's Action Park
1700 Recreation Drive
Springfield, IL (217) 546–8881

The name Action Park aptly describes this 56-acre participatory amusement and waterpark. Everywhere you look, there's activity going on—for example, bumper boats, paddleboats, batting cages, go-karts, 6 water slides, a pair of 18-hole miniature golf courses, a golf driving range, several water activity pools, and an action river ride.

Admission to the action park is free, with rides and activities on a pay-as-you-go basis. Admission to Caribbean Adventure water area is pay-one-price, under $15.

The Amusement Park Guide

Six Flags Great America
I–95 & Route 132
Gurnee, IL (847) 249–1776
http://www.sixflags.com

American patriotism is the theme at this park, built in 1976 during America's bicentennial. The park is divided into six areas, each representing a different era in the nation's growth: Orleans Place, Yankee Harbor, Yukon Territory, Hometown Square, Southwest Territory, and County Fair. Rides, games, and food in each section have been designed with a corresponding theme.

Included in the 35 rides, the park's double-decked carousel is listed in the *Guinness Book of World Records* as one of the two tallest carousels in the world; the other carousel is at Paramount's Great America in Santa Clara, California. Although both parks were built in 1976 by the Marriott Corporation as exact duplicates, both have subsequently been sold to other concerns and have expanded in completely different ways.

The Looney Tunes characters are the official mascots of this, as well as the other, Six Flags parks and make their home in the children's play area, Bugs Bunny's Yukon Adventure.

Extras: The Southwest Territory is an 11-acre tribute to the Old West. There's a high-tech Western Stunt Show, the Viper wooden roller coaster, and 4 other rides.

Special events: FrightFest, weekends in October.

Season: The end of April through October.

Operating hours: 10:00 A.M. to 9:00 or 10:00 P.M.

Admission policy: Pay-one-price, under $33. Parking charge.

Top rides: Giant Drop, free-fall; Space Shuttle America, a simulated trip to the moon; Sky Trek Tower, a 330-foot-tall observation ride; Sky Whirl, a 3-armed Ferris wheel; Splashwater Falls, shoot-the-chute; Ameri-Go-Round, a circa-1910 Dentzel carousel; Roaring Rapids, a raging-rapids ride; Logger's Run, a log flume.

Roller coasters: Batman The Ride, inverted (S); Demon, loop/corkscrew (S); American Eagle, twin racing (W); Iron Wolf, stand-up (S); Shock Wave, multi-element (S); Viper (W); Whizzer, speedracer (S).

 Plan to stay: 8 hours.

 Best way to avoid crowds: Come midmorning or midafternoon on Friday, Wednesday, or Thursday.

 Directions: Located between Chicago and Milwaukee on I–94 at Route 132 East (Grand Avenue).

"The Great Gasp," Six Flags Over Georgia

THE AMUSEMENT PARK GUIDE

Three Worlds of Santa's Village
Racing Rapids
Routes 25 & 72
Dundee, IL (847) 426–6751

Santa Claus shows up to work here every day the park is open. He can be found in his air-conditioned summer cottage. Close by, you'll find a frozen North Pole, which provides a great photo spot!

The 55-acre, heavily wooded park has three distinct areas, of which Santa's Village, with its Christmas decorations and lollipop architecture, is the oldest and most picturesque. The other two areas are Old MacDonald's Farm, containing a large petting zoo and animal rides, and Coney Island, where most of the park's 28 family-oriented rides are located.

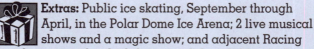 **Extras:** Public ice skating, September through April, in the Polar Dome Ice Arena; 2 live musical shows and a magic show; and adjacent Racing Rapids waterpark, which features slides, children's play areas, Grand Prix go-karts, lazy river, and bumper boats.

 Season: Mid-May through September.

 Operating hours: 10:00 A.M. to 6:00 P.M. or dusk.

 Admission policy: Pay-one-price, under $15. A combination ticket for both parks is available, under $20. Free parking.

 Top rides: Fire Trucks, a full-size antique fire engine pulling tramlike cars into a neighborhood where a house is on fire; the kids have water hoses and put the fire out while squirting at it from their seats. Additional rides of note include a horse-powered carousel and the Snowball, a Cuddle-Up ride with a winter theme; and a Galleon Pirate Ship.

 Roller coaster: Galaxy, compact family ride (S).

 Plan to stay: 5 hours.

Best way to avoid crowds: Visit on weekdays and after Labor Day.

 Directions: Located 45 minutes from downtown Chicago among the tall timbers of the Fox River Valley area. Take the Route 25 exit off I–90 at Elgin; go north 2 miles to the intersection of Routes 25 and 72.

INDIANA

Adventureland
Highway 13
North Webster, IN
(219) 834–2554 (800) 566–2551

In a resort area that boasts 101 lakes, one can only imagine how many people come directly from the beaches or their boats to this park in order to experience additional fun and adventure. Founded as a miniature golf course in 1966, the 12-acre park has added attractions regularly. It now offers 13 rides, plus bumper boats, trampolines, 3 arcade buildings, batting cages, a go-kart track, a pair of 18-hole miniature golf courses, and a 50-minute sternwheel paddleboat ride on Lake Webster aboard the Dixie.

 TIM'S TRIVIA

There are three Adventurelands in the United States: in East Farmingdale, New York; in Des Moines, Iowa; and in North Webster, Indiana.

 Season: May through September.

 Operating hours: Noon to 11:00 P.M.

 Admission policy: Free gate, with rides and attractions on a pay-as-you-go basis. Pay-one-price also available from 6:00 to 11:00 P.M., under

THE AMUSEMENT PARK GUIDE

$10 (but does not include miniature golf, Dixie, or go-karts). Free parking.

 Top rides: Roll-O-Plane; Rock-O-Plane; Octopus; Tilt-A-Whirl; bumper boats; The Little Dipper, small kiddie coaster.

 Plan to stay: 3 hours.

 Best way to avoid crowds: Come during the afternoon, when most of the others are enjoying the lakes. Big business here is after dark.

 Directions: Take Highway 13 north out of Webster. The park is located 8 miles north of Highway 30, on your right.

Bear Creek Farms
Off Route 67
Bryant, IN (800) 288–7630

Deep in the heart of Indiana farm country, this resort provides all sorts of old-fashioned country fun for all members of the family. The Country Fair area is where the 9 rides are located, including 5 for the little ones. Don't miss the miniature train, which takes visitors around the entire complex.

In addition to the rides, Bear Creek Farms features shopping at more than a dozen unique shops, 2 sit-down restaurants, animal displays, farming demonstrations, and several live shows. There are also overnight lodging and RV facilities.

Admission is free, with all rides on a pay-as-you-go basis. Pay-one-price available on Wednesdays and Fridays, under $5. Rides operate May through September, with the rest of the resort open February through December.

Columbian Park
1915 Scott Street
Lafayette, IN (317) 771-2220

The activities offered here are basically what you'd expect in a large municipal park—swimming pool, tennis courts, a small zoo, playing fields, a playground, and a picnic area. But what makes this park excel over most other city parks is that you'll also find an amusement area here with 15 rides.

Among the more popular rides are the Dark Ride and the Turnpike. The 6 kiddie rides, along with the train and carousel, are located in their own fenced area, allowing you to turn the kids loose to enjoy themselves without worrying about them wandering off. Other attractions include a petting zoo and a miniature golf course.

Free admission, with rides on a per-ride basis, or a pay-one-price is available, under $10, including the use of the swimming pool. The park is open year-round; the rides run May through September. Hours vary, so call first.

Fort Wayne Children's Zoo
3411 Sherman Boulevard
Fort Wayne, IN (219) 427-6800

In reality, this place is more of an animal theme park than a traditional zoo facility. There are three themed areas, including the Australian Adventure, the Indonesian Rain Forest, and the African Veldt.

Among the 5 rides are a miniature train journey through the woods, a Log Ride through the Australian outback, and a Jeep Ride through the African Veldt. Of particular interest is the Endangered Species Carousel, one of the few hand-carved wood carousels manufactured in the past 70 years. Rather than horses, the carousel features 17 different endangered species such as elephants, pea fowl, giant pandas, and tapirs.

There are a gift shop, several snack bars, and a lot of nicely shaded areas to sit and rest for awhile. Admission to the zoo is under $5, with each of the rides costing $1 to ride. Open daily 9:00 A.M. to 5:00 P.M., late-April through mid-October.

THE AMUSEMENT PARK GUIDE

Fun Spot Amusement Park
County Road 200W
Angola, IN (219) 833-2972

A relatively new park, this 68-acre facility has much to offer and, according to the owner, is only going to get bigger and better in the years to come.

With an eye to history, the owner is building a traditional family park here, one distinguished by quality, color, and traditional values. In creating the landscaping, special care is being taken to add color and texture to the existing rides and buildings.

The park offers 19 rides, including a special children's area in which 4 of the smaller rides are under a covered pavilion. There are 2 arcades and a beach volleyball area, as well as Alec's Ark, a petting zoo.

Extras: Go-karts, miniature golf, and batting cages, all at extra charge. A big neon sign points out the arcade, a facility, the owner says, that is the largest air-conditioned arcade in the state.

Special events: 2 major fireworks shows each year: Memorial Day and July 4.

Season: May through Labor Day.

Operating hours: Opens daily at 10:00 A.M.; closes at 10:00 P.M., or between 6:00 and 8:00 P.M., depending on weather and crowds. Closed Mondays.

Admission policy: Small gate admission, with rides on a pay-as-you-go basis. Pay-one-price also available, under $10. Free parking.

Top rides: Tilt-A-Whirl; Ferris wheel; Paratrooper; dual-flume water slide; Scrambler; bumper cars.

Roller coasters: Afterburner, shuttle loop (S); Zyklon, family (S).

Plan to stay: 4 hours.

Best way to avoid crowds: Come during the week. Lines are usually long only on holidays.

Directions: Take Exit 150 off I-69, and follow County Road 220W ¾ mile to the park. Located 40 miles north of Ft. Wayne.

Holiday World and Splashin' Safari
Routes 162 and 245
Santa Claus, IN
(812) 937–4401; (800) GO-SANTA

Opened in 1946 as Santa Claus Land, this park has evolved into a unique salute to some of the biggest holidays of the year. The three sections of the 100-acre park—Christmas, Halloween, and Fourth of July—are loaded with rides, attractions, architecture, and eateries representative of those holidays.

Nine of the 21 rides are kiddie rides, located in a children's area called Rudolph's Reindeer Ranch; each of the rides is named after one of Santa's reindeer.

 Extras: Splashin' Safari is a 15-acre waterpark, with 7 water attractions, including a wave pool, action river, and the 60-foot-tall Watubee, a family raft ride. Free, with park admission. A petting zoo, a wax museum, an antique toy collection, and an opportunity to meet Santa Claus, all for no additional charge. The Santa Claus Post Office, located just outside the gates of the park, is a wonderful place from which to send your postcards or Christmas cards, stamped with a unique postmark.

 Season: May through October.

 Operating hours: 10:00 A.M. Closing times vary.

 Admission policy: Pay-one-price, under $20. Free parking.

 Top rides: Raging Rapids, a raging-rapids ride with a western theme; Frightful Falls, a log flume; Banshee, a 360-degree pendulum ride in which riders stay upright.

 Roller coaster: Raven (W); Firecracker (S).

 Plan to stay: 5 hours.

 Best way to avoid crowds: Because the front section, Santa Land, is usually less crowded, start your day in the other areas and then work your way back to the front. Less crowded times are midweek and fall and spring weekends.

THE AMUSEMENT PARK GUIDE

Directions: Located in the southwestern part of the state about 7 miles off I–64. Take the U.S. 231 or Indiana 162 exits off the interstate and head south to the park entrance, where the two roads meet.

Indiana Beach
306 Indiana Beach Drive
Monticello, IN (219) 583–4141
http://dcwi.com/~IB/welcome.html.

A traditional lakeside resort complex, Indiana Beach features a 32-ride amusement park, a motel, cottages, and campgrounds. The park, situated next to the 1,400-acre Lake Shafer, has been run by the same family since its founding in 1926.

The rides and attractions are along the ½-mile boardwalk that runs beside the lake. A large Ferris wheel is located at the end of the boardwalk on a point out in the lake; at night, the lights from the wheel can be seen for miles. The waterpark has 6 slides and a 1,670-foot-long action river, and the large swimming pool has a sand beach.

Extras: Miniature golf, Skycoaster; jet skis; Dr. Frankenstein's Castle (a great spooky walk-through), boat tag, all at extra charge. Waterpark and beach, extra charge.

Special events: Fireworks, July 4; Anniversary Sunday, closest Sunday to June 18, when all rides are 25 cents each from 4:00 P.M. to closing.

Season: May through Labor Day.

Operating hours: Rides are open 11:00 A.M. to 11:00 P.M. daily. The beach opens at 9:00 A.M.; the waterpark, at 10:00 A.M.

Admission policy: General admission, plus rides, waterpark, and beach on a pay-as-you-go basis. A 7-hour, pay-one-price ticket also available, under $13. Free parking.

Top rides: Superstition Mountain and Mystery Mansion, 2 dark rides; *Shafer Queen*, a paddle-wheel excursion on Lake Shafer; Flume, a log flume; Falling Star, a 360-degree looping ride in which the rider always stays upright; Gondola Wheel, a Ferris wheel with gondola cars.

Roller coasters: Hoosier Hurricane (W); Tiger, family (S); Galaxy, family (S).

 Plan to stay: 8 hours, if you use the waterpark.

 Best way to avoid crowds: Come midweek or anytime in early June or late August.

 Directions: Take Route 24 to the 6th Street exit in Monticello. Go north through town to the lake; the park is on your right. Located 95 miles north-west of Indianapolis and 120 miles from Chicago.

 # TIM'S TRIVIA

The Raven at Holiday World, Santa Claus, Indiana, is the only Edgar Allan Poe themed roller coaster in the world.

Indianapolis Zoo
1200 West Washington
Indianapolis, IN (317) 630–2001

In addition to the fun and excitement the zoo itself provides, this facility has a beautifully restored, 1910 Parker carousel, a train ride, bumper boats, and camel, pony, and elephant rides. It's located on 64 acres, a few blocks from downtown.

The zoo and rides are open every day of the year, weather permitting, with peak season hours of 9:00 A.M. to 6:00 P.M. Pay-one-price, under $10. Parking charge. Small additional fee for the rides.

THE AMUSEMENT PARK GUIDE

River Fair Family Fun Park
Indoors at the River Falls Mall
I–65 and Route 131
Clarksville, IN (812) 284–3247

Turn-of-the-century southern Indiana is the theme here, and there's plenty for all to do in that nostalgic atmosphere. In addition to the 6 kiddie rides, there's an 18-hole minia-ture golf course, remote-control boats, and Indy cars. Hooper and Hanna Belle Hound are the costumed character mascots, with one being around most weekdays, and both being present on weekends.

A grand carousel is the park's centerpiece; a train ride takes you under a waterfall, around the golf course, and through a tunnel; and the River Belle Fun Boat is a custom-created participatory play area for the kids.

For the hungry, there's a 10-merchant food court adjacent to the park. Free admission, with rides and attractions on a pay-as-you-play basis. Pay-one-price tickets also avail-able, under $7, not including golf. Open during mall hours.

"Raptor," Cedar Point, Ohio

IOWA

Adventureland
I–80 & Highway 65
Des Moines, IA (515) 266–2121

As you walk into the park and under the railroad tracks, you'll be looking at historical Iowa. Every building along Main Street is a replica of an actual building from somewhere in the state at the turn of the century. Add to that nostalgic feeling the 15,000 flowering plants, the majestic trees, and the large expanses of well-groomed grass areas and you've got yourself the most visited amusement park in the state.

Adventureland has 32 rides in six areas: Farm, Alpine, Old Frontier, River City, Dragon Island, and Outlaw Gulch.

 Extras: A nice picnic area lies next to the parking lot, outside the gate. A hotel and RV camping facilities are also on the property. Don't miss the distorted mirror maze, located at the exit of the Dragon roller coaster in the back of the park; as people get off the coaster, they look at the mirrors and are dismayed to see what the Dragon did to them.

 Season: May through September.

 Operating hours: 10:00 A.M. to 10:00 P.M.

 Admission policy: Pay-one-price, under $20. Parking charge.

 Top rides: Lady Luck, a roulette wheel–themed Trabant, a spinning platform ride; Silly Silo, a rotor inside a silo; Raging River, a raging-rapids ride; the Log Flume; Galleon Pirate Ship; Giant Gondola Wheel; Falling Star.

 Roller coasters: The Underground, indoor (W); Dragon, 2-loop (S); The Outlaw (W); Tornado (W); Galaxy, compact (S).

 Plan to stay: 6½ hours.

THE AMUSEMENT PARK GUIDE

Best way to avoid crowds: Tuesday is the least crowded day. Once you leave the Main Street area, go through the park in a clockwise fashion.

Directions: Take Exit 142A (Highway 65) off I–80, east of Des Moines. The park is at that intersection.

Arnolds Park
Highway 71 & Lake Street
Arnolds Park, IA (712) 332-2183

The good-time feelings of yesteryear will be with you once you enter this lakeside resort amusement park. Your visit here will be nothing short of first-class fun.

Located on the shores of Lake Okoboji, the park has 20 rides, including 9 for kids that are set off in their own kiddieland. If you wish, come by boat, there's plenty of dockside parking available.

The park, which has been completely restored, is especially beautiful at night, with all its lights and sounds. It also has one of the most interesting parking-lot entrances around. To enter, you drive under a sign mounted on the side of a section of reconstructed roller coaster, complete with two coaster trains climbing the hill. The sign proclaims that you're entering AN IOWA CLASSIC.

Extras: Go-karts and miniature golf, available for extra charge. The Tipsy House and the Haunted House of Mirrors are unusual walk-through attractions that shouldn't be missed; both are included in the admission fee. Officials say the Pirate's Cove Sandbox is the world's largest; a McDonald's franchise and a Godfather's Pizza are inside the park.

Special events: July 4 fireworks; monthly car shows; a monthly concert series.

Season: Mid-May through early September.

Operating hours: Opens at noon daily; closes at 9:00 P.M. on weekdays and at 11:00 P.M. on Fridays and Saturdays.

Admission policy: Pay-one-price, under $15. Free car and boat parking.

Top rides: Gondola Ferris wheel providing a splendid view of the lake; bumper cars; Paratrooper; Tilt-A-Whirl; and the Bug House.

Roller coasters: The Legend (W).

Plan to stay: 5 hours.

Best way to avoid crowds: This is a compact park, involving not too much walking, but during peak times, the midways can get crowded. Early June, before the resort cabins fill up, is a good time to visit; during the season, Wednesdays are usually less crowded.

Directions: Take the Jackson Mountain exit off I–90 and go south on Route 71 to the park.

KANSAS

Carousel Park
95th Street & Metcalfe
Metcalfe South Shopping Center
Overland, KS (913) 385–7275

Rejoice parents, there is life on a rainy day! Bring the kids and have some fun, no matter what the weather is like outside. All the action here is indoors. There are 8 rides, including bumper cars, a carousel, and the Dragon Coaster. Also featured is a children's play area.

Admission is free, with rides on a pay-one-price system, under $9. Open Wednesday through Sunday during the summer months, and Friday through Sunday year-round, 10:00 A.M. to 9:00 P.M.

THE AMUSEMENT PARK GUIDE

Joyland
2801 South Hillside
Wichita, KS (316) 684-0179

If you're looking for a well-run traditional park in this neck of the woods, you've found it here. A family-owned and -operated park, Joyland finds that most of its business is local, including various company and industrial picnics.

The park has lots of shade, colorful landscaping, and 23 rides, including 10 for kids.

 Extras: Go-karts, extra charge. Turn-of-the-century, restored Wurlitzer Band Organ, "played" daily by Louie the Clown.

 Special events: Easter Egg Hunt, April.

 Season: April through mid-October.

 Operating hours: 2:00 to 10:00 P.M. on weekends and holidays and 6:00 to 10:00 P.M. on weekdays. Closed Monday and Tuesday.

 Admission policy: General admission charge, with rides on a pay-as-you-go basis. Pay-one-price "Ride-a-Rama" ticket also available, under $10 for weekdays, under $13 for weekends. Free parking.

 Top rides: Log Jam, a flume ride; Wacky Shack, a dark ride; Paratrooper.

 Roller coaster: Roller Coaster (W).

 Plan to stay: 4 hours.

 Best way to avoid crowds: Come during the week.

 Directions: Take Exit K15 off the Kansas Turnpike; go east on Route 15 to 31st Street. Then go east to Hillside Avenue and north 5 blocks to the park.

Theel Kiddieland
103 Central at Spruce
Leavenworth, KS (913) 682–4351

Theel Manufacturing Company, a builder of amusement rides, set up this little park of 9 rides in 1951 as a display showcase for its own products and found that the neighborhood loved it. Since then, it has become a traditional place to take the kids. In addition to the mechanical rides, there are Shetland pony rides. And a miniature train takes riders under "the world's largest Dinosaur Rex" for added thrill.

Open daily Memorial Day through Labor Day, 6:00 to 9:00 P.M. Free admission, pay-as-you-go on rides.

TIM'S TRIVIA

Amusement parks are alive and well on the Internet! There are more than 300 parks and amusement ride related pages. To find them, search http//www.yahoo.com for "Amusement Parks" or for a link to more than 30 official and unofficial Disney sites, search for "Disney Parks."

KENTUCKY

Guntown Mountain
I–65 & Highway 70
Cave City, KY (502) 773–3530

The Old West comes alive at the top of a mountain here in middle Kentucky. The 10 rides are at the base of the mountain, and the entertainment and the western town are at the top, via a chair lift. If the ride to the top looks too scary, a bus will transport you.

 Extras: Onyx Cave lies beneath the property; guided tours are given hourly. Admission to the traditional old haunted house is included in the all-day pass.

Season: May through mid-October.

 Operating hours: Daily, 10:00 A.M. to 9:00 P.M.

 Admission policy: General admission, plus rides, or a pay-one-price ticket, under $15. Free parking.

 Top rides: Tilt-A-Whirl; a train that takes you on a scenic ride around the mountain, with a stop at a petting zoo deep in the woods; Kiddie Whip, a classic kiddie ride; and a Haunted House walk-through.

 Plan to stay: 3 hours for rides and shows, 4 hours if you go on the cave tour.

Directions: Located within view of I–65. Take Exit 53 (Highway 70), west to the entrance.

Kentucky Kingdom
Hurricane Bay Waterpark
Kentucky State Fairgrounds
Louisville, KY
(502) 366–2231/(800) SCREAMS

Because of its arsenal of huge, world-class rides, this place is often referred to as the "biggest small amusement park in America." Originally confined only to a small corner of the fairgrounds, the park has expanded beyond the boundaries and now offers a great lineup of rides and attractions, including 5 roller coasters, 33 rides, and Hurricane Bay waterpark with a wave pool and 11 different water activities.

Even before you enter, you'll see the tall rides looming over the shaded midways. As you come through the front gate, you'll see the Hellavator, the world's first new generation free-fall ride. Behind that, King Louie's Playground, the kiddieland, has a daily live stage show and several distinct rides, including the Concert Carousel. Instead of riding animals, you ride oversized orchestra instruments, including tubas and drums.

 Extras: The Top Eliminator Dragster attraction allows you to drag race against five others in a full-size dragster. You'll race 400 feet, achieving

speeds of 75 mph in 2.8 seconds. There is an extra fee.
The Day 5 Alive Teen Dance is held each Friday night,
with special admission price after 6:00 P.M.

 Special events: Halloscream, weekends in
October.

 Season: April through October.

 Operating hours: Opens daily at 11:00 A.M., closes
Sunday through Thursday at 9:00 P.M.; Saturday
and Sunday, at 11:00 P.M. Waterpark opens daily
at 11:00 A.M., and closes at either 6:00 or 7:00 P.M.

 Admission policy: Pay-one-price, under $25.
Waterpark is included in park admission.
Parking charge.

 Top rides: The Hellavator, a free-fall with your
feet dangling below your chair; Mile High Falls,
shoot-the-chute; Giant Gondola Wheel; Squid, a
four-slide, wet/dry water ride.

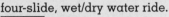

 Roller coasters: Chang, stand-up (S); T2, inverted
(S); Thunder Run (W); Vampire, Boomerang (S);
Roller Skater, family (S).

 Plan to stay: 6 hours.

 Best way to avoid crowds: Come early during the
week. Go directly to the back of the park, and
ride the big rides first and work your way to the
front. Because of its location near the main gate, the
Hellavator has the longest lines early and just before the
park closes.

 Directions: Take the Watterson Expressway
(I–264) exit off I–65, south of downtown Louisville.
Follow the signs to the Kingdom.

 # TIM'S TRIVIA

*Two American amusement parks have
cave tours as part of their offerings.
Guntown Mountain, in Cave City, Kentucky, has Onyx
Cave, and Silver Dollar City, in Branson, Missouri, has
Marvel Cave.*

LOUISIANA

Blue Bayou
18142 Perkins Road
Baton Rouge, LA (504) 753-3333

As Louisiana's largest waterpark, the 40-acre Blue Bayou has quite a selection of family rides, slides, and water activities.

There are 11 adult slides; the Hurricane Bay wave pool, an action tubing river; and Polliwog Pond, a children's activity pool area. In addition, a large family activity pool features many play elements including diving platforms and rope climbs. Two restaurants serve up fun-food, Louisiana style, and the picnic pavilion is the largest in this part of the state.

Open June through Labor Day, from 10:00 A.M. to 6:00 P.M.; admission is under $15.

Carousel Gardens
City Park, #1 Dreyfous
New Orleans, LA (504) 482-4888

Tucked away in a shaded corner of the huge City Park lies this small family amusement park, mostly hidden by the large oak trees. Restored in 1988, the park looks like a turn-of-the-century facility, complete with brick sidewalks. It has 8 rides, including a 1910 Carmel/Looff antique carousel that's housed in a vintage, beautifully renovated carousel building. A 20-minute train ride takes you out of the amusement park, around the large City Park, and across several of its bayous.

Adjacent to the amusement park is Storyland, a storybook park with puppet shows, roving entertainers, and costumed characters.

Gate admission fee, plus rides on a pay-as-you-go basis. Hours vary; call first.

Fun Fair Park
8475 Florida Boulevard
Baton Rouge, LA (504) 924-6266

At one time, this cozy park was surrounded by woods. Now it's across the street from one of the city's major malls and surrounded by commercial developments.

The 7 kiddie rides, covered by a large pavilion, form the centerpiece of a booming birthday party business. The 8 other rides are located on the other side of the 6-acre park.

 Extras: Midway offering games of skill.

 Season: Mid-March through mid-October for all rides. The kiddie rides are also open during winter.

 Operating hours: Major rides open at 6:00 P.M. on weekdays and 1:00 P.M. on weekends. Kiddie rides open at 10:00 A.M. on weekdays and 1:00 P.M. on weekends. All rides close at 10:00 P.M. nightly.

 Admission policy: Free gate, with a pay-as-you-play policy. Pay-one-price also available, under $10. Free parking.

 Top rides: Pirate Ship; Tilt-A-Whirl; bumper cars; Paratrooper; Spider.

 Plan to stay: 2 hours.

 Best way to avoid crowds: Come during the week.

 Directions: Take the Airline Highway exit off I-12. Follow the highway north until you cross the Florida Boulevard overpass. Make the first exit to your left and you'll see the park.

THE AMUSEMENT PARK GUIDE

Hamel's Park
3232 East 70th Street
Shreveport, LA (318) 869-3566

If you appreciate large oak and elm trees in the amusement parks you frequent, you'll love this 30-acre family facility. Located across the parkway from the Red River, the 20 rides are built into the environment, thereby offering a great deal of green and open spaces throughout. The well-maintained park has a nice selection of rides for the entire family, with 6 kiddie rides located inside a 12,000-square-foot building.

 Extras: The go-kart track here may be one of the best at any amusement park in the country. The carts run down between tall, landscaped levees, not only making the track interesting to run but also keeping the noise away from the rest of the park.

 Special events: JuneTeenth, black cultural celebration, Father's Day; Country Music Festival, late June; Labor Day Outing, a labor-union event sponsored by the local newspaper.

 Season: Mid-March through mid-October.

 Operating hours: Open 6:00 to 10:00 P.M. Wednesday through Friday, 11:00 A.M. to 10:00 P.M. Saturday, and 1:00 to 6:00 P.M. Sunday. Closed Monday and Tuesday.

 Admission policy: Small gate fee, with rides on a pay-as-you-go basis. Pay-one-price also available, under $12. Special pay-one-price promotions offered during the week. Free parking.

 Top rides: A Ferris wheel; bumper cars; a train ride around the park and through a tunnel; a log flume; Gravitron.

 Roller coaster: Thunderail, Zyklon family (S).

 Plan to stay: 3 hours.

Best way to avoid crowds: Come during the week or in early June or late August, when the crowds are smallest. Even on weekends, though, unless there is a major promotion going on, the lines here are rarely long.

Directions: Located in the southeast corner of the city on the north side of the 70th Street Bridge. Take the Market Street exit off I–20; then take Highway 1 South to 70th Street (Route 511) and turn left. Go 2 miles to the park.

MAINE

Funtown USA
Splashtown
774 Portland Road
Saco, ME (207) 284–5139

Myriad attractions will keep you busy in this small, nicely maintained family park that has been around since 1967. Plenty of shaded picnic areas are well spaced among the 17 adult and family rides and 11 kiddie rides.

Splashtown is located adjacent to the amusement park and offers 10 water attractions, including a heated swimming pool.

 Extras: A large game arcade; go-karts, extra charge.

 Special events: Mother's Day, May; Father's Day, June; Shriner's Day, June; Boy Scout Day, June.

 Season: May through mid-September.

 Operating hours: 10:30 A.M. to 11:00 P.M.

 Admission policy: Free gate at Funtown, with rides and attractions on a pay-as-you-go basis. Pay-one-price also available, under $20. A combination pass for unlimited use of both parks, under $25. Splashtown only, under $15. Free parking.

 Top rides: Thunderfalls, a log flume; Astrosphere, an indoor Scrambler with a light show and music; Flying Trapeze, flying swings; Ferris wheel; Tea Cups; and a carousel.

The Amusement Park Guide

 Roller coaster: family (S).

 Plan to stay: 4 hours.

 Best way to avoid crowds: The slowest days of the week are Monday, Tuesday, and Friday.

 Directions: Take I–95 to Exit 5, which is a spur of the interstate. Take that to Exit 2B (Highway 1) and go north about 1 mile.

Palace Playland
Old Orchard Street
Old Orchard Beach, ME (207) 934–2001

The present owners have built a top-notch, well-maintained amusement park here, following a disastrous fire in 1972 that destroyed much of the original oceanfront park. Colorful flags, plenty of flower boxes, and a boardwalk separating the beach from the ride area makes this a nice, relaxing place to visit. Besides the 26 rides and a 3-flume water slide, the park has a large arcade building that houses more than 200 video games and games of skill.

 Extras: The fun house is a noteworthy walk-through attraction. Fireworks every Thursday night at 9:30.

 Season: Late-May through Labor Day.

 Operating hours: 11:00 A.M. or noon to 11:00 P.M.

 Admission policy: Free admission, with rides and attractions on a pay-as-you-go basis. Pay-one-price also available, under $18. Paid parking on the street and at various city lots.

 Top rides: A circa-1910 Philadelphia Toboggan Company carousel, in beautiful condition; Pirate, a swinging pirate ship; Matterhorn. A 72 ft. Gondola Ferris wheel provides a gorgeous view of the ocean and the long stretch of beach.

Roller coaster: Galaxi, family (S).

 Plan to stay: 5 hours.

 Best way to avoid crowds: The park is least crowded on Mondays, with just enough people and just enough sun to make the outing fun.

 Directions: Exit 5 (Route 195) off I–95 at Old Orchard Beach. Follow to the Route 5 intersection, go north to Old Orchard. The park is located on the beach at the dead end of Old Orchard Street.

York's Wild Kingdom Zoo and Amusement Park
Route 1
York Beach, ME (800) 456–4911

You'll find a wild time here. From wild and hairy animals to wild and scary rides, this 100-acre complex contains not only the state's largest zoo but also a great little ride area. There are 15 rides, including 9 just for the little members of the family.

 Extras: Miniature golf and paddleboats, free with ride package purchase. Go-karts, elephant and pony rides, extra fee. Elephant show three times a day.

 Season: Rides, Memorial Day through Labor Day. Zoo, May through Columbus Day.

 Operating hours: Rides: Noon to 10:00 P.M.; zoo: 10:00 A.M. to 5:00 P.M.

 Admission policy: Admission to the rides part of the park is free, with a pay-one-price ticket available. Zoo admission extra. Combination ride and zoo tickets also available, under $15.

 Top rides: Ferris wheel; Scrambler; merry-go-ground; go-karts; bumper cars.

 Roller coaster: Flitzer, family (S).

THE AMUSEMENT PARK GUIDE

 Plan to stay: 2 to 3 hours to visit the zoo and ride the rides.

 Best way to avoid crowds: Come on weekdays during July and August.

 Directions: Take the York exit off I–95; go east on Exit Road to Route 1 and proceed 2½ miles north.

MARYLAND

Adventure World
Paradise Island Waterpark
13710 Central Avenue
Largo, MD (301) 249–1500

Originally operated by naturalist Jim Fowler and called the Wildlife Preserve, the park now consists of 7 different areas with 31 adult rides and 15 kiddie rides. You'll find a nice mix of activities spread out over 68 wooded, rolling acres, including the Paradise Island Waterpark. Skull Island, the newest area in the park, is pirate-themed and has a new, unique flume ride that reverses direction several times during the ride.

 # TIM'S TRIVIA

Adventure World in Largo, Maryland, is a real sweetheart of an amusement park. Three couples have gotten married on its Wild One wooden roller coaster; one couple got married in its wave pool; and one couple tied the knot on Paradise Island, the park's waterpark.

Purchased by Premier Parks in 1994, the park has undergone wonderful changes, including a name change from Wild World.

 Extras: There are several shows, including the Crazy Horse Saloon, where you'll also find a buffet, featuring tasty BBQ; The Sahara Speedway, go-kart track, for additional fee; the themed Monsoon Lagoon wave pool in the waterpark; and the Wild West Stunt Show.

 Special events: Christian Youth Day, Memorial Day weekend; Gospel Day, early June; Fireworks, July 4; and Hallowscream, throughout October.

 Season: May through October.

 Operating hours: Opens at 10:30 A.M. daily; closes at 9:00 P.M. during the week, later on weekends.

 Admission policy: Pay-one-price, under $25. All waterpark attractions are included in park admission. Parking charge.

 Top rides: Skull Island Flume, a reversing flume/river rapids ride; Rainbow Zoom Flume; Flying Carousel, swing ride; Renegade Rapids, river rapids; Tower of Doom, 150-foot-tall-free fall; Shipwreck Falls, shoot-the-chute.

 Roller coasters: Mind Eraser, inverted (S); Python, shuttle loop (S); Wild One (W); Cannonball, junior (S).

 Plan to stay: 7 hours.

 Best way to avoid crowds: Monday is the slowest day. Most people enjoy the waterpark during midday when it's the hottest, and ride the rides in the morning and evening. To avoid lines, do the opposite.

 Directions: Take Exit 15A off I–95; follow the signs to the park. Located 15 minutes from Washington, D.C., and 30 minutes from Baltimore.

The Baltimore Zoo
Druid Park Lake Drive
Baltimore, MD (410) 396–7102

This wonderful zoo is the third oldest in the country, but its new children's zoo is state of the art and is considered the best of its kind in the country. In addition to the animals and exhibits here, you'll find 2 rides, an antique carousel, and a train.

Admission to the zoo is pay-one-price, under $7.50. Rides are extra. Hours of rides vary; call first.

THE AMUSEMENT PARK GUIDE

Frontier Town Western Park
Route 611
Ocean City, MD (410) 289-7877

The Old West comes back to life here each summer when the sounds of the train whistle and gunfire fills the air. Besides the train, stagecoach, and horseback rides (extra fee), there are pony rides, paddleboat rides on the lake, and a lot of action throughout the park. Live shows include gunfights, a can-can musical show, an Indian show, and a rodeo.

Pay-one-price, under $10. Call for hours and days of operation.

Jolly Roger Amusement Park
Splash Mountain
30th Street & Coastal Highway
Ocean City, MD (410) 289-3477

Don't let the name fool you—you won't find too many pirates around here, at least not the bad kind. What you *will* find is a 38-acre park providing plenty to keep you and your family busy. The park is divided into three areas: the ride section, including 36 rides for the entire family; Splash Mountain, a waterpark containing 15 slides and activities; and Speed World, featuring gas-powered cars and boats. With 16 tracks and 400 go-karts, Speed World is the largest go-kart complex on the East Coast.

Note: The facility is quite flat and offers little shade; be sure to dress appropriately. And the walkways between the rides are crushed stone; thus, if you're with someone in a wheelchair, or are using a stroller for your small child, you'll want to plan accordingly.

 Extras: 2 miniature golf courses: Jungle Golf and Treasure Hunt, extra charge. Bumper boats and speedboats, extra charge.

 Season: The ride section and waterpark are open Memorial Day through Labor Day; other facilities, open Easter through Labor Day.

 Operating hours: Noon to midnight.

 Admission policy: Rides and attractions on a pay-as-you-go basis. Pay-one-price for rides available. Free parking.

 Top rides: Water Flume, a log flume; Tilt-A-Whirl; bumper cars; Swing Ride, a wave swinger; Himalaya; Pirate Ship; Spider.

Roller coaster: Zyklon, family (S).

 Plan to stay: 8 hours.

 Best way to avoid crowds: The least busy days are Friday and Saturday.

 Directions: Follow Route 50 across the bridge into Ocean City. When the highway ends, take Philadelphia Avenue north (it becomes the Coastal Highway) to 30th Street; the park is on the left.

Ocean Pier Rides
401 South Boardwalk
Ocean City, MD (410) 289–3031

Talk about a multipurpose pier! As you walk off the boardwalk onto this pier, you'll pass the games, then the rides, and at the very end, you'll find an area set aside for fishing.

Located in the heart of the Old Town section of the city, the park started out as a ballroom-dancing pavilion in the early 1900s; the rides were added in the 1930s. Currently there are 11 major rides.

 Extras: A walk-through fun house, and The Ghost, a 2-level ride through haunted house.

 Season: Easter through the third week of September.

 Operating hours: Rides open at 1:00 P.M., with closing times depending on crowds and weather.

 Admission policy: Free admission, rides on a pay-as-you-go basis. Pay-one-price available during the week, under $10.

 Top rides: Hurricane, a Himalaya with pictures of Ocean City storms of the past; Giant Wheel, a Ferris wheel; 1001 Nights, a 360-degree platform ride; Venetian Carousel, an Italian double-deck carousel; Venturer motion-based simulator.

 Roller coaster: Looping Star, 1-loop (S).

THE AMUSEMENT PARK GUIDE

 Plan to stay: 4 hours.

 Best way to avoid crowds: Tuesdays and Wednesdays are the slowest days.

 Directions: Follow Route 50 across the bridge into Ocean City. When Route 50 ends, turn right onto Philadelphia Avenue and follow the signs to "Inlet Parking." Park is adjacent.

Trimper's Rides and Amusements
South 1st Street & Boardwalk
Ocean City, MD (410) 289–8617

The first thing you'll see here is the big steel roller coaster soaring high above the other area attractions. With 37 rides, this park, founded in 1890, is still owned by the same family.

The park is spread out over a 3-block area on the land side of the boardwalk, and its 15 kiddie rides are all indoors.

 Extras: Miniature golf, tank tag, and gallery guns, extra charge. Also offered are an unusual mirror maze and an interesting walk-through called Pirates Cove, both included in pay-one-price admission. Be sure to look over the display (near the carousel) of old photos of the park.

 Season: Indoor rides run on weekends year-round. The entire park is open Easter Sunday through October.

 Operating hours: Opens at 1:00 P.M. on weekdays and at noon on weekends; closes at midnight every night.

 Admission policy: Free admission, with rides and attractions on a pay-as-you-go basis. Pay-one-price also available, under $10. Parking at meters and paid lots nearby.

 Top rides: Wipe Out; Tilt-A-Whirl; tank tag; a circa-1902 Herschell-Spillman carousel; Zipper; Double Sky Wheel. The Haunted House, which you ride through sitting in minicoffins made of wood, is located along the boardwalk, away from the park proper.

 Roller coaster: Tidal Wave, Boomerang (S).

Plan to stay: 3 hours.

 Best way to avoid crowds: Mondays and Tuesdays are the slowest days.

 Directions: Follow Route 50 across the bridge into Ocean City. The highway ends at Philadelphia Avenue; turn right and go 5 blocks to Division Street. Then turn left and go 2 blocks to the boardwalk.

MASSACHUSETTS

Pirates Fun Park
Route 1A
Salisbury Beach, MA (508) 465-3731

A short distance from the oceanside boardwalk, this busy little park is the hub of the entertainment area of the town. It's a popular spot not only with tourists but also with locals.

Along with its 16 rides, including 6 for kids, the park offers a variety of water rides, midway games, and an arcade. Two food outlets provide traditional amusement park "fun" food. The Pirate's Den is a nice ride-through haunted house, and the Island Adventure is a walk-through fun house.

Admission is pay-as-you-go; pay-one-price available, under $8. Hours vary; call first.

Riverside Park
Route 159
Agawam, MA (413) 786-9300

What a wonderful traditional family park this is! With more than 125 rides, games, and attractions, it's New England's largest amusement park. Founded in 1940, the park rests on 170 acres, and its landscaping is mature and colorful.

Two kiddielands contain 16 rides, while the arsenal of 30 major rides includes 4 roller coasters and a giant wheel that provides a view of the park and the Connecticut River. Premier Park purchased the park in late 1996.

 Extras: Miniature golf and Skycoaster, additional charge. NASCAR races every Saturday at 6:00 P.M. at the park's speedway. Admission to races sepa-

THE AMUSEMENT PARK GUIDE

rate, but a combo ticket with park is available. Concert series runs all season.

 Season: April through October.

 Operating hours: 11:00 A.M. to 11:00 P.M. Closing times vary during the season, depending on crowds and weather.

 Admission policy: Pay-one-price, under $25. After 5:00 P.M., under $15. Parking charge.

 Top rides: Shipwreck Falls, shoot-the-chute; Chaos; Sea Dragon; antique cars; bumper cars; Colossus, a 150-foot-tall Ferris wheel; Red River Rapids, a log flume; a circa-1909 Mangels-Illions carousel with original band organ; a monorail.

 Roller coasters: Mind Eraser, Inverted (S); Riverside Cyclone (W); Black Widow, shuttle-loop (S); Thunderbolt (W); Rolling thunder, family (S).

 Plan to stay: 6 hours.

 Best way to avoid crowds: Mondays, Tuesdays, and Thursdays are the slowest days.

 Directions: Take Exit 4 off the Massachusetts Turnpike and follow Route 5 south 5.8 miles to Route 57 (Agawam–Southwick). Follow Route 57 to Route 159 South (Main Street) and go south 3 miles.

Whalom Park
Route 13, Whalom District
Fitchburg, MA (508) 342–3707

The picturesque drive to the park gets you ready for the beauty you'll see once you enter the front gates. This century-old lakeside amusement facility bills itself as the "cleanest, greenest amusement park in New England."

The heavily wooded park has picnic areas situated throughout, and much of the architecture reflects its past heritage as a trolley park at the turn of the century. There are 24 adult and 11 kiddie rides.

 Extras: Swimming in Lake Whalom, with bathhouses for changing, no additional charge. Miniature golf, paddle boats, and aqua cycles, extra charge. Dancing nightly in the beautifully restored 1930s-era ballroom.

 Special events: Park birthday party, every August 18; Fireworks Party, July 3–4; Kid's Fest, Labor Day weekend.

 Season: Easter Sunday through Columbus Day.

 Operating hours: Rides open at noon, close at 9:00 or 10:00 P.M.

 Admission policy: General admission, plus rides and attractions, or pay-one-price, under $17.50, including beach and the 2 waterslides.

 Top rides: The Prism, a unique walk-through featuring experiences in each of the colors of the prism; Tumble Bug, an old favorite (only a few left in operation); Turnpike, antique cars; Giant Slide; a circa-1909/1910 Looff carousel.

 Roller coaster: Flyer Comet (W).

 Plan to stay: 5 hours.

 Best way to avoid crowds: Come early in the season anytime or during the season midweek.

 Directions: Located on Route 13, 3 miles off Route 2, in Lunenburg.

MICHIGAN

Crossroads Village
Bray Road, South of Stanley
Flint, MI (810) 789–8500

Enter the world of a Michigan village as it would have been in the late 1800s. This historic village features 30 re-created structures from that era, including a lumber yard, a cider mill, a blacksmith shop, a doctor's office, and a law office.

Although not all dating back to the 1800s, the village offers 5 amusement rides. The Huckleberry Railroad is a genuine Baldwin steam locomotive that takes passengers on 35 minute, 8-mile excursions, while the *Genesee Belle* paddle-wheel riverboat provides scenic 45-minute cruises on Mott Lake.

At the Lakeside Park amusement area, there's an 85-year-old carousel, a Ferris wheel, and the Venetian Swings, a vintage attraction that only exists in two other North American amusement parks.

There are two different admission plans, both for under $10. There is an extra fee for the *Genesee Belle*. Open daily, late-May through early-September and selected weekends through the fall and early winter when special Harvest, Halloween, and Christmas festivals take place.

 TIM'S TRIVIA

The first Corkscrew roller coaster was made by Arrow Development and opened to the public at Knott's Berry Farm, Beuna Park, California, on May 21, 1975. That coaster is now at Silverwood amusement park in Athol, Idaho.

Dutch Village
12350 James Street
Holland, MI (616) 396–1475

Here's a reproduction of what a quaint Dutch burg would look like if you found it in the Netherlands. The park offers 20 acres of canals, Dutch architecture, and gardens, as well as 3 rides, a circa-1924 Herschell-Spillman carousel, a Dutch swing ride, and a giant wooden-shoe slide. Also on hand are plenty of authentic crafts and foods, plus dancers and other entertainers. In operation, too, is an authentic witch's scale from the Museum of the Netherlands: It weighs you and presents you with a certificate that proves you aren't a witch or warlock—unless, of course, you are.

Pay-one-price, under $7. Open from the end of April through mid-October, 9:00 A.M. to 6:00 P.M.

 TIM'S TRIVIA

In late 1996, Gena Romano, president of Nellie Bly Park, in Brooklyn, New York, became the first female president in the seventy-eight year history of the International Association of Amusement Parks & Attractions, the largest amusement park trade group in the world.

Interlochen Fun Country
9320 U.S. 31 South
Interlochen, MI (616) 276–6360

This is a great place for a small family fun park. The well-shaded facility features 9 rides, including a Scrambler, Himalaya, 2 kiddie rides, carousel, bumper boats, go-karts, and water slides. Available as well are an 18-hole adventure golf course and 2 games arcades.

The park is open Memorial Day through Labor Day, 11:00 A.M. to 11:00 P.M. daily. Activities and rides are on a pay-as-you-play basis, with an all-day pass available, under $13.

THE AMUSEMENT PARK GUIDE

Michigan's Adventure
WhiteWater Adventure
4750 Whitehall Road
Muskegon, MI (616) 766–3377

Ride the state's only 2 wooden roller coasters, and then take a short stroll along a well-landscaped path to the state's largest waterpark. There's a great deal to do here in Michigan's largest wet/dry park. That's a lot of superlatives, but this 80-acre park, just 6 miles from Lake Michigan, fills the bill on all accounts. With more than 20 mechanical rides, including 5 for the kids, the park added WildWater Adventure, a waterpark, and doubled its size. The park is surrounded by trees and offers ample shade and resting areas for sitting and watching, if you so choose.

 Season: May through Labor Day.

 Operating hours: 11:00 A.M. to 6:00, 7:00, or 8:00 P.M.

 Admission policy: Pay-one-price, under $17. Parking charge.

 Top rides: Adventure Falls, shoot-the-chute; Chaos; Logger's Run, flume; Falling Star, a 360-degree platform ride that keeps riders upright at all times; Sea Dragon, a swinging pirate ship; antique cars; a 90-foot-tall, gondola-type Ferris wheel; Grand Carousel.

 Roller coasters: Corkscrew (S); Wolverine Wildcat (W); Zach's Zoomer, junior (W).

 Plan to stay: 7 hours.

 Best way to avoid crowds: June is the slowest month of the season.

 Directions: Take the Russell Street exit off Route 31 and go north to Riley Thompson Road. Go west on Riley Thompson for about 2 miles; the park is on the right at Whitehall Road.

MINNESOTA

Como Park Amusement Park
Hamlin & Midway Parkway
in Como Park
St. Paul, MN (612) 484-6565

You have to be looking for this wonderful little park to find it. Nestled in city-owned Como Park next to the zoo, the facility displays no signs, no fences, nothing fancy. You'll know you're there when you see the rides and a lone ticket booth.

With 15 rides, including 10 for kids, this is the perfect place for a family to visit for an hour or two and let the kids play. Expect to see new rides and attractions each time you visit. The owners, the O'Neil family, enjoy changing things around quite often.

Open daily from Palm Sunday through Labor Day, 10:30 A.M. to 8:00 P.M. There is no admission charge; you pay as you play.

Family Funways
2100 North Frontage Road
Burnsville, MN (612) 894-9782

When they built this park in 1980, the owners wanted to make sure they offered something for everyone. And they were successful: With a large kiddieland of 20 rides and about a dozen additional family rides, the park has a nice mix of attractions for the entire family.

Here you'll find a miniature golf course, 4 go-kart tracks, batting cages, a haunted mine-shaft elevator ride, a petting zoo, games, and a small video arcade. The park is filled with individual animatronic scenes that are activated by token. Among other activities, you can watch a cowboy getting a shave, a surgeon during a very bloody operation, or the goings-on at an early blacksmith shop.

Admission is free, and attractions are on a pay-as-you-go basis. Hours vary; call first.

THE AMUSEMENT PARK GUIDE

Knott's Camp Snoopy
Indoors, Mall of America
5000 Center Court
Bloomington, MN (612) 883-8500

Under a glass roof in the middle of the largest shopping mall in the United States, this state-of-the-art, 7-acre facility is the country's largest indoor theme park.

It's hard to believe you're indoors when standing in the middle of the park. To achieve the grandeur of Minnesota's northwoods, nearly 400 trees, standing from 10 to 35 feet high, and more than 30,000 plants were brought in and planted in the deep, rich soil when the park was built in 1992.

 TIM'S TRIVIA

Knott's Camp Snoopy, in the middle of the Mall of America, Bloomington, Minnesota, is located on the site of the Old Metropolitan Stadium. There's a brass replica of the stadium's home plate, exactly where it sat, on one of the pathways of the indoor park.

The 1.2 miles of clear glass skylights, 100 feet above the floor, allow natural light to flow into the park. A 9-foot gradation in the rolling landscape gives the flowing streams and the banks of evergreens an even more natural appearance.

The Peanuts cartoon gang, including Snoopy and Charlie Brown, live here as costumed characters and appear regularly throughout the park.

There are 17 rides and several daily shows, including an animal presentation in the Wilderness Theater. Mrs. Knott's famous fried chicken is available here as well.

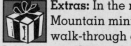 **Extras:** In the mall, adjacent to the park: Golf Mountain miniature golf; Underwater World, a walk-through aquarium attraction; Lego Imagination Center; Laser Tag; Amazing Space interactive adventure play center; 8-nightclubs/themed restaurants; and more than 400 retail stores.

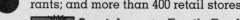 **Special events:** Family Fun Nights, every Tuesday after 5:00 P.M., September through May, discounted rides; Dinner with the Peanuts Gang, every Friday at Mrs. Knott's Restaurant, September

through May; Easter Egg-stravaganza, Easter Sunday; Camp Spooky, 1 weekend in October; and Knott's Camp Santa, Thanksgiving through December 24.

 Season: Year-round.

 Operating hours: 9:30 or 10:00 A.M. to 9:30 or 10:00 P.M.

 Admission policy: Free admission, with rides and attractions on a pay-as-you-go basis. Pay-one-price available at certain times of the year. Automated admission system permits you to buy tickets from machines, with cash or credit cards, without standing in lines.

 Top rides: Paul Bunyan's Log Chute, log ride through a mountain of animated scenes; Mystery Mine Ride, a ride simulator; Skyscraper Ferris Wheel, 74 feet tall; American Carousel; bumper cars; and the Snoopy Bounce, a play bounce inside a huge, inflated Snoopy.

 Roller coaster: Ripsaw Roller Coaster, family (S).

 Plan to stay: 3 hours.

 Best way to avoid crowds: Crowds tend to grow as the mall becomes busier. Come early during the week, and avoid the Christmas-shopping crowds.

 Directions: Inside Mall of America. Take 24th Avenue South exit off I–494.

 # TIM'S TRIVIA

Like to read about Amusement Park history? You should join the National Amusement Park Historical Association. Write them at P.O. Box 83, Mt. Prospect, IL 60056

The Amusement Park Guide

Paul Bunyan Amusement Center
Highways 210 & 371
Brainerd, MN (218) 829-6342

For nearly 50 years, this amusement park has served as the home of the legendary lumberjack of the Northwoods. Paul Bunyan, in the form of a 26-foot-high talking, moving statue, entertains visitors throughout the day. Babe, his famous blue ox, also towers over the grounds.

Scattered throughout the 8-acre park are 17 amusement rides, including 8 for the little ones. Among the more popular rides are the Ghost Mine, the Himalaya, miniature train, Mystic Mine walk-through, WWII Bomber, miniature golf, picnic grounds, and lumbering exhibits.

Additional rides outside the park gates include bumper boats, tank wars, and the unique Space Probe, where a rider sits in a ball as it is shot up a tube by an air current.

Admission is under $10 for rides and attractions within the gates. There are separate charges for those outside the gate. Open daily Memorial Day through Labor Day at 10:00 A.M.; closing times vary.

Valleyfair!
Whitewater Country
1 Valleyfair Drive
Shakopee, MN (612) 445-7600

If you appreciate great neon artistry, the fun starts here before you even leave the highway. The park's unique and colorful neon sign is one of the best in the country. The sign depicts 3 moving rides—a Ferris wheel, a roller coaster, and a carousel—in neon.

Inside the gates eye-catching gardens and a wealth of hanging plants dominate the 68 acres of landscape. There's much to keep you busy, or if you choose, you can find a nice shady spot, grab yourself a cold drink, and watch the world—and the roller coasters—go by.

Five roller coasters and 7 kiddie rides are among the park's 32 rides.

Entrance to Whitewater Country is included in the park's admission. In all, there are 10 water activities. Unlike most waterparks, all water is heated.

Extras: Challenge Park is adjacent to the front gate, with all activities on a pay-as-you-play basis. No admission to Valleyfair! is required. Attractions include Grand Prix go-karts; two 18-hole miniature golf courses; bumper boats; and a skycoaster.

Special events: Fireworks, July 4; a 3-day corn feast over Labor Day weekend.

 Season: May through September.

 Operating hours: Opens at 10:00 A.M. and closes at either 10:00 P.M. or midnight.

 Admission policy: Pay-one-price, under $25. Special starlight admission after 5:00 P.M. every day saves $9. Parking charge. Children under 48 inches tall, and those over 60 years of age, get in for $4.95.

 Top rides: The Wave, shoot-the-chute; Hydroblaster, a dry ride down an enclosed water chute; Thunder Canyon, a raging-rapids ride; a circa-1915, Philadelphia Toboggan Company carousel; a log flume; a gondola-style Ferris wheel from which you can see the Minnesota River Valley.

 Roller coasters: The Wild Thing (S); High Roller (W); Excalibur (S); Corkscrew (S); The Rails, family (S).

 Plan to stay: 9 hours.

 Best way to avoid crowds: Come on weekdays, early in the day.

 Directions: Located southwest of Minneapolis on Highway 101, 9 miles west of the intersection of Highways 13 and 35 West.

TIM'S TRIVIA

General admission was $3.50 per person when Walt Disney World, near Orlando, opened on October 2, 1971. An eleven-ride pass cost an extra $5.75. On February 25, 1996, the cost to enter the park, including tax, was nearly $43.00 per person.

MISSISSIPPI

Fun Time USA
Highway 90 & Cowan Road
Gulfport, MS (601) 896-7315

Located on the beach, halfway between Gulfport and Biloxi, this small, clean park offers miniature golf, go-karts, a large arcade with video games, and Skee-ball. It also has 11 rides, including bumper boats, Tilt-A-Whirl, a small steel roller coaster, and 6 kiddie rides.

Admission is free, with rides on a pay-as-you-go basis. The park is open daily until midnight during the summer, and until 4:00 P.M., weather permitting, during the rest of the year.

Funtricity Family Entertainment Park
1444 Warrenton Road
Vicksburg, MS (601) 631-0303
http://www.southernet.com/funtricity/

If the big park chains were to build family entertainment centers, this is what they would look like. In fact, it was the Six Flags Theme Park chain that designed, built, and now manages this prototype fun park.

The indoor-outdoor facility has a lineup of activities to please the entire family, including: Bayou Bumpers, bumper boats; Dixie Demo, krazy kars; Vicksburg 500, go-karts; and Kidtricity Kingdom children's play area with 3 rides, a train, swings, and a small roller coaster.

Kidtricity Kastle is a Medieval-themed participatory play area for the little ones; Space Shuttle America is a motion-based simulator; and there are batting cages and miniature golf. Free admission, with rides on a pay-as-you-go basis, or an all-day, unlimited ride and attractions pass is available, for under $15.

Open Sunday through Thursday, 11:00 A.M. to 10:00 P.M., and Friday and Saturday, 11:00 A.M. to midnight. Free parking.

Magic Golf/Biloxi Beach
Amusement Park
1785 Beach Boulevard
Biloxi, MS (601) 374–4338

The Gulf of Mexico provides a great backdrop for this family park with a fairyland theme. The beachside park has 13 rides, "magical" miniature golf, go-karts, and a games arcade. The Ferris wheel; Dragon, a roller coaster; and bumper cars are the most popular rides. A small kid-dieland features 6 rides for the wee ones.

There is no charge to get in, and everything is on a pay-as-you-play basis. Hours vary; call first.

Wonderland Entertainment Park
5800 Martin Bluff Road
Gautier, MS (601) 497–2570

The world's oldest operating Ferris wheel calls this little park its home. The 75-foot-tall wheel was originally constructed in 1895 at Casino Amusements in Asbury Park, New Jersey. When that park closed in 1988, the wheel was brought here, completely restored, and reopened in 1990.

Another antique ride is the 1904 German carousel. In all, the park has 12 rides, including bumper boats, a waterpark with 5 slides, a large swimming pool, and several smaller kid's pools, and a miniature golf course.

Admission is under $10, including the waterpark and train ride. Other activities cost extra. Open daily, mid-May through early-September, 10:00 A.M. to 9:00 P.M.

THE AMUSEMENT PARK GUIDE

MISSOURI

Oceans of Fun
4545 Worlds of Fun Avenue
Kansas City, MO (816) 454-4545

Situated next to Worlds of Fun theme park, this 35-attraction waterpark offers a full day of cool fun and adventure. There are 7 slides, the Surf City wave pool, the Caribbean Cooler lazy river, and an adults-only pool with a swim-up bar where alcoholic beverages are available.

Coconut Cove is a children's play area with small slides and pools, and another kid's area, Crocodile Isle, offers a bevy of fun water activities for the little ones. A lagoon offers bumper boats and kayak rides.

Park guests also have access to The Monsoon shoot-the-shoot ride, located between the waterpark and the theme park. Open daily at 10:00 A.M., closing at dusk, Memorial Day through Labor Day. Admission is under $20. A 2-day combination pass with the theme park is available, under $37.

Silver Dollar City
Off Highway 76
Branson, MO (417) 338-2611

Far from the glitter, glitz, and country music sounds of nearby Branson, this turn-of-the-century theme park started out as a place that offered tours of Marvel Cave and has grown to be an oasis for frontier craftspeople. The park's resident crafts colony now numbers more than 100, with many demonstrating their talents at any one time among the hilly, well-shaded acreage.

Among the quaint architecture, you'll find 13 rides, including 6 for kids.

Extras: A 55-minute guided tour of Marvel Cave is free with admission to park. Geyser Gulch is a 2-acre participatory play area billed as "the world's largest treehouse."

Special events: World Fest, featuring international performers, May; National Crafts Festival, September and October; Old Time Country Christmas, November through December.

Season: Mid-April through December.

 Operating hours: 9:30 A.M. to 6:00 or 7:00 P.M. during peak season.

 Admission policy: Pay-one-price, under $26. Free parking.

 Top rides: Great Shoot-Out, a ride-through shooting gallery; Lost River of the Ozarks, a raging-rapids ride; Great American Plunge, a log flume; Frisco, a steam train; Wilderness Waterboggan, an 8-story toboggan ride down a water chute; Fire in the Hole, an indoor themed action dark ride.

 Roller coaster: Thunderation, mine train (S).

 Plan to stay: 7 hours.

 Best way to avoid crowds: The park is laid out in a circle; pick up a map and follow the circle without doubling back or crossing over. Weekdays, as well as spring and fall weekends, entail fewer people.

 Directions: Located off Highway 76, 9 miles west of Branson, 40 miles south of Springfield.

 # TIM'S TRIVIA

Wonderland Entertainment Park in Gautier, Mississippi, has the world's oldest operating Ferris wheel. The 75-foot tall wheel was originally built in 1895 for Caino Amusements in Asbury Park, New Jersey.

THE AMUSEMENT PARK GUIDE

Six Flags St. Louis
Six Flags Outer Road
Eureka, MO (314) 938–4800
http://www.sixflags.com

Nicely landscaped and full of action, this 200-acre park formerly known as Six Flags Over Mid-America, is a member of the Six Flags family and has many of the same accoutrements, including the Looney Tunes characters and a children's area built around the cartoon bunch.

Spread out among the trees and the theming of the eight areas are 31 rides. In each area, the rides, architecture, and activities all carry out the theme of the area—1904 World's Fair, Gateway to the West, Warner Bros. Backlot, Chouteau's Market, Illinois, Brittania, Spain, and Looney Tunes Tour.

You enter the park through the 1904 World's Fair section, which has a turn-of-the-century theme and includes the magnificent Palace Music Hall, where the major musical productions are held.

 Extras: Food may not be brought into the park; however, adjacent to the parking lot is a fantastic picnic area, just for guests. It has plenty of shaded tables, a nice lake in the middle (with lots of hungry ducks), and bathrooms.

 Special events: Celebrate St. Louis, April; Cheerleading Festival, April; Country Fair, September; Fright Fest, October.

 Season: April through October.

 Operating hours: Opens at 10:00 A.M. every day and closes at 9:00 P.M. on weeknights, midnight on Fridays, and 11:00 P.M. on Saturdays and Sundays.

 Admission policy: Pay-one-price, under $30. Second-day admission available for under $5 additional. Parking charge.

Top rides: Thunder River, raging rapids; Log Flume, a double-trough ride with great capacity; Colossus, a giant Ferris wheel; Enchanted Carousel, a circa-1915 Philadelphia Toboggan Company carousel.

Roller coasters: Mr. Freeze, LIM Shuttle (S); Batman The Ride, inverted (S); River King Mine Ride (S); Ninja, multi-element (S); Screamin' Eagle (W).

Plan to stay: 8 hours.

 Best way to avoid crowds: The least busy days are Tuesdays, Wednesdays, and Thursdays. Otherwise, come early, get a map, plan the shows you want to see, and try to avoid doubling back.

 Directions: Take the Allenton exit off I–44, 30 minutes southwest of St. Louis. The park is located there on the service road.

TIM'S TRIVIA

The Screamin' Eagle wooden roller coaster at Six Flags St. Louis, Eureka, Missouri, was painted with Sears Weatherbeater paint and featured in Sears's 1990 commercials

White Water
West Highway 76
Branson, MO (417) 334–7487

Aloha. The tropical attitude is alive and well here at White Water, a twelve-attraction waterpark in the midst of the Ozark Mountains. There are 6 slides and flumes, including the popular Paradise Plunge, a 207-foot-tall, triple-drop slide, and the Bermuda Triangle and the Typhoon Tunnel, both enclosed body flumes.

Other activities and attractions include the Paradise River, lazy river; Surf Quake wave pool; Splash Island, kid's activity pool; live entertainment, including dive-in movies and beach dance parties; sand volleyball courts; food service; and a beach shop.

Located 5 miles from its sister park, Silver Dollar City, the park is along the "strip" in this busy tourist area, full of country music theaters, restaurants, and family activities. Silver Dollar City also owns the White Water park in Marietta, Georgia, adjacent to its American Adventure park. See the listings for Georgia.

The Amusement Park Guide

Worlds of Fun
4545 Worlds of Fun Avenue
Kansas City, MO (816) 454-4545

Jules Verne's *Around the World in Eighty Days* is the theme of this 170-acre park, with each of its five areas representing different parts of the world—the Orient, Scandinavia, Europe, Africa, and America.

All food, rides, games, and architecture in each area reflect its theme. The park has 39 rides, including 14 for kids and Pandamonium, a kids' play area. After crossing the gangplank and entering the park, you'll find that the rides and attractions are laid out in a big circle, making the park easy to get around in. You'll never be too far from anything.

 Extras: RipCord, Skycoaster, extra. The Forum Amphitheatre presents top-name entertainment throughout the season, extra charge. Shaded picnic areas are located outside the park, adjacent to the parking lot. Oceans of Fun waterpark is adjacent, extra fee. Berenstain Bear Country, based on the children's book series of the same name, is a one-acre play area.

 Special events: Christian Music Festival, spring; Boo! Blast, October.

 Season: Mid-April through mid-October.

 Operating hours: Opens daily at 10:00 A.M., closing varies from 8:00 P.M. to midnight.

 Admission policy: Pay-one-price, under $27; discount after 4:00 P.M. Parking charge.

 Top rides: Detonator, twin space shots; Fury of the Nile, a raging-rapids ride; Python Plunge, a wet/dry water slide using 1-person boats; Viking Voyager, a log flume; The Monsoon, shoot-the-chute.

Roller coasters: Timber Wolf (W); Orient Express, multielement (S); Wacky Worm, junior (S); Zambezi Zinger, speedracer (S).

Plan to stay: 9 hours.

Best way to avoid crowds: Come on weekdays during the peak season or on Sundays in spring and fall. Go to the farthest distance from the gate and work toward the front.

 Directions: Located in I–435 at Exit 54, just north of the Missouri River.

NEBRASKA

Fun-Plex
7003 Q. Street
Omaha, NE (402) 331-8436

Don't expect to be in and out of here in an hour! This diversified entertainment complex truly has something for all members of the family. You can choose from 2 go-kart tracks, bumper boats, 5-kiddie rides, a Tilt-A-Whirl, batting cages, the Cabana Arcade, 2 waterslides, the Ocean Motion wave pool, and a lazy river.

Open daily noon to 8:00 P.M. during the summer, and on weekends in the spring and fall. Rides are available on an individual basis, or a combination waterpark and rides unlimited-use ticket costs under $17. A separate waterpark-only pass is available, under $11.

 # TIM'S TRIVIA

As they were just starting out, the Beach Boys would travel to Salt Lake City, Utah, on weekends to play at Lagoon Park.

The Amusement Park Guide

NEVADA

In Nevada, many of the finest rides and attractions are not located in amusement parks, but in Casino Hotels instead. Following is a sampling of such facilities that have note-worthy rides and attractions.

Buffalo Bill's
Primadonna
Whiskey Pete's
I–15 at the California border, Jean, NV (702) 679–7433

This three-casino complex features a lot of gambling opportunities in fun, themed casinos, as well as great fun on world-class amusement rides. Inside Buffalo Bill's, you'll find the loading station for the 209-foot-tall Desperado steel roller coaster, one of the tallest roller coasters in the world. As you go up the lift hill, you'll travel through the roof of the casino to the top of the first hill, where you'll get quite a view of the mountains and desert. Also inside is the Adventure Canyon Log Flume and the Ghost Town motion-based simulator ride. Outside, there's a train, Ferris wheel, and carousel.

Luxor Las Vegas
3900 Las Vegas Boulevard South, Las Vegas, NV (702) 262–4555

On the attractions level of this huge, pyramid-shaped hotel, you'll find several fun things to do. There's an IMAX 3-D theater, a motion-based simulator attraction, and a third theater attraction. You'll get a chance to visit both a life-sized replica of King Tut's tomb and the museum. The Sega VirtuaLand is an 18,000-square-foot entertainment center, featuring Sega's most advanced commercial games and activities. A major, themed water-ride attraction is set to open in late 1997 or early 1998.

New York, New York Hotel and Casino
3155 West Harmon Avenue
Las Vegas, NV (702) 740–6969

As the name implies, this 2,119 room hotel/casino has New York City as its theme. The only ride is the Manhattan Express, a 203-foot-tall roller coaster that loads and unloads inside the casino. Once it goes out the roof of the building, it works its way across the roof and around the towers of the hotel. The coaster cars resemble taxi cabs. The Coney Island Emporium is a large fun center with laser tag, bumper cars, shooting gallery, 22 midway games, and nearly 200 coin-operated games.

Stratosphere Tower
2000 South Las Vegas Boulevard
Las Vegas, NV (702) 383–4752

Located near the top of the 1,149-foot-high tower, the High Roller is the highest roller coaster in the world. Starting at the 909-foot level, the coaster makes several laps around the top of the tower. At the 921-foot level, the Space Shot free-fall ride propels riders approximately 160 feet straight up. (In case you missed it, that's 160 feet up from the loading platform, which is already located nearly 1,000 feet above the Las Vegas Strip far below . . . Yikes!) The Sky-Bound Arcade (at the bottom) features a large selection of midway and video games.

Grand Slam Canyon
2880 South Las Vegas Boulevard
Las Vegas, NV (702) 794-3939

Located under the big pink dome next to the colorful Circus Circus Hotel Casino, this 5-acre indoor theme park offers some of the best climate-controlled fun in the city.

The theme is the Southwest. Designed to resemble a classic desert canyon, artificial rock gives way to caverns, pinnacles, and steep cliffs. A stream flows gently through the landscape, cascading over a 90-foot-tall waterfall. Dinosaurs certainly aren't extinct here. There are 8 life-sized animatronic creatures loudly making their presence known between two 140-foot-tall peaks.

There are 9 rides, including The Canyon Blaster, the only indoor double-loop, double-corkscrew roller coaster in the United States. The Rim Runner shoot-the-chute ride takes passengers on a scenic journey before dumping them over a 60-foot-tall waterfall. The Sand Pirates is a pirate ship, The Canyon Cars are bumper cars and the Thunderbirds is a family plane ride.

 Roller coaster: Canyon Blaster, loop/corkscrew (S).

The Fossil Dig is a children's sand play area; the Cliff Hangers is a participatory play area full of balls and nets, and the place is full of strolling clowns, mimes, and jugglers. Hot Shots is a 7,500-square-foot black-lit, graffiti-filled laser tag arena, and the Grand Slam midway features games of skill and the Sega Arcade with 72 games.

Open daily, year-round with gates opening on most days at 11:00 A.M., closings vary with the season. Currently admission to the park is free, with all rides and attractions on a pay-as-you-play basis, but a small general admission fee may be added in 1997. Call first to make sure.

Inside the Circus Circus Casino in the center stage area of the grand carnival midway, free circus acts begin performing daily at 11:00 A.M. From tight wire performers to the flying trapeze, several acts are booked each hour.

MGM Grand Adventure Theme Park
3799 Las Vegas Boulevard South
Las Vegas, NV (702) 891–1111

Located behind the behemoth MGM Grand Hotel & Casino, the 33-acre theme park is themed to replicate a backlot movie set and features 10 rides, several live shows, and 4 major fun-filled festivals a year. The 250-foot-tall SkyScreamer Skycoaster is the tallest of its kind in the world and provides passengers a flight pattern over the lake.

In addition to the coaster and the Skycoaster, the park features Deep Earth Exploration, a motion-based simulator ride; Backlot River Tour, riverboat excursion through a simulated movie set; Grand Canyon Rapids, river-rapids ride; Over the Edge, log flume; and the Parisian Taxis, bumper cars.

 Roller coaster: Lightning Bolt, family (S).

There are restaurants, numerous gift shops, and a wedding chapel. Admission to the park is free, but to see any of the shows or ride any of the rides, a wristband, under $19, is needed. There is no charge to come in and shop or to dine at the restaurants. Open year-round at 10:00 A.M. During the peak summer, closes at 10:00 P.M., during the off season, 6:00 or 7:00 P.M. A separate entrance is next to the parking lot behind the hotel, or one can enter through the rear of the hotel.

Playland Park
In Idlewild City Park
1900 Cowon Drive
Reno, NV (702) 329–6008

Billing itself as the "biggest little playground in the world," this neat little amusement area is located next to the Truckee River in Idlewild Park, about a mile from downtown Reno.

It has 8 rides that almost everyone in the family can enjoy together, including a Tilt-A-Whirl, a train ride, tea cups, and a small steel roller coaster. A public swimming pool is also located in the city park. Adjacent to the rides is a large playground operated by the Reno Arch Lions Club.

Playland is open daily from mid-May through October, 11:00 A.M. to 6:00 P.M., and on weekends during the rest of the year, weather permitting.

Admission is free, with rides on a pay-as-you-play basis.

New Hampshire

Canobie Lake Park
North Policy Street
Salem, NH (603) 893–3506
http://world.std.com/fun/clp.html

The screams and the clickety-click from the big old wooden roller coaster greet you as you enter this wonderful old traditional park. The coaster runs out into the parking lot and past the main entrance, providing a great preview of things to come.

Unlike most traditional parks, this one has almost all the original buildings, dating back to 1902, still standing and in use. The tranquil lakeside setting forms the backdrop for 45 rides, including 16 for kids. The Old Canobie Village area of the park has a turn-of-the-century theme and offers a rustic look at early New Hampshire.

The big stone fountain was in operation when the park opened, as was the carousel building, just inside the main entrance. The picnic pavilions are almost always packed with local parties and company picnics—a sure sign of a popular park.

 Extras: A swimming pool and a 20-minute excursion on the lake aboard the 150-passenger *Canobie Queen* paddle-wheel boat, both included in park admission.

 Special events: Hot Rod Show, July; Fireworks, every Saturday night during July and August.

 Season: Mid-April through September.

 Operating hours: Noon to 10:00 P.M.

 Admission policy: Pay-one-price, under $18. Discount after 6:00 P.M. Free parking.

 **Top rides:** Boston Tea Party, shoot the chutes; The Log Flume; Mine of Lost Souls, a dark ride; Psycho-Drome, an indoor Scrambler with lights and sound effects; Canobie Express, a steam train; a 90-foot-tall, gondola-style Ferris wheel with a computerized,

nighttime light show; a 1906 Looff/Dentzel antique carousel, with some horses dating back to the 1880s.

 Roller coasters: Canobie Corkscrew (S); Yankee Cannonball (W); Galaxi (S); Dragon, kiddie (S).

 Plan to stay: 7 hours.

 Best way to avoid crowds: Come early in the day or late afternoon during the week. The weekends are quite busy with commercial picnics and party groups.

 Directions: Take the Salem exit (Exit 2) off Route 93 and turn left at the light. Follow Policy Street down about 1 mile to the park. Located 35 minutes from Boston.

 # TIM'S TRIVIA

Disneyland's famed Main Street Electrical Parade made the final run of its twenty-four-year history on November 26, 1996. The light bulbs used in the parade were sold as nostalgic souvenirs and the $720,000 raised by their sale was donated to eighteen Southern California children's charities.

Santa's Village
Route 2
Jefferson, NH (603) 586–4445

It's always Christmas here, where you can visit Santa, feed his reindeer, enjoy live holiday shows, shop at the unique shops, and ride the rides from May through mid-October.

In addition to all the fun shows and the colorful Christmas displays and decorations, there are 10 rides the entire family can enjoy together. The favorites include the Yule Log Flume, Rudy's Rapid Transit roller coaster, and the Santa's Sky Sleigh monorail. You'll even find a unique reindeer carousel.

During the summer months, open 9:30 A.M. to 6:30 P.M. On fall weekends, open 9:30 A.M. to 5:00 P.M. Admission, under $15, includes all rides, shows, and activities.

The Amusement Park Guide

Story Land
Route 16
Glen, NH (603) 383–4293

Fairy tales do come true, and it could happen to you if you visit this magical, child-size world where well-known tales come to life. The heavily wooded, beautiful grounds appeal as much to adults as the activities do to children.

There are 16 family rides.

 Extras: Picnics may be brought into the park. The Farm Follies, featuring an animated vegetable variety show.

 Season: Father's Day through Columbus Day.

 Operating hours: 9:00 A.M. to 6:00 P.M.

 Admission policy: Pay-one-price, under $16. Pay to enter after 3:00 P.M., next day admission free. Free parking.

 Top rides: Dr. Geyser's Remarkable Raft Ride, a tamed-down version of the raging-rapids ride; *Story Land Queen*, a boat ride on the lake in a large swan; Pirate Ship, a participatory ride on the lake, wherein the 30 passengers all row the boat; Pumpkin Coach Ride, taking the rider up to Cinderella's Castle; Voyage to the Moon, a dark ride in a bullet-shaped rocket ship with a Jules Verne theme; Octopus Sprayground, a water cool-down play area.

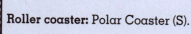 **Roller coaster:** Polar Coaster (S).

 Plan to stay: 6 hours. A park official says the "park usually outlasts the kids."

 Best way to avoid crowds: The park is least busy on weekends, due to the travel patterns of this part of New England.

 Directions: Located in the White Mountain National Forest area, 6 miles north of North Conway, on Route 16, just north of the intersection of Routes 16 and 302.

NEW JERSEY

The following seven parks are grouped together because they all share one big attraction—the Atlantic Ocean. They are located on the boardwalk, along with many other attractions, restaurants, and activities. They are not theme parks, and most have no entertainment within the park itself. They are good, old-fashioned seafront parks. Go to each one and enjoy!

Casino Pier
Waterworks
Boardwalk at Grant Avenue
Seaside Heights, NJ (908) 793–6488

If only the old-time fisherman could see this pier now. Though Casino Pier was used as a fishing pier until 1933, the old salts left quickly when the rides moved in. The pier has the best selection of rides and attractions in Seaside Heights, with a total of 30 rides, including 13 just for the tykes.

Don't miss the wonderful, circa-1910 Dentzel/Looff carousel, called the Dr. Floyd Moreland Carousel; some of its hand-carved animals date back to the 1890s. Other rides include the Nightmare Manor, a ride-through haunted house; the Poltergeist, an indoor Scrambler; White Water, log flume; Evolution; Sea Dragon; Gravitron.

 Roller coasters: Wizard's Cavern, indoor (S); Jet Star, family (S).

Make sure you eat at Meatball City or play a round of miniature golf on the rooftop course. Waterworks, a water-park owned by the same people, is located across the street and has 27 attractions.

Free admission, with rides and attractions on a pay-as-you-go basis (no pay-one-price available). Open from mid-April through September. Opens during the summer months at noon and closes at various times.

THE AMUSEMENT PARK GUIDE

Fun City Amusement Park
Boardwalk at 32nd Street
Sea Isle City, NJ (609) 263–3862

A good array of rides can be found at this block-long seaside park, which is open daily from 6:30 to 11:00 P.M. There are 18 rides, including 11 for kiddies. Among the highlights are a beautiful 1949 Allan Herschell carousel in mint condition, a Tilt-A-Whirl, Flying Bobs, and Big Valley, a music ride.

The park is open Memorial Day through Labor Day and has free admission, with rides on a pay-as-you-go basis.

Fun Town Pier
Boardwalk at Porter Avenue
Seaside Heights, NJ (908) 830–1591

What a unique log-flume ride they have here! It's quite an experience to be riding a water ride high above the park and to look out onto the Atlantic Ocean and see a seaworthy freighter chugging by not much faster than you're going.

In addition to the flume ride, this park features 23 other rides, including 13 for children. Here you'll find the popular tank-tag ride/game, and the Giant Wheel, a ride that also provides a great view of the oceanfront.

 Roller coaster: Roller Coast Loop, looping (S).

Opening for limited operation on Easter Sunday, the park remains in operation until the third week of September. Closing times vary, depending on weather and season, but rides crank up daily at noon. Admission is free, with rides and attractions on a pay-as-you-go basis. An unlimited-ride pass is available weekdays from 1:00 to 6:00 P.M., under $14.

 TIM'S TRIVIA

Singer John Denver wanted to be a musician for Six Flags Over Texas, but officials said he wasn't good enough.

Gillian's Island Waterpark
Boardwalk at Plymouth Place
Ocean City, NJ (609) 399–7082

http://www.clever.net.wwwmall/gillians

The sister park of the Gillian family's Wonderland Pier, this park has 8 water slides, a lazy river, and a pirate-themed interactive children's play area called Li'l Buc's Bay. One of the nice things about this place is that you don't have to pay for an all-day ticket if you only want to play for a few hours! After all, the world's largest waterpark (the Atlantic Ocean) is just across the street.

There's a big discount if you play anytime from the 8:30 A.M. opening until noon, and you can also buy a 2-hour, 3-hour, or an all-day ticket (under $17). Closes at 7:30 P.M. A discounted 18-hole miniature golf ticket is in effect before 5:00 P.M. on weekdays. One block south from Wonderland Pier, between 7th and 8th streets.

Jenkinson's Beach Boardwalk & Aquarium
3 Broadway
Point Pleasant, NJ (908) 892–0844

Stretched out along a mile-long boardwalk, this facility has 30 rides and a wide selection of just about anything you'd ever want while on a boardwalk, including 2 miniature golf courses, batting cages, and many gift and souvenirs shops.

There is also a modern, state-of-the-art aquarium.

There are many walk-up eateries, including the Pavilion Restaurant, seating up to 1,200; a candy shop; a bar; and a nightclub. Live musical entertainment occurs nightly, with a free concert on the beach every Wednesday night, and fireworks take place every Thursday. Events are scheduled year-round at the pavilion.

Among the more popular rides are the Himalaya; Spider; and 24 kiddie rides.

 Roller coaster: Flitzer, family (S).

The park is open April through October, and the 4 games arcades are open every day of the year. There's no admission charge, with all rides and attractions on a pay-as-you-go basis.

THE AMUSEMENT PARK GUIDE

Playland Park
1020 Boardwalk at 10th Street
Ocean City, NJ (609) 399–4751

Partly indoors, partly outdoors, this boardwalk entertainment complex has 28 rides, including 11 for kids. The carousel and arcade games are inside, whereas the larger rides are behind a large, circa-1940 expo building.

Rides include a merry-go-round; Tilt-A-Whirl; a Ferris wheel; a train ride; kiddie and adult go-karts; bumper cars.

 Roller coasters: Wild Mouse, family (S); Flitzer, family (S); Dragon, kiddie (S); Python, 1-loop (S).

Free admission, with rides and attractions on a pay-as-you-go basis. The arcade opens at 10:00 A.M., the rides at 2:00 P.M., and everything closes at midnight.

Wonderland Pier
Boardwalk at 6th Street
Ocean City, NJ (609) 399–7082
http://www.clever.net.wwwmall/gillians

This is one of the nicest seafront parks on the East Coast. Family operated, the park offers a clean, well-supervised entertainment area, with 33 rides, including 12 for kids. Two costumed characters, Wonder and Landy, walk the park daily.

Part of the complex is indoors, so don't let the bad weather keep you away from the boardwalk. The circa-1925 Philadelphia Toboggan Company carousel, in beautiful condition, is the focal point of the rest of the rides, which include a monorail; a giant Ferris wheel; the Zugspitze, a Himalaya ride; Canyon Falls, log flume; and the Raiders, a kid's participatory play unit.

Roller coaster: City Jet, family (S).

The season runs from Memorial Day through mid-September and is open from noon to midnight daily. Admission is free, with rides and attractions on a pay-as-you-go basis (no pay-one-price available). The same family also owns Gillian's Island, a waterpark, 1 block south on the boardwalk.

Action Park
Route 94
Vernon, NJ (201) 827–2000

If you're a passive type of parkgoer who likes things done for you, you're out of luck here—this is a unique, "self-operated" park in which you do the work . . . and you have the fun.

As part of the 200-acre Great Gorge Ski Area, the park is located in a lovely mountainside setting with abundant trees and landscaping. There are three distinct areas: Water World, Alpine Center, and Motor World.

Bring your bathing suit—park officials say theirs is the world's largest waterpark.

 Extras: Miniature golf and Grand Prix raceway, extra charge.

 Special events: Polka Festival, Memorial Day; Latin Festivals, late July and late August.

 Season: Memorial Day through Labor Day.

 Operating hours: 10:00 A.M. to 8:00 P.M.

 Admission policy: Pay-one-price, under $30. Parking fee.

 Top rides: Space Shot, a quick ascent, then a free fall; Aerodium, in which a DC-3 jet engine provides enough uplift for people to float midair; Transmobile, a people mover resembling a sideway monorail; Colorado River, a raging-rapids ride; Roaring Springs, an 8-acre water-activity area with spas; speedboats; auto races; a chair lift; Tidal Wave, a wave pool; bungee jumping; alpine slides.

 Plan to stay: 8 hours.

 Best way to avoid crowds: Tuesdays are the slowest; weekends are packed!

 Directions: Take the Route 23 exit off I–80 and go north to Route 94 for 2 miles. The park spans both sides of the highway. Located between McAfee and Vernon.

THE AMUSEMENT PARK GUIDE

Bowcraft Amusement Park
Route 22
Scotch Plains, NJ (908) 233-0675

This well-kept, little park is located in the foothills of the Watchung Mountain and caters to young families with kids from age 3 through the midteen years. With 19 rides that the entire family can enjoy together, as well as plenty of games and other activities, the park offers something for everyone.

 Extras: 18-hole miniature golf course and a 129-game arcade, with redemption.

 Season: Palm Sunday through Thanksgiving. The arcade is open year-round.

 Operating hours: 10:00 A.M. to 10:00 P.M.

 Admission policy: Free admission, with rides and attractions on a pay-as-you-play basis (no pay-one-price available). Free parking.

 Top rides: Bumper cars; Tilt-A-Whirl; a train ride around the park; Elephant Tower, a pink pachyderm kiddie ride; kiddie go-karts; gas powered car ride around the lake.

Roller coaster: Flying Dragon, family (S).

Plan to stay: 4 hours.

Best way to avoid crowds: Come during the week, any time of day.

Directions: Take Exit 140 (Route 22) off the Garden State Parkway and go west 7 miles to the park. Located 15 miles from Newark.

Casino Pier, see page 119.

Clementon Amusement Park
SplashWorld Waterpark
Route 534, Berlin Road
Clementon, NJ (609) 783-0263

The 15-acre Clementon Lake provides the centerpiece for this well-kept traditional park. Several old buildings date back to the park's founding in 1907 and give the 50-acre park a nostalgic ambience.

Among the 22 rides is the second oldest operating wooden roller coaster in North America. There are 5 kiddie rides in an appealing little shaded kiddieland.

 Extras: SplashWorld Waterpark has 4 large slides, a lazy river, and a children's activity pool. Softball; volleyball and basketball courts; many large picnic pavilions. Food baskets may be brought into amusement park, but not the waterpark.

 Special events: Fireworks, July 4.

 Season: Late April through Labor Day.

 Operating hours: Noon to 10:00 P.M., Tuesday through Sunday; closed Monday.

 Admission policy: Pay-one-price for either park, under $15. Discount after 5:00 P.M. A combination ticket for unlimited use of both parks available, under $19.

 Top rides: Circa-1919 Philadelphia Toboggan Company carousel; a Whip; Neptune's Revenge, a log-flume in the lake; Sea Dragon, a pirate ship; Ferris wheel; train ride around the lake.

 Roller coaster: Jack Rabbit, circa 1919 (W).

 # TIM'S TRIVIA

The cost to paint the Jackrabbit—the wooden roller coaster in Clementon Park, Clementon, New Jersey—in 1988 was more than double the cost to build it in 1919.

The Amusement Park Guide

 Plan to stay: 5 hours.

 Best way to avoid crowds: Tuesdays are least crowded.

 Directions: Take Exit 3 off the New Jersey Turnpike. Go south 4 miles on Route 168 to Route 534. Go east on 534 for 4 more miles; the park is on the right.

Dinasaur Beach, see page 130.

Ed Brown's Playground
Highway 34
Allaire Airport
Allaire, NJ (908) 938–3188

This family-oriented amusement park might very well have the most unusual location of any park in the country. It's located on the grounds of the largest privately owned airport in the United States. And I don't mean hidden off in a corner either!

Owned by the same person who owns the airport, the park is adjacent to the terminal and has 12 rides, several of which are beneath a large canopy to allow for operation during inclement weather. A beautiful carousel, with a band organ, is located in its own building.

The gondola Ferris wheel provides a great view of the grounds, while the railroad takes passengers on a 20-minute tour around the edge of the runways, back into the woods, and past a small convention center, also owned by Ed Brown. There's a children's playground, miniature golf course, and a concession stand. Talk about a nice way to kill time while waiting for your flight!

Open daily, mid-June through August, 1:00 to 9:00 P.M., and on weekends through the fall, 1:00 P.M. to dusk. Admission is free, rides on a pay-as-you-go basis.

(Editor's Note: This park did not open for the 1996 season, due to zoning problems; however, it is expected to open again for the 1997 season. To be safe, call first.)

Fantasy Island
320 West 7th Street
Beach Haven, NJ (609) 492–4000
http://www.fantasyislandpark.com

Victoriana—that's what this pleasant park is all about. From the brick sidewalks and immaculate landscaping to the Tiffany lights in the arcade, the atmosphere here is Victorian.

Occupying an entire block just 2 blocks from the beach, the park has 21 rides, including 11 for kids.

 Extras: Various live acts perform on a daily basis; Fantasy Delights, a Victorian-era ice-cream parlor serves up great frozen concoctions; Casino activities are aimed for adults and includes slot machines, poker machines, and blackjack machines.

 Special events: Every Friday night, a pay-one-price special discount; Fireworks, July 4.

 Season: Park is open Memorial Day through Labor Day; the arcade, year-round on weekends and daily during summer.

 Operating hours: The park opens at 5:00 P.M. during the week and at 2:00 P.M. Friday through Sunday; it closes at varying times, depending on crowds and weather. The arcade opens at noon.

 Admission policy: Free admission, with rides and attractions on a pay-as-you-play basis. Pay-one-price specials on Friday night. Free parking.

 Top rides: Sea Dragon, a swinging pirate ship; bumper cars; kiddie boats; a train ride; a carousel; Giant Wheel.

 Plan to stay: 4 hours.

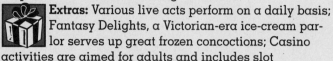 **Best way to avoid crowds:** Come on a sunny day; everyone else is at the beach.

Directions: Take the Garden State Parkway to Exit 63 (Route 72). Take Route 72 east until it dead-ends on Long Beach Island. Turn right and go 7 miles; the park is on the right. Follow the 65-foot-tall Giant Wheel to the park.

THE AMUSEMENT PARK GUIDE

Fun City Amusement Park, see page 120.

Fun Town Pier, see page 120.

Gillian's Island Waterpark, see page 121.

Jenkinson's Beach Boardwalk & Aquarium, see page 121.

TIM'S TRIVIA

Six Flags Great Adventure, in Jackson, New Jersey, has the largest drive-through safari outside Africa.

Keansburg Amusement Park Runaway Rapids
75 Beachway
Keansburg, NJ (908) 495-1400

This neat little waterside park, overlooking Raritan Bay, is a mecca for the entire family. With 25 of the 41 rides especially for kids, it's no wonder the park is a favorite among local families. In all, there are more than 150 rides, games, eateries, and attractions located along the ¼-mile walkway adjacent to the beach.

Runaway Rapids waterpark features 9 different slides and a lazy river.

 Extras: Go-karts, batting cages, and a mirror maze, extra charge.

 Special events: Fireworks, July 3; Anniversary Celebration, featuring discounted prices and a fireworks show on a Monday in August.

 Season: Palm Sunday through mid-October.

Operating hours: Opens daily at noon; closes at 11:00 P.M. during the week and at midnight on weekends.

 Admission policy: All rides and attractions on a pay-as-you-play basis (no pay-one-price available). Each Friday is Family Day, with all rides discounted 50 percent. Admission to waterpark, pay-one-price, under $16. Parking charge in lot or park at meters on street.

 Top rides: Spook House, a ride-through dark ride; bumper cars; a Himalaya ride; Trabant; Skydiver; Pharoah's Fury.

 Roller coaster: Screamin' Demon, family (S).

 Plan to stay: 4 hours.

 Best way to avoid crowds: Mondays are the slowest; spring weekends are very seldom crowded.

 Directions: Take Exit 117 off the Garden State Parkway. Follow Route 36 east for 4 miles. Turn right at the sign for Keansburg Beach and go 1½ miles; the park is on the left. Located just south of the New York State line.

 # TIM'S TRIVIA

With 12 roller coasters, and 57 rides, Cedar Point in Sandusky, Ohio, has more coasters and more rides than any other amusement park on the planet.

The Amusement Park Guide

The following seven seaside amusement and waterparks are all located along the wooden boardwalk in Wildwood. Like similar boardwalk parks, they are surrounded by many restaurants, arcades, and shops.

Dinosaur Beach
Boardwalk at Poplar Avenue
Wildwood, NJ (609) 523–1440

Dinosaurs are alive and well and living on this amusement pier! The family amusement park has a dinosaur theme with more than 24 of the life-sized creatures looming in and among the 33 family rides. There are 15 rides just for the wee ones.

Raptor Rapids is a white-water rapids ride that takes riders through a tunnel and up close to several scary raptors, Golden Nugget Mine is an East Coast classic among dark rides, and the Long Neck River is a refreshing log flume ride. Guests ride through The Escape From Dinosaur Beach dark ride in jeeplike vehicles, across rickety bridges, past falling trees and sparking power lines. While in there, you'll experience the up-close antics of 11 animatronic dinosaurs.

An outdoor amphitheater features magic shows throughout the day, and there are several interactive educational displays, as well as a sand-filled fossil dig area.

Open daily, noon to 1:00 A.M., Easter through October. Free admission, with rides on a pay-as-you-go basis. A pay-one-price wristband is available, under $20.

Mariner's Landing
Boardwalk at Schellenger Avenue
Wildwood, NJ (609) 522–3900

The park's huge Ferris wheel, located halfway out on the pier, has become a Wildwood landmark, and at night, when its lights are on, it can be seen for miles. This 6½-acre park, high above the sandy beaches of the Atlantic, has 35 rides, including a Skyship, pirate-themed monorail, and a Cycle Monorail, which riders pedal at their own speed. In addition, the park has bumper cars and a nice family carousel.

Because space is at a premium along the coast, every inch is used, which accounts for a unique structure here that houses a miniature golf course, water slides, and a go-kart track, all intertwined. It's a great use of space and adds a different experience to all three attractions.

Roller coasters: Zyklon, family (S); Sea Serpent, Boomerang (S).

The park is owned by the same family that runs the other two Morey's Piers (see below); the prices, hours, and season are the same as listed for those entries.

TIM'S TRIVIA

The best rock & roll amusement park lyrics ever written: "You'll never know how great a kiss could feel, when you're stuck at the top of a Ferris wheel, where I fell in love ... down at Palisades Park" were recorded by Freddy "Boom Boom" Cannon and penned by Chuck "Gong Show" Barris. Originally titled Amusement Park, it was changed to salute the now defunct popular park, across from Manhattan on New Jersey's palisades.

Morey's Pier
Boardwalk at 25th Street
Wildwood, NJ (609) 522–3900

It's amazing how many fun things a person can squeeze into a small space. Here you'll find the widest variety of attractions on any amusement pier in the United States, including a three-tiered log flume and a multilevel waterpark at the ocean end of the facility. Counting all three built-up levels, there are about 6½ acres of usable space on the pier.

A total of 31 rides includes a dark ride called Dante's Inferno, a high-flying Condor, and a giant slide. The theme of the miniature golf course is the history of Wildwood.

Open from Easter Sunday through mid-October. Admission is free, with rides and attractions on a pay-as-you-go basis. The pier is transformed into a haunted pier during Spooktober Fest, held during October each year.

 Roller coasters: The Great Nor'Easter, inverted (S); Jet Star, family (S).

A Splash & Ride pay-one-price ticket, good for all 3 Morey's ride parks and 2 waterparks (Raging Waters, see page 134), is available, under $30. A ride-only ticket for the 3 amusement piers is also available, under $24. In all, there are more than 100 rides (not counting waterparks), and again that many attractions on the 3 piers.

THE AMUSEMENT PARK GUIDE

Morey's Wild Wheels Raceway & Adventure Pier
Boardwalk & Spencer Avenue
Wildwood, NJ (609) 522-3900

As the southernmost of the Morey's family of boardwalk parks, this one has a different appeal and attitude. It has an exciting blend of rides, adventure activities, and the country's only wooden roller coaster built on a seaside pier. In all, there are 30 rides and attractions, with about half being amusement park rides.

The Great White roller coaster drops you immediately down a 25-foot hill, and the first 150 feet of your journey are in a tunnel under the pier; it then goes up the lift hill and takes you 250 feet beyond the end of the pier, nearly up to the waters of the Atlantic Ocean.

Among the offerings here are a carousel, batting cages, Skycoaster, climbing wall, a maze built under the coaster, a chair lift that takes you beyond the end of the pier and back, and 2 go-kart tracks.

The hours, prices, and operating procedures here are the same as Morey's Pier (see page 131). Tickets purchased for any Morey's property are good at the others as well.

Roller coaster: The Great White (W).

"Great White Shark," Raging Waters, California

Nickel's Midway Pier
Boardwalk at Schellenger Avenue
Wildwood, NJ (609) 522–2542

On the land side of the boardwalk, this pier has the state's only remaining walk-through haunted castle, complete with flaming torches at the entranceway. Called Castle Dracula, the place is also one of the most popular attractions along the boardwalk. Under the Castle, the Dungeon Boat Ride takes you along a blood-colored river to myriad scares and surprises.

The 23 rides consist of 18 for kids and 5 that the entire family can enjoy, such as the bumper cars; Jurassic Adventure; Tilt-A-Whirl; and 3 go-kart tracks.

Open during peak season from noon to midnight, the operation begins each spring on Easter Sunday and closes at the end of September. Free admission, with rides and attractions on a pay-as-you-go basis. Pay-one-price also available, under $12. Every Wednesday is "Wacky Wednesday," when pay-one-price passes are discounted.

 Roller coaster: Python, family (S).

Raging Waters at
Mariner's Landing
Boardwalk at Schellenger Avenue
Wildwood, NJ (609) 522–3900

At the end of the pier offering a view of the Atlantic Ocean and the massive, sandy beaches, this compact waterpark offers 12 slides and flumes; the Little Dipper children's area with slides and activity pool; lazy river; adult activity pool with nets, rings, crawls, and swings; food service; and a beach shop. Open daily during summer 9:00 A.M. to 7:30 P.M.

Admission options include a 2-hour pass, under $14; a 3-hour pass, under $16; and an all-day pass, under $20. A 3½ hour session for under $14 is in effect each morning up to 12:30 P.M. A pay-one-price combo ticket, which includes a 3-hour waterpark session as well as more than 100 rides at Morey's Pier, Mariner's Landing, and Morey's Wild Wheels Raceway & Adventure Pier, is available, under $30.

The Amusement Park Guide

Raging Waters at Morey's Pier
Boardwalk at 25th Street
Wildwood, NJ (609) 522-3900

Providing a magnificent view of the Wildwood beaches, this park is not only a cooling oasis of fresh, clear water with a lot of activity and fun, but it's also an engineering marvel. How did they fit it on the already crowded pier? Planning, they say.

Built amid, below, and over the rides and attractions of the pier amusement park, the waterpark contains 9 slides and flumes, an adult activity pool, lazy river, Little Dipper children's activity pool, a large hot tub, food service, and a beach shop. Hours and admission prices are same as Raging Waters at Mariner's Landing, see above.

Mariner's Landing, see page 133.

Morey's Pier, see page 131.

Morey's Wild Wheels and Adventure Pier, see page 132.

Nickel's Midway Pier, see page 133.

Raging Waters at Mariner's Landing, see page 133.

Raging Waters at Morey's Pier, see above.

Six Flags Great Adventure
Route 537
Jackson, NJ (908) 928–1821
http://www.sixflags.com

This is the largest amusement park facility along the East Coast and gets much of its business from the New York and Philadelphia markets.

The 1,100-acre park has no overall theme, but some of the individual sections do, including the Old Country, Bugs Bunny Land, Movietown, and a games area called Good Times Square. In addition to the ride park, with 43 rides, is a drive-through safari, considered the largest such facility in the world.

Several fantasy buildings were constructed when the park was built in 1974, including the Yum Yum Palace, a giant Tepee and a huge covered wagon. These are unique and make great photos—especially the Great Character Cafe, shaped like an ice-cream sundae.

 Extras: The adjacent Six Flags Wild Safari Animal Park is the world's largest drive-through safari outside Africa. A 4½-mile, self-guided drive takes you past more than 1,200 animals who call this 350-acre complex their home.

 Special events: Spring Breakout Extreme, April; Fright Fest, October.

 Season: Late March through Halloween weekend in October.

 Operating hours: Opens at 10:00 A.M.; closes at 10:00 P.M. on weekdays and at 11:00 P.M. on Saturdays and Sundays.

 Admission policy: Pay-one-price, under $35. A safari ticket may be purchased for $3 more. An evening discount goes into effect at 4:00 P.M. Make sure you get your ticket validated for $11, and it will be good for another admission anytime during the season. Parking charge.

 Top rides: The Right Stuff Mach I Adventure, simulated jet ride; Movietown Water Effect, shoot-the-chute; Roaring Rapids, a raging-rapids ride; Parachute Training Center–Edwards AFB Jump Tower, a 250-foot-tall parachute drop; a circa-1890 Savage Gallopers carousel that runs clockwise; Adventure Rivers, a series of 10 wet/dry raft-ride experiences.

THE AMUSEMENT PARK GUIDE

Roller coasters: Batman & Robin: the Chiller, Twin LEM Shuttles (S); Skull Mountain, indoor (S); Batman The Ride (S); Great American Scream Machine, multi-element (S); Viper, heartline (S); Runaway Mine Train (S); Rolling Thunder (W).

Plan to stay: All day and into the evening, 8–10 hours.

Best way to avoid crowds: Avoid weekends if you want to stay out of crowds. Come early during the week or just before dinnertime. Ride the big rides first. Pick up a free park map when you enter, and plot your course.

Directions: Take Exit 7A off the New Jersey Turnpike, go east on I-195 to Exit 16, and head south on Route 537 for 1½ miles. Follow signs to the park. Located 50 miles from Philadelphia and 60 miles from New York City.

Steel Pier
Boardwalk at Virginia Avenue
Atlantic City, NJ (609) 345–4893

In the early part of the century, Atlantic City's Steel Pier was internationally famous for its dance halls, exhibitions, and attractions. The pier fell on hard times and closed in 1977 but was reopened as an amusement pier in 1992.

Now full of life and excitement, the park features 20 rides, including the Giant Ferris Wheel, Wildcat roller coaster, go-karts, and 9 kiddie rides. There is also a Skycoaster, midway games, and a video-games arcade. Food can be found at the International Food Court.

No admission charge to the pier, with rides and activities on a pay-as-you-go basis. Pay-one-price is available on weekdays, under $20. Open daily, June through mid-September, weekends in spring and fall.

Storybook Land
Black Horse Pike
Cardiff, NJ (609) 641–7847

You'll be greeted by a 25-foot-tall statue of Mother Goose as you approach this intriguing 20-acre park. Opened in 1955, it has become a tradition in the area. Kids who came here long ago are now bringing their own children to enjoy the fun.

This wonderful world of fantasy has 10 kiddie rides, including a train, a carousel, antique cars, and a flying elephant. A special month-long "Fantasy with Lights" Christmas celebration features more than 200,000 lights in the park and Mr. and Mrs. Santa in their home to welcome the kids.

Admission is pay-one-price, under $10. Hours vary; call first.

Wonderland Pier, see page 122.

NEW MEXICO

Cliff's Amusement Park
4800 Osuna NE
Albuquerque, NM (505) 881-9373

Pinks, tans, and browns—the traditional Southwest colors are the dominant shades here, as is adobe architecture with a touch of frontier motif. Located in the middle of the city, in the middle of the desert, this 15-acre park doesn't have to work too hard to achieve its southwestern theme.

There are 21 rides, including 10 just for the wee ones, set in a separate kiddieland.

 Extras: A large game room and a midway lineup of carnival games.

 Season: Mid-April through mid-October.

 Operating hours: Weekdays, 6:00 to 10:00 P.M.; weekends, opens at noon and closes at 10:00 P.M. on Saturday and 9:00 P.M. on Sunday.

 Admission policy: General admission fee includes all entertainment, with rides and attractions on a pay-as-you-play basis. Pay-one-price available, under $12. Free parking.

 Top rides: Rocky Mountain Rapids, a log flume; Yo-Yo, flying swings; Sea Dragon; Scrambler; bumper cars.

 Roller coaster: Galaxy, family (S).

The Amusement Park Guide

 Plan to stay: 4 hours.

 Best way to avoid crowds: Come on weeknights early in the week.

 Directions: Take the San Mateo exit off I–25, and go south on San Mateo for a short distance to Osuna. Turn right on Osuna; the park is a short distance on the left.

NEW YORK

Adventureland
2245 Broadhollow Road, Route 110
East Farmingdale, NY (516) 694–6868

The last thing you expect to see as you're driving along this crowded highway, known as the "downtown area of Long Island," is a first-class major amusement park.

Located on 10 acres, this beautifully landscaped park has decorative brick sidewalks and is especially pretty at night. A large kiddieland is at one end of the park and offers 12 rides. In addition, there are 13 major rides and an 18-hole miniature golf course, with a unique floating hole.

 Extras: The large arcade and restaurant are open year-round.

 Season: Palm Sunday through mid-September

 Operating hours: 11:00 A.M. or noon to 11:00 P.M. or midnight.

 Admission policy: Free admission, with rides and attractions on a pay-as-you-go basis. Pay-one-price also available, under $16. Parking is free.

 Top rides: 1313 Cemetery Way, a ride-through haunted house; Capt. Willy's Wild Water Ride, bumper boats; Looping Star; Surf Dance; Ferris wheel.

 Roller coaster: Hurricane (S).

Plan to stay: 4 hours.

 Best way to avoid crowds: Come any weeknight during the season, and you'll rarely have a long wait.

 Directions: Take Exit 49 (Route 110) off the Long Island Expressway and head south for 2 miles. The park is on the left.

Astroland Amusement Park
1000 Surf Avenue
Brooklyn/Coney Island, NY
(718) 265–2100

Ahh, Coney Island. This is where it all started, a long, long time ago. Amusement park roots lie under these sandy beaches. Today the entertainment area of Coney Island is comprised of this park and various other clusters of rides, games, and attractions along the boardwalk.

Astroland consists of 23 rides, including 11 for kids. Among the 12 adult rides is the world-renowned Cyclone wooden roller coaster, which holds a New York Historic Landmark designation. Built in 1927, it's the last operating wooden coaster of the many that used to be along these boardwalks, including the Switchback Railway, the first roller coaster built in the United States, in 1884.

 Special events: Air Show, during the July 4 holiday period; Mermaid Parade, sponsored by a local historical group, June.

 Season: Palm Sunday through September.

 Operating hours: Noon to midnight, during summer.

 Admission policy: Free admission with rides on a pay-as-you-go basis. Pay-one-price also offered, under $15. Though parking is available at meters along street, recommended parking is in the New York Aquarium parking lot adjacent to the park; the parking fee during the day includes admission to the aquarium.

 Top rides: A log flume; Dante's Inferno, a dark ride; Music Express; Breakdance; Enterprise; Pirate Ship; Astrotower, a 200-foot-tall observation tower providing a magnificent view of the entire Coney Island area.

 Roller coaster: Cyclone, circa 1927 (W).

 Plan to stay: 3 hours.

 Best way to avoid crowds: The last 2 weeks in June are the least crowded during the season. Come early to avoid the big after-work crowd.

 Directions: Take Exit 7 South (Ocean Parkway South) off the Belt Parkway. Ocean Parkway curves onto Surf Avenue. Follow Surf to West 10th Street; the park is on the left.

Darien Lake Theme Park
Barracuda Bay
Route 77
Darien Center, NY (716) 599–4641

http://www.darienlake.com

Billing itself as the state's largest entertainment and recreational complex, this park is located on more than 1,000 acres, which includes a 2,000-site campground.

There are 43 rides here, including 12 for kids, located in two separate kiddie areas, Popeye's Seaport and Adventureland. The park is clean, easy to get around in, and offers a great deal of activity.

Barracuda Bay is included in park admission and features 20-plus activities, including a 40,000-square-foot family activity pool.

 Extras: The campground is an original: You can bring your own RV or rent one of theirs. A general store is located within the camping area. Paddleboats, Skycoaster, miniature golf, and go-karts are available for an additional fee.

 Special events: Custom Car Show, early June; July 4 fireworks and activities; Kingdom Bound, Christian Music Festival, late August; International Festival, Labor Day weekend.

 Season: Memorial Day through Labor Day.

Operating hours: 10:00 A.M. to 10:00 P.M. daily, except in June, when the park closes at 5:00 P.M. on weekdays.

 Admission policy: Pay-one-price, under $20. Discount tickets available at Tops Markets throughout the area. Parking charge.

 Top rides: Grizzly Run, a raging-rapids ride; Giant Wheel, a 165-foot-tall Ferris wheel; and Ranger, a looping ship ride.

 Roller coasters: Mind Eraser, inverted (S); Nightmare at Phantom Cave, indoor Jet Star (S); Predator (W); Viper, multielement (S).

 Plan to stay: 4 hours—6 if you go to Barracuda Bay.

 Best way to avoid crowds: Come early in the day on all days. Mondays and Tuesdays are the slowest.

 Directions: Located midway between Rochester and Buffalo. Take Exit 48A off the New York State Thruway and head south 5 miles on Route 77.

 # TIM'S TRIVIA

The 80s teen idols, the New Kids on the Block, filmed their first music video at Deno's Wonder Wheel in Coney Island, Brooklyn, New York.

Deno's Wonder Wheel Park
1025 Boardwalk
Brooklyn/Coney Island, NY
(718) 372-2592

The giant Wonder Wheel is another survivor of the old Coney Island rides lineup and has been officially declared a New York Historic Landmark. There are 23 rides here, 18 of them for kids. The circa-1920, 135-foot-tall, oceanside Wheel is the main attraction and the only one of its kind in the world. Although most of the additional rides and attractions are relatively new, the Spook-a-Rama is an old dark ride. Located along the boardwalk and adjacent to Astroland,

THE AMUSEMENT PARK GUIDE

the park is close to all other Coney Island attractions, rides, and food outlets. Admission is free; rides are on a pay-as-you-play basis. The park is open from noon daily and is in operation from mid-April through October.

The Enchanted Forest
Water Safari
Route 28
Old Forge, NY (315) 369-6145

If there's an amusement park in America that can be described as "way off the beaten path," this is it. Nestled in the heavily wooded hills of the Adirondack Mountains in the upstate area, the park can't be seen from the parking lot, because of the dense woods.

The 50-acre facility is a wet/dry park with a combination of waterpark and amusement park rides. It's divided into four themes: Water Safari, the waterpark; Storybook Lane, a walk through the land of several storybook characters; Animal Lane, a petting zoo; and the Yukon, a western village.

There are 14 mechanical rides, including 7 for kids, and 24 water slides and activities, including a wave pool. All water is heated!

 Extras: A large statue of Paul Bunyan, plus narrated visits to the cottages of some of the most famous storybook characters of all times, free with admission.

 Season: Mid-June through Labor Day.

 Operating hours: 9:30 A.M. to 6:00 P.M.

 Admission policy: Pay-one-price, under $20. "Siesta Savings" plan allows for next day free when you pay after 3:00 P.M.

 Top rides: Tilt-A-Whirl; Ferris wheel; bumper cars; carousel; and Scrambler.

 Plan to stay: 8 hours if you play in the waterpark.

Best way to avoid crowds: Come during early summer or midmorning during the peak season.

Directions: Located 1 hour north of the New York State Thruway (I–90). Take Exit 31 (Route 12) off I–90 near Utica, and go north on Route 12 for about 25 miles to Alder Creek. Take Route 28 north to Old Forge; the park is on Route 28, on the north side of the village.

Great Escape and Splashwater Kingdom Fun Park
Splashwater Kingdom
Route 9
Lake George, NY (518) 792–6568
http://www.thegreatescape.com

Nestled into the Adirondack Mountains, this park is one of the prettiest in the country. In addition to the colorful landscaping, a clear river, numerous bridges, and huge shade trees, the 140 acres hold 31 rides, including 10 just for kids; a participatory play area; and several walk-through attractions.

There are seven separate areas: Fantasy Rides, where most of the rides are located; Ghost Town, an Old West area and one of the oldest sections in the park; International Village, offering shopping from around the world and including a Tiffany shop and a quality toy shop; Jungle Land, a tropics-oriented area; Arto's Small World, a child-size version of a town, with walk-through buildings; Alice in Wonderland, where one enters the area through the famed rabbit hole that Alice fell through to reach her dream; Splashwater Kingdom offering 3 slides, a lazy river, wave pool, and Noah's Playground, a water activity pool for children.

 Extras: Miniature golf, no additional charge. The Cinderella Carriage Coach is a horse-drawn coach ride during which a princess tells stories. Also, a high-dive show, 4 daily circus performances, and a petting zoo.

 Special events: Scout Month, June; Oktoberfest, late September.

 Season: May through mid-September.

 Operating hours: 9:30 A.M. to 6:00 P.M.

THE AMUSEMENT PARK GUIDE

 Admission policy: Pay-one-price, under $23. Come in after 3:00 P.M., next day free. Free parking.

 Top rides: Giant Wheel, a gondola-style Ferris wheel; Desperado's Plunge, a log flume; Raging River, a raging-rapids ride; Condor; Tornado dark ride.

 Roller coasters: Comet (W); Steamin' Demon, 2-corkscrew, loop (S).

 Plan to stay: 5 hours.

 Best way to avoid crowds: Come during the middle of the week.

 Directions: Located a few miles outside Lake George on Route 9, between Exits 19 and 20 of the Adirondack Northway (I–87).

Hoffman's Playland
Route 9
Latham, NY (518) 785–3842

With its small family park, the Hoffman family caters to the local market and it's not unusual, especially during the day, for most of the people in the park to know one another.

The 16 rides include a 1952 Allan Herschell carousel, an iron horse (train), a Ferris wheel, a compact steel roller coaster, and extremely well-maintained bumper cars. A large arcade and a video-game room feature a diversity of games including Skee-ball. And both a miniature golf course and a driving range are adjacent to the park.

Open from Easter Sunday through mid-September. Park hours are noon to 10:00 P.M. daily; admission is free, with rides and attractions on a pay-as-you-go basis.

Kids Kingdom
3351 Route 112
Medford, NY (516) 698–3384

This Long Island kiddieland birthday park has its parties under a giant tent next to the rides midway. In addition to its 15 kiddie and family rides, the park offers costumed characters, live music, puppet shows, and a good selection of fast food, including gyros.

Open daily, from April through October, noon to 6:00 or 8:00 P.M. The park has a free gate, with rides and attractions on a pay-as-you-go basis; pay-one-price ticket is also available, under $15.

Lake George Action Park
Route 9
Lake George, NY (518) 668-5459

As the name implies, action is the emphasis at this well-maintained park on the edge of the village, close to Lake George. The 7½-acre park is full of willow and maple trees, and has lots of grassy areas.

With 7 rides, the park is very attractive after dark, with its neon signs and many traveling lights on the rides and buildings. Among the rides and activities are a Tilt-A-Whirl, bumper cars, bumper boats, kiddie airplanes, a beautiful double-deck Italian carousel, go-karts, miniature golf, and a large arcade.

Open daily, Memorial Day through Labor Day, from 2:00 to 10:30 P.M. There is a $2 admission fee, with each paying guest receiving $2 worth of tokens. All rides and attractions are on a pay-as-you-play basis. The park is owned by the legendary Charles R. Wood, founder of The Great Escape and Splashwater Kingdom Fun Park,which is now owned by Premier Parks, just outside of Lake George.

 TIM'S TRIVIA

Talk about recycling! Through the years, the owners of Knoebels Amusement Resort in Elysburg, Pennsylvania, have purchased used rides and equipment from other parks and have carefully reconditioned and rebuilt them and put them back into use. Today the history of more than thirty parks, many now defunct, lives on at Knoebels.

Magic Forest
Route 9
Lake George, NY (518) 668-2448

Set in a pine forest a few miles from Lake George, Magic Forest is a family park with a Christmas and holiday atmosphere. It's divided into three areas: Christmas Village, Storybook, and a ride section. In addition to the bird show, the magic show, and a high-diving horse, the park offers 19 family and kiddie rides, and 6 adult rides, including a Tilt-A-Whirl and a Ferris wheel.

Open daily from Memorial Day through early September; call for hours. Admission is pay-one-price, under $11.

Martin's Fantasy Island
2400 Grand Island Boulevard
Grand Island, NY (716) 773–7591

It's hard to pinpoint the exact theme of this "something for every member of the family" park. A lot of parks claim it, but this 80-acre facility truly does have something for everyone.

It's a ride park, a waterpark, a western town, a storybook park, and a fantasyland all tied together. Each of the five areas has a theme: Fantasyland, Western town, Midway, Water World and Festival Picnic Grounds. There's a great children's area, containing many of the 18 kiddie rides. In total, the park offers 36 rides.

Extras: Cinema 180; miniature golf, paddleboats, and a petting zoo are all included in the admission price.

Special events: Sneak-a-Peak, a park preview, with special rates, Memorial Day weekend.

Season: Late-May through mid-September.

Operating hours: 11:30 A.M. to 8:30 P.M. Closed Mondays.

Admission policy: Pay-one-price, under $15. Free parking.

Top rides: Chaos; Old Mill Scream, a log flume; Splash Creek, an active lazy-river raft ride.

Roller coaster: Wildcat, family (S).

Plan to stay: 6 hours.

Best way to avoid crowds: Come during the week and plan your visit around the show schedule.

Directions: Take Exit N19 off Highway 190, go west on Whitehaven Road to Baseline Road, turn left, and go to Grand Island Boulevard. The park can be seen from the highway.

Midway Park
Route 430
Maple Springs, NY (716) 386–3165

When this turn-of-the-century park opened in 1898, William McKinley was president and there had never been a World Series. People came by steamboat, train, and trolley car. Today, that nostalgic, trolley park atmosphere is being preserved, and a step into this park is a step back in time. Midway Park is a scenic, well-designed facility on the banks of Lake Chautauqua. It has 16 rides, including 8 for kids, and features a roller-skating rink—complete with a view of the lake—on the second floor of a circa-1915 ballroom building.

Extras: Museum highlighting the park and the trolley and railroad companies that started it, free. Roller skating, miniature golf, go-karts, bumper boats, and family paddleboat excursions on the lake, all for extra charges.

Special events: July 4 picnic and celebration.

Season: Memorial Day weekend through Labor Day weekend.

Operating hours: 1:00 P.M. until dusk.

Admission policy: Free admission to the park, with rides on a pay-as-you-go basis. Pay-one-price available on weekends. Wednesdays are 25-cent kiddie days, when popcorn and most rides cost a quarter.

Top rides: Tubs of Fun, a spinning ride; Tilt-A-Whirl; a giant slide; and 7 Allan Herschell kiddie rides.

Roller coaster: Dragon Coaster, family (S).

THE AMUSEMENT PARK GUIDE

 Plan to stay: 2 hours.

 Best way to avoid crowds: Come during the week and be there when the rides open.

 Directions: Located on Route 430 on Lake Chautauqua in Maple Springs.

Nellie Bly Park
1824 Shore Parkway
Brooklyn, NY (718) 996–4002

Other than the beach, this may well be the most delightful place in Brooklyn to take the kids. It's a compact, friendly, family park with 17 rides, including 9 just for the wee ones.

Located 5 blocks from the Coney Island district, the park was named after the country's first female newspaper reporter. The theme of the fun house is Bly's world travels.

 Extras: Go-karts and miniature golf, extra charge.

 Season: Easter through October, or as long as the weather holds out.

 Operating hours: Noon to 10:00 or 11:00 P.M.

 Admission policy: Admission is free, with rides and attractions on a pay-as-you-play basis. Pay-one-price available on Tuesday and Thursday from 11:00 A.M. to 2:00 P.M. and on Wednesday evenings, 7:30 to 10:00 P.M. , under $10. Free parking.

 Top rides: Flying School Bus; Panda, spin-about; train ride; water slide; giant slide; Convoy, a kiddie truck ride; Red Baron, a kiddie plane ride; a carousel; Tilt-A-Whirl.

 Roller coaster: Flash, family (S).

 Plan to stay: 2 hours.

Best way to avoid crowds: Wednesdays are the slowest days.

 Directions: Take Exit 5 off the Belt Parkway and travel ½ mile to 25th Street; the park is on the right.

Playland Park
Playland Parkway and the Beach
Rye, NY (914) 921–0370

There's so much preserved nostalgia here that the entire park (built in 1928) has been listed as a National Historic Landmark. The combination of original Art Deco elements of the late 1920s with rides of the 1990s provides a wonderful experience.

This 279-acre, county-owned complex features a boardwalk along Long Island Sound, a large beach, an 80-acre lake, picnic groves, and a nicely shaded and landscaped ride park. The 45 rides include 7 original, circa-1929 rides that are still in great working shape. The 20 kiddie rides are located in a separate kiddieland.

 Extras: Olympic-size swimming pool, miniature golf, paddle boats, beach swimming, all extra. Nature preserve, free.

 Special events: Fireworks and marching-band performance every Wednesday, plus shows and concerts throughout the summer on the outdoor stage.

 # TIM'S TRIVIA

The American Coaster Enthusiasts (ACE) publishes a glossy magazine and a monthly newsletter all about roller coasters. Both publications are free with membership. Write them at P.O. Box 8226, Chicago IL 60680.

 Season: Mid-May through mid-September.

 Operating hours: Opens at noon and closes at various hours during the evening, depending on crowds and weather. Closed Mondays.

THE AMUSEMENT PARK GUIDE

 Admission policy: Free admission, with all rides and attractions on a pay-as-you-go basis. Parking charge.

 Top rides: The Log Flume, with 2 drops; go-karts; Giant Gondola Wheel; Auto Scooter, bumper cars; Derby Racer carousel, one of only two still operating in the nation (the other is at Cedar Point in Ohio).

 Roller coasters: Hurricane (S); Dragon Coaster (W); Kiddy Coaster, junior (W).

 Plan to stay: 4 hours.

 Best way to avoid crowds: Tuesdays are the slowest, but Wednesdays are the most fun. Come early, have dinner, hear the band concert, and see the fireworks. You'll have small crowds to contend with but will have a great, old-fashioned time.

 Directions: Take Exit 19 (Playland Parkway) off I–95. Follow the parkway 1½ miles to the beach where the road dead-ends at the park.

Seabreeze Amusement Park
Raging Rivers Waterpark
4600 Culver Road
Rochester, NY (716) 323-1900

High on the bluffs overlooking Lake Ontario, this is a beautiful, well-kept traditional park. Founded in 1879, this 30-acre step back into time offers 23 rides, plus a waterpark. It's also a good place to be on a hot day—the temperature is usually 10 degrees cooler up here than in the city.

With many of its buildings dating back to the turn of the century, the park provides a fine blend of nostalgia and technology, the latter evident in the sophisticated water rides within Raging Rivers waterpark.

 Extras: A 1994 fire destroyed several original buildings and a circa-1915 carousel. In 1996, a new hand-carved carousel, with 46 horses and 2 chariots, opened in a beautifully reproduced Victorian building. Many other buildings were also rebuilt in a Victorian style.

 Special events: Grand Opening celebration, highlighting fireworks, opening day weekend in May.

Season: Early May through Labor Day.

 Operating hours: Noon to 10:00 or 11:00 P.M.

 Admission policy: General admission, includes entrance and 2 rides, under $6. Pay-one-price available; includes all rides and waterpark, under $15. Discounted Night Rider pass available every night after 4:00 P.M. Free parking.

 Top rides: Sea Dragon; Gyro-Sphere, a dome with a Scrambler, complete with sound and light show; a log flume; bumper cars; Tilt-A-Whirl.

 Roller coasters: Jack Rabbit (W); Quantum Loop, 2-loop (S); Bobsleds (S).

 Plan to stay: 6 hours.

 Best way to avoid crowds: Come Mondays through Wednesdays.

 Directions: Take I–490 off the New York State Thruway (I–90) to I–590. Go north toward Lake Ontario. Take a left at the Seabreeze traffic circle; then take the next right onto Culver Road. The park is a few blocks down on the right.

Splish Splash
Exit 72W off the Long Island Expressway
Riverhead, NY (516) 727–3600

Situated deep in the Long Island pine forest, you'll find this beautiful 100-acre waterpark, the state's largest. And it keeps getting bigger and more diverse every year!

Among its vast offerings are 16 adult slides, with such descriptive monikers as the Cliff Diver, an 85-foot-high speed slide down a chute, through a house, and into the splash pool. The Abyss is a tube slide through an enclosed flume that goes through a shipwreck and a waterfall. The Barrier Reef slide dumps you out next to a shark, and Shotgun Falls drops you out several yards above the splash pool.

Additionally, there's a 1,300-foot-long lazy river with waves; a wave pool; Kiddie Cove, a children's activity area

THE AMUSEMENT PARK GUIDE

featuring 3 different pools and a kiddie carwash; and 2 daily shows, a combination sea lion/high-dive show, and a tropical bird presentation.

There are 2 restaurants, 2 gift shops, and plenty of parking. Open 9:30 A.M. to 7:00 P.M., daily, Memorial Day through Labor Day, under $20.

Sylvan Beach Amusement Park
Park Avenue, Route 13
Sylvan Beach, NY (315) 762–5212

Some of the best amusement parks in our history were established near summer resorts, as was this one. These early parks were important gathering places for the community and provided an entertainment constant in the area.

This one, on the east shore of Oneida Lake, has survived pretty much intact and is a good example of a traditional Northeast resort park. A village park and a public swimming beach are located next door.

A 1940 Art Deco building houses traditional midway games such as Fascination and Skee-Ball and imparts a sense of nostalgia. There are 21 rides, including 10 for kids and a super slide.

Extras: Every Wednesday, a clown roams the park passing out gifts and doing face painting. Ride prices are reduced all day.

Special events: Old-Fashioned Weekend, observed opening weekend in April, with all rides 25 cents each; Thank-You Weekend, last weekend of the season, with all rides 25 cents each.

Season: Late April through mid-May.

Operating hours: Noon to 11:00 P.M.

Admission policy: Free gate, with rides and attractions on a pay-as-you-go basis. A pay-one-price special, under $9, is available every Friday night after 6:00 P.M.

Top rides: Bumper cars; Bumper boats; Laffland, a classic Pretzel dark ride; Tilt-A-Whirl; and a classic Philadelphia Toboggan Company teacup ride.

Roller coaster: Galaxi, family (S).

 Plan to stay: 2 hours.

 Best way to avoid crowds: Since rides are on a pay-as-you-go basis, there usually isn't a crowd rushing from one ride to another. The pace is slower here; the park is very seldom crowded, especially during the week.

 Directions: Located in the Village of Sylvan Beach on Route 13, 4 miles north of Route 31 and 8 miles north of Exit 34 (Route 13) off I–90, the New York Thruway. About halfway between Utica and Syracuse.

NORTH CAROLINA

Emerald Pointe Waterpark
3800 South Holden Road
Greensboro, NC (910) 852–9721

Surfs up! The Tsunami Wave Pool produces individual, 6-foot-tall breakers, some of the largest man-made waves in the world, and that translates into big-time fun for action seekers visiting this top-notch park. Although the waves are big and powerful enough for surfing, no boards are allowed in the pool, but body surfing is permitted and encouraged, as are tube riders.

In addition to the 40,000-square-foot wave pool, there are 13 slides, 2 kiddie activity pools, 3 family activity pools, the Lazee River, and the fast-moving Cyclone Zone circular river for the toddlers of the family.

There are 3 sand volleyball courts, 5 snack stands, a beach and gift shop, and a 3-point basketball court. Open mid-May through mid-September, 10:00 A.M. to 7:00 P.M. An "All-Day Splash" ticket is under $20; an after 4:00 P.M. ticket, good until closing, is available, under $13.

THE AMUSEMENT PARK GUIDE

Ghost Town in the Sky
U.S. Route 19
Maggie Valley, NC (704) 926-1140
(800) 446-7886

What an amazing place this is! To get to the park, you have to take a chairlift or an incline railway to a plateau most of the way up the side of a mountain. Then you climb aboard a bus that takes you the rest of the way up to the attractions.

Begun in 1961 as a ghost-town attraction, the facility has added rides and other elements through the years. There are 20 rides, including 8 for children. But the best attraction of all is the splendid view of the Great Smoky Mountains.

Divided into four sections, the park offers the original Ghost Town, Fort Cherokee, Mining Town, and the Mile-High Ride area.

 Extras: Sunday church services are held in Ghost Town. The Mystery Shack is a unique gravity house, free with admission. Five different shows, including cancan dancers, gunfights, and Cherokee Indian dancers.

 Season: May through October.

 Operating hours: 9:00 A.M. to 6:00 P.M. The chairlifts and incline quit taking guests up to the park 2 hours before the official closing time.

 Admission policy: Pay-one-price, under $18. Free parking.

 Top rides: Global Swings, flying swings in a metal globe; Black Widow, an indoor Scrambler; Sea Dragon; Tilt-A-Whirl; bumper cars; carousel.

 Roller coaster: Red Devil, looping (S). (Built on side of mountain. You leave loading station and immediately drop off the side of the mountain.)

 Plan to stay: 4 hours.

 Best way to avoid crowds: The smallest crowds come in late May and late August. Monday is the slowest day of the week.

Directions: Located on Highway 19, west of Maggie Valley. The park is 35 miles from Asheville via I-40 and 90 miles east of Knoxville, Tennessee, via I-40.

Goldston's Beach and Pavilion
White Lake Road at the Beach
White Lake, NC (910) 862–4064

The major draw here is the white, sandy beach. Located on 15 acres, the park offers 12 rides, miniature golf, a large video-game and games-of-skill arcade, cottages, and a motel.

In addition to 2 restaurants, the park has a Dairy Queen franchise.

The entire facility is open from 9:00 A.M. to 11:00 P.M., with the rides in operation only during the evening. Admission is free, with a pay-as-you-play policy for the rides, attractions, and beach facilities.

Jubilee Park
Highway 421
Carolina Beach, NC (910) 458–9017

Located 3 blocks from the oceanside boardwalk, this 7½-acre park has 18 rides, including 7 for kids. Flat, paved walkways between the rides makes this an easy park to get around in.

Extras: Go-karts; water slides, speed slides, and a kiddie play pool; large arcade with pool tables; gift shop.

Special events: Fireworks, July 4.

Season: Easter through mid-October.

Operating hours: July is considered peak season, with hours 10:00 A.M. to 11:00 P.M. Slides open first and close first; rides open later and close last.

Admission policy: Free admission, with rides on a pay-as-you-go basis. Pay-one-price also available, under $15.

Top rides: Carousel, Tilt-A-Whirl; Ferris wheel; bumper cars; Scrambler; Swings; Octopus; Viking Ship.

Plan to stay: 3 hours.

Best way to avoid crowds: Tuesdays are the slowest days. July is the busiest month.

The Amusement Park Guide

 Directions: Located on Highway 421, about 1 mile past the Pleasure Island Bridge, 17 miles south of Wilmington.

Paramount's Carowinds
Riptide Reef
Carowinds Boulevard
Charlotte, NC (704) 588–2600
http://www.thegreatescape.com

The Old South is alive and well and living in this park. You enter through Plantation Square, and everywhere you look you see the traditional South. You'd swear you were on a Charleston waterfront.

This 83-acre park can also claim something no other park can. It has the North Carolina–South Carolina state line running right down the middle of its main street. There's a marker on the street, where you can catch some great photos of you and yours standing in both states at the same time.

 # TIM'S TRIVIA

Carowinds, located just south of Charlotte, North Carolina, has the North Carolina–South Carolina state line going right through the middle of the park. Although a unique distinction for the park, it creates its share of headaches, including different state-mandated break times, employment procedures, and state income tax rules.

In addition to the park's 40 rides, including 18 for kids, the 12-acre Riptide Reef waterpark contains a number of speed slides, activity pools, family slides, a wave pool, and several family tube slides. There is no additional fee to enter the waterpark.

 Extras: The Paladium Amphitheatre books in top-name entertainers throughout the summer, extra charge. There are also 207 campground sites adjacent to the park.

 Special events: 5 Christian Music Festivals, throughout the summer; Math, Science and Physics Day, May.

NORTH CAROLINA

 Season: Mid-March through the first weekend of October.

 Operating hours: 10:00 A.M. to 8:00 P.M. Stays open until 11:00 P.M. on Fridays and Saturdays.

 Admission policy: Pay-one-price, under $30. Reduced rates after 5:00 P.M. Parking charge.

 Top rides: Drop Zone, free fall; Days of Thunder, motion-based simulator; and White Water Falls, shoot the chute.

 Roller coasters: Goldrusher mine train (S); Scooby Doo's Ghoster Coaster, junior (W); Carolina Cyclone, 2-loop/corkscrew (S); Hurler (W); Thunder Road, racer (W); Vortex, stand-up (S).

 Plan to stay: 10 hours.

"The Hurler," Paramount's Carrowinds, North Carolina

The Amusement Park Guide

 Best way to avoid crowds: Come on weekends during the morning hours and ride the popular rides before the midday crunch arrives.

 Directions: Take Exit 90 (Carowinds Boulevard) off I–77, 10 miles south of Charlotte.

Santa's Land
Route 1
Cherokee, NC (704) 497–9191

Santa is always on duty at this cool, 16-acre park, located in the Great Smoky Mountains. Flower and vegetable gardens throughout the facility add a great deal of color, and the large shade trees and grassy areas enhance comfort. Bring your Christmas shopping list—there's terrific shopping here, in addition to the 9 rides.

 Extras: 6 shows, including a chance to meet Santa; paddleboats, playground equipment, a petting zoo, all free. Don't miss the Nativity scene or the giant snowman. And the employees wear what may be the neatest costumes of any park in the country . . . some are dressed as elves.

 Special events: Harvest Festival, weekends in October and the first weekend in November.

 Season: May through the first weekend of November.

 Operating hours: 9:00 A.M. to 5:00 P.M.

 Admission policy: Pay-one-price, under $13. Free parking.

 Top rides: A train ride, a mile-long jaunt; paddleboats; a Ferris wheel; carousel.

 Roller coaster: Rudicoaster, Rudolph-themed family ride (S).

 Plan to stay: 3 hours.

Best way to avoid crowds: Weekdays are least crowded. Park officials say the best time to visit is during the Harvest Festival.

 Directions: 3 miles north of Cherokee, on U.S. Highway 19.

Tweetsie Railroad
Highway 221/321
Blowing Rock, NC (704) 264–9061

Billing itself as the state's first theme park, this unique place opened in 1956 as a train excursion. Today, not only is that train ride aboard a full-size, coal-fired steam locomotive just as popular as ever, but also the owners have created a neat little theme park around it.

The overall atmosphere is one of an Old West railroad town. You enter the park through an old depot building and proceed down a western-style street. Specific areas include Tweetsie Square, Miner's Mountain, and Country Fair, where the 7 family rides are located.

Apart from the rides and the train, a chairlift takes you up to Miner's Mountain, where you can pan for gold, visit a petting zoo, or take a miniature train ride through Mouse Mine and see small, animated mice busy at work.

 Extras: Wild West, a coin-operated shooting gallery, and the Railroad Museum. During the 3-mile train ride, guests get robbed by bandits and attacked by Indians. Shows include a clogging show, saloon cancan, and a Bluegrass music band.

 Special events: Railroaders Day, late June; July 4 Week celebration; Clogging Jamboree, June; Halloween Festival and the Ghost Train, October.

 Season: Mid-May through October.

 Operating hours: 9:00 A.M. to 6:00 P.M. daily.

 Admission policy: Pay-one-price, under $16. Free parking.

 Top rides: A chair lift to Miner's Mountain; bumper cars; Ferris wheel; bumper boats; train ride; carousel.

THE AMUSEMENT PARK GUIDE

 Plan to stay: 5 hours.

 Best way to avoid crowds: Come at opening time on a Monday or a Friday. Try to avoid weekends and holidays if you can.

 Directions: Located 3 miles from Blowing Rock and 3 miles from Boone, on Highway 321/221.

NORTH DAKOTA

Lucy's Amusement Park
Highway 83 South
Minot, ND (701) 839–2320

With a slogan of "Fun is our business," how can you pass up Lucy's? Located on 3 acres, ½ mile outside the city limits, the park has 6 kiddie rides, a giant slide, an 18-hole miniature golf course, and a circular go-kart track with intersecting crossroads.

Although you'd think the park would be mainly for kids, 75 percent of its business comes from adults playing miniature golf.

Nicely laid out in a treed, grassy area, the park has free admission, with all rides and attractions on a pay-as-you-play basis. It is open daily, from midmorning to 10:00 or 11:00 P.M. The golf course stays open later than the rides.

OHIO

Americana Amusement Park
5757 Middletown–Hamilton Road
Middletown, OH (513) 539–7339

Surrounding a 22-acre, man-made lake, this traditional park is southeast Ohio's premier corporate picnic park, hosting several hundred outings per year. This fact alone says something about the local reputation the park enjoys. Founded in 1921 as LeSourdsville Lake, the facility was renamed in 1978. The owners of Cincinnati's Coney Island park purchased Americana in 1996 and have vowed to rebuild it to its former splendor.

The shaded picnic grove is directly inside the gate to your right, with most of the 32 rides to your left and across the lake.

 Extras: Miniature golf, paddle boats, and an Olympic-size swimming pool, free with park admission; Jolly Roger children's participatory play area, with nets, ball craws, swings, and 11 kiddie rides.

 Special events: July 4 celebration.

 Season: May through Labor Day weekend.

 Operating hours: 11:00 A.M. to 9:00 P.M., Sundays thru Fridays; 11:00 A.M. to 11:00 P.M., Saturdays.

 Admission policy: Pay-one-price, under $15. After 4:00 P.M., half-price special. Parking charge.

 Top rides: Raging Thunder, a log flume; The Galleon, a swinging pirate ship; Demolition Derby, bumper cars; Speedway, turnpike cars; Rock-O-Plane; Flying Scooters; carousel.

 Roller coasters: Screechin' Eagle (W); The Serpent (S).

 Plan to stay: 5 hours.

 Best way to avoid crowds: Come during the week; mornings are the least busy.

 Directions: Take Exit 29 (Monroe–Lebanon) off I–75 to Route 63 West, proceeding to the intersection of State Route 4; the park is at the intersection, about 5 miles from the interstate. Located 30 miles north of Cincinnati, 30 miles from Dayton, 100 miles from Columbus.

THE AMUSEMENT PARK GUIDE

The Beach
Kings Mill Road (Exit 25) at I-71
Mason, Ohio (513) 398-7946
http://www.thebeachwaterpark.com

Constantly voted by various fan organizations as one of the best waterparks in the world, The Beach has no problem living up to that reputation. You'll find 35 acres of activities for sand and sun here among the park's 30 waterslides and rides, 2 million gallons of water, and more than 40 activities.

The Aztec Adventure is the Midwest's first water coaster

"Magnum XL-200," Cedar Point, Ohio

and is set amid Aztec ruins. The Cliff is a 5-story free-fall slide, and Thunder Beach is the popular wave pool. The Banzai is a twin speedslide, and The Lazy Miami River is the tranquil, lazy river ride. There are 3 sand volleyball courts and 2 basketball courts, plus all the action in the Pirates Den Video Arcade. A Reggae Music Concert Series is held each season.

The park is located across the interstate from Paramount's Kings Island. Open mid-May through early September, it opens at 10:00 A.M. and closes at 7:00 or 9:00 P.M. Admission is under $20, with a special after–5:00 P.M. price of under $11. Parking charge.

Cedar Point
Soak City
On a Lake Erie Peninsula
Sandusky, OH (419) 626–0830
http://www.cedarpoint.com

Overlooking Lake Erie, this turn-of-the-century park is the finest traditional amusement park in the country. With its 56 rides, including 12 roller coasters, it is also the largest ride park on the continent.

Although some areas have themes, Cedar Point is not a serious theme park. It is a good, old-fashioned ride park, with a great deal of nostalgia.

The 364-acre park, with its tall rides presenting a bird's-eye view of Lake Erie, is heavily wooded and spread out. A walk to Frontier Town in the back of the park is about a mile hike. Along the Frontier Trail you'll find numerous craftspeople and log cabins.

Utilize the park's transportation system to get around and save a few steps. The skyride provides a one-way trip between the front and back of the park, and the Cedar Point and Lake Erie Railroad has a stop in Frontier Town.

Soak City Waterpark and Challenge Park are located between the park and resort hotels. Soak City offers a full-size waterpark with slides, rides, and pools. Admission is on a 2-hour, under $12, or all-day, under $17, basis. Challenge Park has two 18-hole miniature golf courses, go-karts, and a Skycoaster. Attractions are on a pay-as-you-go basis.

Extras: The park's 900-slip marina is one of the finest on Lake Erie. Docking for boats of all sizes is available just 500 feet from the park's entrance. Swimming in Lake Erie, with lifeguard supervision and bathhouse facilities, is included in admission. The park's history is chronicled in the Town Hall Museum, free.

The Amusement Park Guide

There are 2 hotels offering modern rooms and suites, and Camper's Village, with 300 equipped RV sites.

 Special events: CoasterMania, a day for enthusiasts, early June; in-water boat show, September.

 Season: May through September.

 Operating hours: Opens 10:00 A.M.; closing times vary through season, from 10:00 to midnight.

 Admission policy: Pay-one-price, under $31, 2-day, under $47; after 5:00 P.M., under $20. Parking charge.

 Top rides: Three antique carousels; Thunder Canyon, a raging-rapids ride; Giant Wheel, a 15-story-tall Ferris wheel with gondola-style seating; Snake River Falls, a shoot-the-chute.

 Roller coasters: Mantis, stand-up (S); Raptor, inverted (S); Blue Streak (W); Mean Streak (W); Corkscrew (S); Disaster Transport, indoor bob-sleds (S); Cedar Creek Mine Ride (S); Iron Dragon (S); Gemini, twin racing (S); Magnum XL200 (S); Jr. Gemini, junior (S); Wildcat (S).

 # TIM'S TRIVIA

Two parks premiered Arrow Development's new Log Flume during the 1963 season: Six Flags Over Texas, Arlington; and Cedar Point, Sandusky, Ohio.

 Plan to stay: A 2-day visit is a must, in order to enjoy the park to its fullest.

 Best way to avoid crowds: Come before mid-June or during the last week in August. Be there early; the causeway leading out to the park becomes a bottleneck once the masses start arriving.

 Directions: Located midway between Toledo and Cleveland. Take Exit 7 off the Ohio Turnpike (I–80), go north on Route 250 into Sandusky, and then follow the signs to the causeway.

"Mean Streak," Cedar Point, Ohio

THE AMUSEMENT PARK GUIDE

Coney Island
6201 Kellogg Avenue
Cincinnati, OH (513) 232–8230

With the name Coney Island, this park along the banks of the Ohio River had a lot to live up to in the early days. Founded in 1886, the park, often referred to as Coney Island West, had little but its name in common with the famous Brooklyn, New York, area. But it was every bit as popular, with thousands of people coming weekly by steamboat to play, swim, dance, and ride.

Most of the park was dismantled in 1972, when Kings Island was developed by the same owner. Today, however, this pretty little park is starting to make a slow comeback. A large swimming pool and water slides have kept its gates open. Officials say Sunlite Pool, measuring 200 x 401 feet, is the largest in the world. Two water slides, the Pipeline Plunge and the Zoom Flume, drop riders into the pool.

There is now a total of 16 family and kiddie rides, a combination turn-of-the-century classic rides and new favorites. An 18-hole miniature golf course was created specifically to accommodate the physically challenged. In addition there is pedal boating on Lake Como and a full range of recreational activities such as tennis, basketball, sand volleyball, and ping-pong.

The historic Moonlite Gardens features hop, bob, and rock concerts on many Friday nights during the season, and the equally nostalgic Moonlite Pavilion plays host several times a year to big-band dances, R&B, and jazz concerts. The popular Appalachian Festival is held on the grounds each May, and features down-home cooking, foot-stompin' music, and arts and crafts dealers.

 TIM'S TRIVIA

In Geneva-on-the-Lake, Ohio, they make their own wine at Erieview Park's Firehouse Winery.

Erieview Park
5483 Lake Road
Geneva-on-the-Lake, OH (216) 466–8650

Located on a bluff overlooking Lake Erie, this 18-ride park may be the best-kept secret in this part of the state: Its rides are "hidden" behind the stores and restaurants on the commercial strip of this resort community.

But that's a plus once you're in the park. The hustle and bustle of the street and real life are left behind, and usually only the sounds of boats on the lake can be heard above the sounds of the rides.

Founded in 1945, the 3-acre park has, in addition to its mechanical rides, a 2-flume water slide and a large arcade.

 Extras: A palm reader and a large shooting gallery are directly adjacent to the park entrance. The Firehouse Winery makes its own wine.

 Special events: Each year, the winery presents a 2-day Polka Fest in June, and a 2-day Celtic Fest in August.

 Season: Mother's Day through Labor Day.

 Operating hours: Opens during the week at 5:00 P.M.; on weekends, 10:00 A.M. Closes nightly at 10:00 P.M.

 Admission policy: Free gate, with rides on a pay-as-you-go basis. An all-day "ride and slide," pay-one-price ticket is available, under $12. Parking free if you buy ride tickets.

 Top rides: Ferris wheel; Roll-O-Plane; dark ride; bumper cars; carousel.

 Plan to stay: If you intend to use both rides and water slides, plan to stay 4 to 5 hours.

 Best way to avoid crowds: Come early in the week or at midday on weekends. The park is busiest in the evening, when the town itself is hopping.

 Directions: Take the Geneva-on-the-Lake exit (Route 534 North) off I–90 and drive north about 7 miles into the village. The park is on your left, with parking next to the water slide and Woody's World Arcade.

THE AMUSEMENT PARK GUIDE

Geauga Lake
Boardwalk Shores
1060 North Aurora Road
Aurora, OH (216) 562-7131

A lakeside location, plenty of old buildings, rides and games, and trees and colorful landscaping make a trip to this traditional park a good fun investment. Today the facility is one of the state's finest parks, offering the latest in rides, shows, and attractions.

Located on Geauga Lake, across from Sea World, the 47-acre park is reminiscent of the old-time family fun parks once so plentiful in this part of the country. The place is also a good example of a wet/dry park, wherein waterpark elements and mechanical amusement rides coexist in a total environment, creating a great entertainment bargain for the whole family. There are more than 43 "dry" rides and 15 "wet" rides, all included in the park admission price.

Boardwalk Shores features The Wave wave pool, 4 body slides, 3 speed slides, and 2 toboggan slides. Turtle Beach is the children's area, offering slides, a kiddie river, and an interactive play area.

 Extras: Large games-of-skill arcade. Go-karts, batting cages, paddleboats available at additional charge.

 Special events: Octoberfest, third and fourth weekend in September; Hallowscream, weekends in October.

 Season: May through September.

 Operating hours: 11:00 A.M. to 10:00 P.M.

 Admission policy: Pay-one-price, under $22. After 5:00 P.M. reduced ticket available. Parking charge.

 Top rides: Shoot-the-Chute; Cuyahoga River Logging Company, log flume; Grizzly Run, rapids ride; The Skyscraper, 210-foot-tall observation tower; The Texas Twister, a top spin; a circa-1918 Illions Supreme Carousel.

Roller coasters: Raging Wolf Bobs (W); Double Loop (S); Big Dipper (W); Mind Eraser, Boomerang (S).

Plan to stay: 6 hours.

 Best way to avoid crowds: Wednesdays and Thursdays are the least crowded days. Take a ride up the observation tower and see what the park layout looks like and where the crowds are congregating; then plan your attack accordingly.

 Directions: Take Exit 13 off the Ohio Turnpike (I–80) and go north 9 miles on North Aurora Road (Highway 43). The park is 30 miles southeast of Cleveland and 26 miles north of Akron.

Memphis Kiddie Park
10340 Memphis Avenue
Brooklyn, OH (216) 941–5995

The manager who helped open this park in 1952 is now the owner, and the 11 rides that were running on opening day are still the only rides in the park. Things haven't changed much here. In fact, the rides still look new, and the cotton candy is still fluffy and delicious.

In a state filled with megaparks, this quaint little traditional kiddie park is a breath of fresh air. Dedicated to the "little people" of the Cleveland area, the facility is adjacent to a metropolitan park and across the street from a drive-in theater.

Open daily from 10:00 A.M. to 9:00 P.M., April through October. It's pay-as-you-go for the rides, games, and miniature golf.

THE AMUSEMENT PARK GUIDE

Paramount's Kings Island WaterWorks Waterpark
Kings Island Drive
Kings Island, OH (513) 573-5800
http://www.pki.com

The people of Ohio love their amusement parks, and they're sure lucky to have this one. With more than 3 million visitors yearly, Kings Island is one of the three most popular seasonal amusement parks in America (Cedar Point, also in Ohio, and Six Flags Great Adventure In New Jersey are the other two). The park's entrance is nothing short of breathtaking: At the end of a 320-foot-long-by-80-foot-wide water fountain stands a magnificent, 330-foot replica of the Eiffel Tower, complete with observation deck. That's a good place to start your visit. With map in hand, search out what you want to do from high atop everything else.

And there's *a lot* taking place on these 288 acres. There are 45 rides, for example, including 16 for children. One of those rides is the Beast, without a doubt the best wooden roller coaster in the world, and with its 4-minutes-plus ride, it's also the longest coaster ride in the United States. There's also WaterWorks, the park's 15-acre waterpark, offering 16 additional rides and activities at no additional charge.

Splat City is a 3-acre Nickelodeon-themed play area with interactive (and messy) activities, and Hanna–Barbera Land is an area full of pint-sized thrills for the little ones.

 Extras: Xtreme SkyFlyer, Skycoaster, extra fee; XS Race Way, miniature race cars with drivers competing against 19 other drivers for a 15 lap race, extra fee. The TimberWolf Amphitheatre offers top-name concerts throughout the summer, additional charge.

 Season: Mid-April through mid-October.

 Operating hours: 9:00 A.M. to 11:00 P.M.

 Admission policy: Pay-one-price, under $30. A specially priced second-day ticket is available. Parking charge. Season passes good at all 5 Paramount parks.

Top rides: Days of Thunder, motion-based simulator theater; Kings Mills Log Flume; Amazon Falls, shoot-the-chute; White Water Canyon, raging-rapids raft ride; Rushing River, an inner-tube wet ride in the waterpark section; a circa-1926 Philadelphia Toboggan Company carousel.

Ohio

Roller coasters: Racer, twin racing (W); The Beast (W); The Beastie, junior (W); King Cobra, stand up (S); Vortex, 6-loop (S); Adventure Express mine train (W-S); Scooby Zoom, kiddie (S); Top Gun, suspended (S); Outer Limits: Flight of Fear, indoor (S).

Plan to stay: 10 hours.

Best way to avoid crowds: Work your way around the circular layout and finish each area as you go; doubling back is time-consuming. Use a map to plan your voyage.

Directions: Located 24 miles north of Cincinnati, 80 miles south of Columbus, off I–71. Take the Kings Island Drive exit and go east to the park entrance.

"The Vortex," Paramount's Kings Island, Ohio

171

The Amusement Park Guide

Sea World of Ohio
1100 Sea World Drive
Aurora, OH (216) 995-2121/
(800) 63-SHAMU
http://www.4adventure.com

Shamu is alive and well, and living in Ohio. This 90-acre marine-life park was the second of the 4 Sea Worlds to be built (1970), and the only "northern" facility of the group. There are 7 live animal shows and 20 exhibits and attractions.

Extras: Dolphin feeding and petting; the Penguin Encounter, an Antarctic exhibit; and sea lion feeding—all free with admission. Pirates, a 3-D film featuring the comedic adventures of a hapless pirate crew.

Special events: A special nighttime celebration offers additional shows, laser-light productions, and fireworks during the peak summer months.

Season: Mid-May through September.

Operating hours: 10:00 A.M. to 11:00 P.M.

Admission policy: Pay-one-price, under $30. Discount after 6:00 P.M. Parking fee.

Top rides: No mechanical rides at park; Shamu's Happy Harbor offers a 3-acre participatory play area for children.

Plan to stay: 5 hours.

Best way to avoid crowds: Come during the week right at opening time, or come at about 5:00 P.M. and stay until closing.

Directions: Located 30 miles southeast of Cleveland on Route 43. Take Exit 13 (Route 43) off the Ohio Turnpike (I–80) and go north 9 miles to Sea World Drive.

Swings 'N' Things
8501 Stearns Road
Olmstead Township, OH (216) 235-4420

Action. That's what you'll find everywhere you look on these 13 acres! Action attractions include an adult and kid's go-kart track, the Fun Junction kiddieland with 6 kiddie rides, bumper boats, 2 miniature golf courses, batting cages, and the popular Kids Corner indoor play area.

Make sure you check out the fresh pizza and the homemade ice cream. Delicious! The 2-story, year-round Gameroom offers the latest in video games and games of skill.

Opens 11:00 A.M. daily, and closes at 11:00 P.M. during the week and at midnight on weekends. Fun Junction closes at 10:00 nightly. Open daily mid-May through August and weekends in the spring and fall. Pay individually for everything as you go, or a Playday Pass, good for unlimited use of all rides, go-karts, miniature golf, and discounts on Gameroom tokens is available, under $17.

Time Out on the Court
Indoors at the Forest Fair Mall
I-275 and Winton Road
Cincinnati, OH (513) 671-8008

Colorful banners, an 18-hole miniature golf course, and the grand carousel let you know when you've entered this nice, clean family entertainment center. With 6 rides total, the area also offers a large video-game room and a games-of-skill midway.

The park, adjacent to the mall's large food court, is open during mall hours. There's no admission charge; rides and attractions are on a pay-as-you-go basis.

 TIM'S TRIVIA

Walt Disney's long time dream, Disneyland, opened at 2:30 P.M. on July 17, 1955.

The Amusement Park Guide

Tuscora Park
Off Tuscora Avenue
New Philadelphia, OH (330) 343–4644

You'll see the colorful Ferris wheel from the road as you drive down Tuscora Avenue, a few blocks from downtown. Other than that, you'd have no idea a small ride park was nestled into the corner of this 37-acre, city-owned recreation area.

The park has a total of 8 family and kiddie rides, including a circa-1929 Herschell–Spillman carousel in beautifully restored condition. And the place offers an 18-hole miniature golf course, a swimming pool, picnic facilities; and batting cages.

Open daily at noon, Memorial Day through Labor Day. The rides are on a pay-as-you-go basis.

Wyandot Lake
10101 Riverside Drive
Powell, OH (614) 889–9283

Don your bathing suit and spend the day—this park exemplifies the way in which wet and dry amusement rides can work together successfully. Here you can ride and scream on a roller coaster and then walk a few yards and go bodysurfing in a wave pool, all for one admission price.

With 18 mechanical rides (including 10 kiddie rides) and 12 major water elements, there's plenty to keep you busy. Swimsuits need not be changed before riding the dry rides, but shoes are required.

The waterpark has 4 tube slides, 5 body slides, wave pool, an action river, and Christopher's Island interactive family play lagoon.

 Special events: Dive-in movies and Teen Dance parties, Friday nights in August; Hallowscream, 3 weekends in October.

 Season: Mid-May through mid-September. Reopens mid-October for Hallowscream.

 Operating hours: 10:00 A.M. to 8:00 or 9:00 P.M.

 Admission policy: Pay-one-price, under $17. Parking charge.

Top rides: A circa-1914 Mangels–Illions carousel; Ferris wheel; Rock-O-Plane; Scrambler; bumper cars.

 Roller coaster: Sea Dragon, junior (W).

 Plan to stay: 7 hours if both wet and dry activities are to be experienced.

 Best way to avoid crowds: Much of the crowd comes and rides the rides first and then hits the water elements to cool off. Reverse this pattern and you'll have no problems with crowds.

 Directions: Located adjacent to the Columbus Zoo on Route 257. Take the Sawmill Road exit off I–270 and follow the signs to the park and to the zoo.

Soak City, Cedar Point, Ohio

OKLAHOMA

Bell's Amusement Park
3900 East 21st Street
Tulsa State Fairgrounds
Tulsa, OK (918) 744–1991

There's a lot of fun packed onto these 10 acres. Robert Bell Sr., who founded the park in 1951, has taken those acres and created a 27-ride family amusement park. Needless to say, it's compact, but it's also well run and quite popular among the locals. There's even room left over for trees, flower beds, and shaded rest areas.

This may also be the only park in the country where senior citizens (age 65 and over) always get in and ride for free. Bell has informed his employees that these special guests are to be treated "just like Mr. Bell."

Extras: Miniature golf, extra fee. Make sure you see where the Zingo roller coaster goes under one side of a concession stand and out the other. The park becomes part of the carnival midway during the Tulsa State Fair.

Special events: Fireworks and Music Festival, July 4.

Season: Mid-April through mid-October. Season ends with the closing of the Tulsa State Fair in October.

Operating hours: Weekdays, 6:00 to 10:00 P.M.; weekends, 1:00 to 11:00 P.M.

Admission policy: Small general admission fee, with rides on a pay-as-you-go basis. Pay-one-price available for all rides, under $15. Free parking.

Top rides: Phantasmagoria, a dark ride; White Lightning, a log flume; Chili Pepper Plunge, a dry ride down a water chute; Himalaya; Tilt-A-Whirl.

Roller coasters: Zingo (W); Wildcat, family (S).

Plan to stay: 3 hours.

Best way to avoid crowds: Mondays through Thursdays are the least busy days. Although this is a small park, its rides are high-capacity and seldom entail a wait of more than 10 minutes, even on the busiest day.

 Directions: Take the Harvard Street exit off I–244, go south 1¾ miles, turn east on 17th Street, and go ⅓ mile and to the fairgrounds.

Frontier City
11601 Northeast Expressway
Oklahoma City, OK (405) 478–2414

You might think you're walking onto a TV-western set when you enter the front gates of this 40-acre park. It's a replica of an 1880s western town, with all architecture and environs reflecting that genre.

In keeping with the image, the owners call the park the "territory of fun." The kiddie rides are located in the O.K. Kid's Korral, as are special games, shows, and activities. Also for the kids is a Paul Bunyan–themed children's area where everything is larger than life. In all, there are 32 rides, including 11 for the young ones.

 Extras: A large games complex houses a full array of video games and games of skill. The Wildcat roller coaster was moved here from the now-defunct Fairyland Park in Kansas City. The Geronimo Skycoaster and Thunder Road Raceway NASCAR-style go-karts, extra fee.

 Special events: Easter Egg Hunt, April; July 4 Extravaganza; Christian Family Nights, August; Back to School Party, mid-August; Oktoberfest, weekends in early October; Hallowscream, weekends in late October.

 Season: Mid-April through October.

 Operating hours: Opens 10:30 A.M. daily; noon on Sundays; closes most nights at 10:00 P.M.

 Admission policy: Pay-one-price, under $20. Parking charge.

 Top rides: Grand Centennial Ferris wheel, located on the highest point in the park; Time Warp, a 360-degree swinging pendulum; Mystery River, a

THE AMUSEMENT PARK GUIDE

log flume; Prairie Schooner, a swinging pirate ship; Renegade, a raging-rapids ride.

 Roller coasters: Silver Bullet, looping (S); Diamond Back, shuttle loop (S); Wildcat (W). Nightmare, indoor family (S); Wild Kitty, kiddie (S).

 Plan to stay: 6 hours.

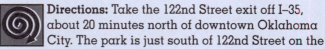 **Best way to avoid crowds:** Come on weekdays or on Sunday afternoons.

Directions: Take the 122nd Street exit off I–35, about 20 minutes north of downtown Oklahoma City. The park is just south of 122nd Street on the west side of the interstate.

"Time Warp," Frontier City, Oklahoma

OREGON

Enchanted Forest
8462 Enchanted Way SE
Turner, OR (503) 363–3060

Truly a child's paradise, Enchanted Forest is a heavily forested park, with storybook characters' homes as the main attraction. Walk through the Seven Dwarfs' Cottage or the Alice in Wonderland area, or take a stroll past a life-size gingerbread house.

In addition to the storybook activities are two other attractions, a walk-through haunted house, the Ice Mountain Bobsleds, and the Big Timber Log Ride.

 Season: Mid-March through September.

 Operating hours: 9:30 A.M. to 6:00 P.M.

 Admission policy: Pay-one-price, under $6. Ice Mountain Bobsleds, Big Timber Log Ride, and Haunted House cost extra.

 Roller coaster: Ice Mountain Bobsled, family (S).

 Plan to stay: 2 hours.

 Directions: Located 7 miles south of Salem, just off Exit 248 of I-5.

The Amusement Park Guide

Oaks Park
Southeast Oaks Parkway
Portland, OR (503) 233-5777

Once you see this 44-acre family park along the banks of the Willamette River, you'll know how its name came about: Huge oak trees are everywhere.

First opened in 1905 to coincide with the Lewis and Clark World Expo, the park now has 28 rides, as well as some of the original buildings, including those housing a roller skating rink, skooters, and a carousel.

 Extras: Go-karts and miniature golf, extra charge.

 Special events: Fireworks, July 4; Sculling Race, collegiate competition, October; plus several other sponsored events during the season.

 Season: Mid-March through October. Roller skating rink is open year-round.

 Operating hours: Open daily at noon; closes at 9:00 or 10:00 P.M. Closed nonholiday Mondays.

 Admission policy: Free admission, with rides and attractions on a pay-as-you-go basis. During July and August, various promotions offer a pay-one-price deal. Free parking.

 Top rides: Sea Dragon; Tilt-A-Whirl; bumper cars; Scrambler; a Ferris wheel; a circa-1924 Philadelphia Toboggan Company carousel; Haunted Mine, a dark ride; a train ride around the park and along the river.

 Roller coasters: Looping Thunder, 1-loop (S); Monster Mouse, family (S).

 Plan to stay: 5 hours.

 Best way to avoid crowds: Visit Tuesday or Friday during the day or on weekends before Memorial Day or after Labor Day.

Directions: Take the Corbett Road exit off I-5 and follow the signs to Lake Oswego, which will take you to Macadam Avenue. Proceed south on Macadam until you get to the Sellwood Bridge. Cross the bridge and make a left on 6th Avenue; the park is on your left. Located 8 miles from downtown.

Thrill-Ville USA
8372 Enchanted Way
Turner, OR (503) 363–4095

Serving the residents of this area of Oregon since 1984, this family-owned amusement park features 17 rides, including a steel roller coaster, a Skycoaster, go-karts, and bumper boats. In addition, there are 2 water slides, several classic older rides, miniature golf, a picnic area, and concession stands.

 Roller coaster: Ripper, family (S).

There are several admission plans. No charge to enter the grounds, with rides on a pay-as-you-go basis. One pass for all the rides, slides, and 2 go-kart rides is available for under $17. Unlimited use of waterslides is $8, and for unlimited use of everything, plus a ride on the Skycoaster, is available, under $30.

Open daily, Memorial Day through Labor Day at 11:00 A.M., with weeknight closing at 6:00 P.M., weekends at 9:00 P.M. Open weekends during spring and fall. A trip to Thrill-Ville, combined with the adjacent Enchanted Forest makes for a diverse, fun day out.

PENNSYLVANIA

Bland's Park
Route 220
Tipton, PA (814) 684–3538
http://www.railroadcity.com/blands/blands.htm

The people of Pennsylvania are indeed lucky—their state is full of wonderful, traditional family parks, and this is one of the finest. Although small, the park packs a lot of fun into its 13 acres. Kids Kingdom is a separate little kiddieland with 11 rides, and 10 additional adult and family rides are spread throughout the park.

 Extras: Live pony rides, included in pay-one-price admission; 2 go-kart tracks and a miniature golf course, extra charge. Don't leave the park without trying Bland's potato salad or the pizza. Delicious!

 Special events: Mother's Day, mothers ride free; Father's Day, fathers ride free; Fireworks, one of the largest displays in the state, July 4; Harvest Festival, with big-name entertainers, late September.

The Amusement Park Guide

 Season: May through September.

 Operating hours: Noon to 9:00 P.M. Closed Mondays.

 Admission policy: Free admission, with rides and attractions on a pay-as-you-go basis. Pay-one-price available, under $7.50.

 Top rides: Space Odyssey, an indoor caterpillar with a sound and light show; Scrambler; bumper cars; a circa-1924 Herschell–Spillman carousel, with a Wurlitzer band organ.

 Roller coaster: Zyklon family (S).

 Plan to stay: 4 hours.

 Best way to avoid crowds: Tuesdays are the least crowded. Small crowds and beautiful weather prevail on weekends in spring and fall.

 Directions: Take Exit 23 (Highway 220) off I–80. Follow Highway 220 south for 35 miles; the park is on the right, 3 miles south of Tyrone.

Bushkill Park
2100 Bushkill Park Drive
Easton, PA (610) 258-6941

Founded in 1902, this 17-acre traditional park offers a lot of shade, nostalgic buildings, classic amusement rides, and antique charm. There are a total of 16 rides, including the Merry Mixer, Tilt-A-Whirl, train, and the Kiddie Land with 8 rides.

The walk-through fun house, dating back to 1902, is known as The Barl of Fun. It's name has been misspelled for as long as anyone can remember, and when the owners restored it, they repainted the sign as it was.

The roller skating rink is open to the public as well as for private parties, and the large picnic grounds have plenty of covered pavilions. Open Wednesday through Sunday, noon to 6:00 P.M., Memorial Day through Labor Day. Rides are priced individually, by an all-day pass, or by the Frequent Rider pass, $25 for 32 rides.

Conneaut Lake Park
Highway 618
Conneaut Lake Park, PA (814) 382–5115

For more than a century, this classic amusement park was an integral part of summertime social activities around here. Rides, attractions, and summer cottages are all mixed together in this traditional resort setting.

It fell into financial problems in the late 1980s, went bankrupt in 1994, and the rides and attractions didn't open in 1995. New owners claimed it, reopened it for part of the 1996 season, with the promise of restoring it to its former place as part of the summer experience when it was called the "Queen of Inland Summer Resorts."

With 24 rides, including the famous Blue Streak wooden roller coaster, the park also offers a waterpark with several slides and a lazy river, a sandy beach on the lake, Camperland camp ground, boat rentals, and the Hotel Conneaut, a classic summer resort hotel.

Open daily, 11:00 A.M. to 10:00 P.M., Memorial Day through Labor Day. Free admission, with rides on a pay-as-you-go basis. Pay-one-price, under $10, includes waterpark.

Dorney Park
Wild Water Kingdom
3830 Dorney Park Road
Allentown, PA (610) 398–7955

There isn't much this park *doesn't* have to offer. From a contemporary, full-scale, top-notch waterpark to a traditional amusement park, Dorney Park and Wild Water Kingdom have a host of activities for the entire family.

Opened as a fish weir and summer resort in the 1860s, the park, which opened in 1884, now has 48 rides, including 14 for kids. The older part of the park still has some of the original buildings left and several of the early classic rides, including a Whip, skyride, and water scooters.

Wild Water Kingdom is included in admission price, and features more than 30 rides, slides, and activities, including 2 lazy rivers, wave pool, 3 children's activity pools, and a beach shop.

 Extras: Miniature golf course, extra.

 Season: May through October.

THE AMUSEMENT PARK GUIDE

 Operating hours: 10:00 A.M. to 10:00 P.M.

 Admission policy: Pay-one-price, under $26, includes both the ride and waterpark. Special after-5:00 P.M. rate saves $12 per admission.

 Top rides: White Water Landing, shoot-the-chutes; Thunder Canyon, rapids ride; antique Dentzel carousel; Skyscraper, a 90-foot-tall Ferris wheel; Thunder Creek Mountain, a log flume; a Zephyr train, offering a classic train ride.

 Roller coasters: Steel Force (S); Hercules (W); Thunderhawk (W); Lazer, 2-loop (S); Little Lazer, junior (S); Dragon, family (S).

 Plan to stay: 10 hours if you visit both parks.

 Best way to avoid crowds: Most people visit the ride park until noon, next go to the waterpark until around 5:00 P.M., and then go back to ride park until closing. To avoid the crowds, do the opposite. Monday is the slowest day of the week.

 Directions: Take Exit 16 (Route 222) east off Highway 309 and follow the signs to the park.

 # TIM'S TRIVIA

Crooner Perry Como was "discovered" while cutting hair at the Hotel Conneaut at Conneaut Lake Park, Pennsylvania.

Dutch Wonderland
2249 Route 30 East
Lancaster, PA (717) 291–1888

Although the name would lead you to believe the park has a strong Dutch theme, don't be fooled. This park *is* in the middle of the Pennsylvania Dutch area, but it doesn't have a major theme—instead, it has several small themed areas, each beautifully landscaped and, all told, containing more than 100,000 exotic plants and shrubs.

The 44-acre park has a great deal of water, lots of trees,

lots of walk-through attractions, and 25 family-oriented rides. You enter the park through a castle. Once you're inside, the paved paths take you through an Indian Village, past the Old Woman's Shoe, the Church in the Dell, and Bossie the Cow, and across a bridge to an international-themed botanical garden.

Among the unique rides is a gondola boat ride that takes visitors on a trip past the Eiffel Tower, Big Ben, and a Japanese pagoda. It also takes riders past another unique ride: a kiddie Ferris wheel built to resemble a Dutch windmill.

 Extras: The Wonder House is a fascinating attraction: The guest sits still while the whole room spins, making you feel like you're tumbling. Other extras, also included in admission, are a giant slide inside a barnyard silo and an opportunity to milk a make-believe cow.

 Special events: Grandparent's Day, late September.

 Season: Easter weekend through Columbus Day.

 Operating hours: Opens at 10:00 A.M., Monday through Saturday and at 11:00 A.M. on Sunday; closes at 7:00 P.M. daily.

 Admission policy: Pay-one-price, under $20. Free parking.

 Top rides: Flying Trapeze, flying swings; skyride, going from the front to the back of the park; Turnpike Ride, antique cars; Monorail, a trip around the park; Tug Boat Ride; River Boat Ride; Pipeline Plunge, a dry ride down a water slide; Double Splash Flume, a log flume with 2 drops.

 Roller coaster: Sky Princess, junior (W).

 Plan to stay: 3½ hours.

 Best way to avoid crowds: Come early in the week; take the skyride to the back of the park and work your way forward.

THE AMUSEMENT PARK GUIDE

Directions: Located on Route 30, 4 miles east of Lancaster.

Hersheypark
100 West Hersheypark Drive
Hershey, PA (717) 534–3900;
(800) HERSHEY

http://800hershey.com/park

Beautiful—that's the word to sum up this 90-acre, well-landscaped park. The wonderful old trees, the rolling terrain, and the myriad shaded resting areas make this park one of the nicest in the country.

Founded in 1907 by Milton Hershey as a recreation area for his chocolate-factory workers, the park now contains 51 rides, including 20 for children. And contrary to expectations, the park does *not* have a chocolate theme!

Yet there *is* intricate theming in eight areas, including: Tudor Square, a seventeenth-century English village; Music Box Way, an 1800s-style Pennsylvania Dutch settlement; Tower Plaza, featuring the 330-foot-tall Kissing Tower observation ride; Rhineland, an early German town; Carousel Circle, a circle of smaller rides around the antique carousel; ZooAmerica, an 11-acre walk-through zoo; and Midway America, a re-creation of an old-time amusement park, complete with classic rides.

Extras: Miniature golf and paddleboats, extra charge. Chocolate World, located next to the park, presents a ride-through tour of how chocolate is made (free). The streetlights in the town of Hershey are shaped like Hershey chocolate kisses. Marine mammal presentation at the Aquatheatre; and top-name concerts at the Hersheypark Stadium and Hersheypark Arena. Show your concert ticket on day of show and get a large discount to the park.

Special events: Literacy Day, September; Creatures of the Night, October; Balloonfest, late October; and the Hersheypark Christmas Candylane, mid-November through December.

Season: May through September.

Operating hours: 10:00 A.M. to 10:00 P.M.

Admission policy: Pay-one-price, under $29, includes admission to ZooAmerica. In fall when park is closed, a separate admission is available for ZooAmerica.

 Top rides: Coal Cracker, a log flume; Canyon River Rapids, a raging-rapids ride; a circa-1919 Philadelphia Toboggan Company carousel, the second largest this company ever made; Giant Wheel, a double Ferris wheel with gondola seating.

 Roller coasters: Wildcat (W); Comet (W); Sidewinder, Boomerang (S); Sooperdooperlooper, looping (S); Trailblazer, mine train (S).

 Plan to stay: 8 hours.

 Best way to avoid crowds: Monday and Tuesdays are the slowest days during the season. Avoid weekends. The park opens a half-hour before the rides do; come early, stake your claim on your favorite ride, and go from there.

 Directions: Take Exit 20 off the Pennsylvania Turnpike to Route 322. Follow Route 322 to Hershey and take Route 39 West to Hersheypark Drive; the park is on the right.

TIM'S TRIVIA

Hersheypark's "Carrousel," in Hershey, Pennsylvania, was spelled wrong by the original sign painter and the name is still used today.

Idlewild Park
Route 30
Ligonier, PA (412) 238-3666

This 90-acre park, located in the mountain woodlands of Central Pennsylvania, is considered America's most beautiful amusement park by most aficionados. It's more than 100 years old and has kept its traditional amusement park flavor.

Yet it has not stood still. The 27 rides, including 11 for kids, are top-notch contemporary rides. The park is divided into

THE AMUSEMENT PARK GUIDE

four sections: H-2-Ohhh Zone, a waterpark; Hootin Holler, Wild West territory; Jumpin Jungle, a participatory play area; and the Story Book section, where kids can walk through Little Red Riding Hood's woods and visit other book stars' homes.

All the kiddie rides are located in Raccoon Lagoon.

Extras: Miniature golf, paddleboats, and row-boats, extra fee.

Special events: Old Fashion Days, mid-July; Ligonier Highland Games, September (the Scottish games are sponsored by an outside group, not the park, but they are held annually).

Season: Mid-May through the first week of September.

Operating hours: 10:00 A.M. to dusk. Closed Mondays.

Admission policy: Pay-one-price, under $15. Free parking.

Top rides: Mister Rogers' Neighborhood, a one-of-a-kind trolley ride through the neighborhood of make-believe popularized by TV's Fred Rogers; Rafters Run, a twin-tube water slide; a circa-1931 Philadelphia Toboggan Company carousel; Black Widow, a Spider ride; Caterpillar, with canvas top.

Roller coasters: Wild Mouse, family (S); Rollo Coaster (W).

Plan to stay: 6 hours.

Best way to avoid crowds: Come early afternoon on any weekday.

Directions: From the Pennsylvania Turnpike, take Exit 9 and go north on Route 711 to Route 30; turn right and go 3 miles west to the park.

TIM'S TRIVIA

The best french fries in the world, inside or outside an amusement park, can be found at the Potato Patch fry stand at Kennywood Park, West Mifflin, Pennsylvania, and its sister facility Idlewild Park in Ligonier, Pennsylvania.

Kennywood
Route 837
West Mifflin, PA (412) 461–0500

http://www.kennywood.com

This popular park is one of the best traditional parks in the country. High on the bluff overlooking the Monongahela River, the park sits on 40 acres and has 50 rides, including 15 for kids.

Founded in 1898 as a trolley park, it has a long-standing reputation as a superb picnic and family park. It's one of two parks in the country that has been listed as a National Historic Landmark. Kennywood received that status for the preservation of traditional park elements. (Playland in Rye, New York, is the other park.)

Two of the original turn-of-the-century buildings are still standing, and the tunnel-of-love ride dates back to 1901.

The park is known nationally for its 3 high-ranking wooden roller coasters and for having the best amusement park french fries in the country.

 Extras: Noah's Ark, a dark, walk-through fun house, free with admission. Available for an extra charge are a miniature golf course and paddleboats. Pittsburg's Lost Kennywood is a re-created area of nostalgic rides and buildings from turn-of-the-century. Food may be brought into the park.

 Special events: Christian Music Weekend, Labor Day; plus a dozen different ethnic and community days throughout the summer. The different nationalities come out, cook and sell food, have their own entertainment, and draw visitors from a three-state area.

 Season: Mid-May through Labor Day.

Operating hours: Noon to 11:00 P.M.

 Admission policy: General admission fee, with rides on a pay-as-you-go basis. Pay-one-price also available, under $20. Free and paid parking.

 Top rides: Pittsburg Plunge, shoot-the-chute; Skycoaster (extra fee); Pitt Fall, a 255-foot-tall free-fall ride, which from the top allows you to see downtown Pittsburgh; Log Jammer, a log flume; Raging Rapids, a raging-rapids ride; Turtle, the classic Tumble Bug ride; Old Mill, a ride-through tunnel of love in wooden boats; a circa-1926 Dentzel carousel with band organ.

 Roller coasters: Steel Phantom, looping (S); Thunderbolt (W); Jack Rabbit (W); Racer (W); Little Phantom, junior (S).

 Plan to stay: 7 hours.

 Best way to avoid crowds: Come on weekdays. This is not a tourist park, so crowd patterns do not reflect tourist patterns. It's wise to call ahead to learn when the major groups are booked, so that you can avoid those days.

 Directions: Take Exit 9 (Swissvale) off I–376 (Penn–Lincoln Parkway). Go south, across the river, until the road dead-ends. Turn left on Highway 837 and go about 1½ miles. The park is on your left; free parking is on your right. Located 8 miles from downtown Pittsburgh. *Note:* The park is famous for its big yellow arrows pointing the way.

Knoebels Amusement Resort
Route 487
Elysburg, PA (717) 672–2572
http://www.knoebels.com/

This family-owned and -operated facility is amazing. Though situated in the middle of nowhere, it offers just about anything you could ever want in an amusement park.

Roaring Creek meanders through a pine forest that shelters most of the 43 rides. It was this creek that started it all back in the early 1900s, when a swimming hole attracted people to Knoebels Groves. The first rides and attractions were added in 1926, and thankfully, the family has not attempted to create a theme for the park. The lovely, natural setting provides its own theme.

Just walking onto the grounds gives one an "old-fashioned" feeling. The shaded, hilly walkways and the old buildings are beautifully maintained, as are both old and new rides. The attractions, plus the state's largest swimming pool, the large picnic grounds, rental cabins, and a campground, make this a true family resort.

 Extras: A crafts demonstration area, the Anthracite Coal Museum, and 5 working band organs are all free. Miniature golf, 4 water slides, and the 750,000-gallon swimming pool are all available for a fee. The Brass Ring Carousel Museum features more than 40 hand-carved figures. There's also a 550-site campground, including 20 cabins.

 Special events: Covered Bridge Festival, first weekend in October; Appreciation Day, September 1; Senior Citizens Day, one in June, one in July; Crafts Fair, fourth week of July.

 Season: Mid-April through mid-September.

 Operating hours: 11:00 A.M. to 10:00 P.M.

 Admission policy: Free gate, with rides and attractions on a pay-as-you-go basis. Pay-one-price available only during the week, under $20 (does not include the Haunted Mansion). After–5:00 P.M. specials. Free parking.

 Top rides: AXIS, rotating ride with a 360-degree spin around 2 axes; Italian Trapeze, swing ride; Skloosh, a 50-foot-tall shoot-the-chute; 110-foot giant Ferris wheel, the tallest in the state; Haunted Mansion, the best haunted ride-through outside the Disney parks; Scooter, bumper cars that still use original Lusse cars; a log flume; and you can still grab for the brass ring on the Grand Carousel, a circa-1913 Kramers Karousel Works/Carmel machine with band organ.

 Roller coasters: Phoenix (W); High Speed Thrill Coaster, junior (S); Whirlwind, split corkscrew (S).

 Plan to stay: 6 hours is the average, but if you plan to swim and eat here, add a couple of hours—you'll probably want to make it an all-day affair.

The Amusement Park Guide

 Best way to avoid crowds: Tuesdays are the slowest, followed by other midweek days. Weekends are busiest, but because of the number of high-capacity rides, most lines move swiftly.

Directions: Located on Highway 487 between Elysburg and Catawissa, in the east-central part of the state. Take Exit 33 (Danville) off I–80 and head to Danville on Highway 54. Follow Highway 54 east through Danville to Elysburg, then 487 North to park.

Lakemont Park
Island Waterpark
Routes I–99 & 36
Altoona, PA (814) 949–7275

Leap The Dips, the country's oldest wooden roller coaster, is located here, and if things go according to plan, it should be renovated and in operating order shortly. Lakemont Park—founded in 1894 and located on the south side of the city—now has about 30 rides, plus the Island Waterpark, with 3 slides, paddleboats, bumper boats, and Pirates Cove, a kid's activity pool.

Roller coasters: Mad Mouse, family (S); Skyliner (W).

The park is open daily, with a pay-one-price admission, under $6. Hours vary during the season.

Sandcastle
1000 Sandcastle Boulevard
West Homestead, PA (412) 462–6666

Situated on the banks of the Monongahela River, this is two parks in one. During the day, it's the area's premier family waterpark. By night, it's one of the most popular hangouts for young adults.

Among its offerings are 15 slides and flumes; a lazy river; Wet Willie's children's area, with slides and interactive activities; an adult activity pool; 3 large hot tubs; marina on the Monongahela River; food service; beach shop; sand volleyball courts; shuffleboard courts; and a 1,400-foot boardwalk overlooking the river. Miniature golf, and adult and kiddie go-karts are available for an extra fee.

An all-day slide and pool pass sells for under $15, and an all-day pool pass, with no slides, goes for under $10. Open Memorial Day through Labor Day weekend, 11:00 A.M. to 7:00 P.M.

At 8:00 P.M., the park turns into an adult entertainment center for ages 21 and over. Five separate bars and clubs are open, as are all water elements except slides. Live entertainment. Admission is $1 during the week, $4 on weekends.

The park is owned by Kennywood Park, located 4 miles away in West Mifflin.

Sesame Place
New Oxford Road
Langhorne, PA (215) 752-7070
http://www.4adventure.com

Big Bird, Ernie, and all the other members of the "Sesame Street" gang are here to greet and entertain you at what is absolutely the finest children's park in the country. The facility has plenty of color, unique activities, and first-rate supervision; its familiar characters make the experience great fun for the kids, especially the younger ones.

Although the park has no mechanical rides, it does offer 13 water attractions and more than 40 outdoor physical

"Sky Splash," Sesame Place, Pennsylvania

THE AMUSEMENT PARK GUIDE

play activities. (Be sure to bring swimsuits for the entire family.) Familiar sights, including scenes from the popular TV show, make this park feel like home to the little tykes.

 Extras: Educational computer games arcade, extra charge. The Sesame Neighborhood is a full-size replica of the storefronts and buildings seen on the TV show. Sesame Studio Science Exhibits, stimulating hands-on scientific activities, free with admission. The Sesame Place Brass Band entertains in various locations throughout the day.

 Special events: Grandparents Day, and Country Fair Days, September.

 Season: May through mid-October.

 Operating hours: 9:00 A.M. to 8:00 P.M.

 Admission policy: Pay-one-price, under $25. Parking charge.

 Top rides: Big Bird's Rambling River, lazy-river raft ride around the facility; Sky Splash, a 5-story-tall raft ride with riders in a large raft gliding down a whimsical water chute; Slimey's Chutes, double inner-tube slide; Sesame Streak, double inner-tube ride down a twisting chute; and the Rubber Duckie Pond, an activity pool for children under 5 years old.

 Plan to stay: 5 hours.

 Best way to avoid crowds: Come early morning or just before dinnertime during the week.

Directions: Located on New Oxford Valley Road off U.S. Route 1 near Oxford Valley Mall, 7 miles southwest of Trenton and 20 miles northeast of downtown Philadelphia.

Waldameer
Water World
Route 832
Erie, PA (814) 838–3591

As you enter this wonderful, traditional park, you'll immediately realize you're in for a nostalgic journey.

Directly adjacent to the gate are 20 heavily wooded picnic groves, and the first signs you see of the ride park itself are the roller coaster and a beautiful carousel off to your right. Waldameer, founded in 1896 as a trolley park, has kept much of its old-time charm.

In addition to the popular waterpark, Waldameer offers 25 rides, including 8 just for the little ones.

Water World can be included in the park's pay-one-price charge, and offers 17 different slides, a giant hot tub, a Tadpole kid's activity pool, and a lazy river.

 Extras: Pirates Cove, a walk-through fun house.

 Special events: Fireworks 6 times a year: July 3 and 4, Sunday and Monday of Memorial Day weekend, Father's Day, and Labor Day Sunday; plus several specially sponsored community days.

 Season: Mother's Day through Labor Day.

 Operating hours: The ride park is open from 1:00 to 10:00 P.M.; the waterpark, from 11:00 A.M. to 7:30 P.M. Both facilities closed Mondays.

 Admission policy: Free gate, with rides and attractions on a pay-as-you-go basis. Pay-one-price also available, good for all rides and attractions in both parks, under $15. Free parking.

 Top rides: Thunder River, log flume; 100-foot-tall gondola Ferris wheel; Sea Dragon; Wipeout; train ride, a scenic, 15-minute ride; Wacky Shack, a 2-decker dark ride; carousel.

 Roller coaster: Comet, junior (W).

 Plan to stay: 4 hours if you only go on the rides; 7 hours if you also visit the waterpark.

THE AMUSEMENT PARK GUIDE

Directions: Take Exit 5N off I–90 and go north on Route 832 for about 8 miles. The park is on the left, just before you enter the parkway to Presque Isle State Park.

Williams Grove Amusement Park
Off Route 74 on Williams Grove Road
Mechanicsburg, PA (717) 697–8266

What does a park that first opened to the public more than 130 years ago look like? Visit this quaint little park and you'll find out. Located in a heavily wooded, rural area, the park has a stream and a small lake on its property. During late August each year, the park is home to the Grange Fair. Between 400–500 steam aficianados display their working steam engines of all sizes. There is a daily steam parade, and the park's steam train is in operation during the fair.

Among the nostalgia and the well-kept old buildings are 20 rides, including 7 just for kids. Also here are a miniature golf course and paddleboats. You can bring in your own food and beverages and enjoy a nice, shaded picnic, or you can eat in the park's cafeteria or one of its fast-food and snack locations.

Roller coaster: The Cyclone (W) currently under reconstruction, set to open 1997 or 1998.

Magic shows are usually scheduled throughout the season. The park is open from Memorial Day through Labor Day. Call for hours and days of operation and admission prices.

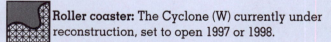

TIM'S TRIVIA

The popular It's a Small World ride was originally created by Walt Disney for the 1964 New York World's Fair. The ride opened at Walt Disney World in Florida on October 2, 1971, Tokyo Disneyland on April 15, 1983, and Disneyland Paris on April 12, 1992.

RHODE ISLAND

Enchanted Forest
Route 3
Hope Valley, RI (401) 539–7711

Founded in 1962 as a kiddie attraction, this 17-acre park has been able to maintain its original storybook theme through the years. A walk along the path through the woods takes you to many storybook characters' homes, including the Three Little Pigs' house and the Little Red Schoolhouse.

In addition, there are 12 rides, all kiddie and family oriented, and a go-kart skid track.

 Extras: Miniature golf is included in admission. Go-kart skid cars and batting cages cost extra.

 Season: May through September.

 Operating hours: The park is open from 10:00 A.M. to 5:00 P.M.; golf, batting cages, and game room, from 10:00 A.M. to 10:00 P.M.

 Admission policy: Pay-one-price, under $10. Free parking.

 Top rides: Airplanes; a merry-go-round; a kiddie roller coaster; kiddie pony carts, originally from Coney Island, New York.

 Plan to stay: 2 hours.

 Directions: Take Exit 2 off I–95 to Route 3; proceed to the park, in Hope Valley. About 30 miles south of Providence.

SOUTH CAROLINA

Boardwalk at the Beach
Between 21st & 29th Streets
Highway 17 Bypass
Myrtle Beach, SC (803) 444–3200

You may have a problem finding the little family entertainment center among the offering at this big (and getting bigger each year) retail and entertainment center, located 10 blocks from the beach.

The 350-acre complex features more than 100 retail stores; an IMAX Theater; Ripley's Aquarium; Planet Hollywood; NASCAR Cafe, and 6 other clubs, all built around a 23-acre lake.

There are 4 kiddie rides, paddle boats, a games arcade, and the Dragon's Lair miniature golf course, featuring a 28-foot-tall animatronic, fire-breathing dragon. All rides and attractions are on a pay-as-you-go basis. Open during store hours, year-round.

Plans call for a new world-class theme park to be built on the 110 acres next to this complex, which is owned by the same people who own the Myrtle Beach Pavilion and Amusement Park. Set to open spring 1999, it will have two major roller coasters and more than 30 other rides. The Pavilion will close following the 1998 season, with all rides being moved to this location.

Family Kingdom
3rd Avenue South
Myrtle Beach, SC (803) 946–9821

South Carolina's only wooden roller coaster, the state's tallest Ferris wheel, and a beautiful antique carousel are the stars at this seaside resort park, located along the popular Grand Strand.

You'll find 29 rides here, including 16 for the little ones in the family. In addition, there are boat rides on the Atlantic, and parasailing. An arcade provides some great video-game fun and a games-of-skill area is located along the midway.

 Roller coaster: Swamp Fox (W).

Admission is free, with rides on a pay-as-you-go basis. Pay-one-price available, under $15. Individual tickets cost 50

cents each, with rides requiring from 2 to 7 tickets each. Open daily, mid-April through September. Hours vary with season.

Myrtle Beach Pavilion and Amusement Park
Ocean & 9th Avenues
Myrtle Beach, SC (803) 448–6456

The largest seaside ride park south of New Jersey, this 11½-acre complex is smack-dab in the middle of the city's downtown area. It serves as the hub of a 5-block area of beachside entertainment attractions, shops, and restaurants.

The park, in business since 1949, is intersected by Ocean Avenue. The pavilion, teenage club, arcade, go-kart track, boardwalk games, shops, and restaurants are located on the beach side of the avenue, whereas the amusement park, including its 37 rides, is located on the other.

Although located on land, not on a pier, this fun spot has the feeling of a traditional seaside park, with more than enough attractions here to keep you active and happy. As you enter the park, one element will jump out at you—the green asphalt. To help keep the heat down in the park, a tennis court coating is put over the blacktop each season. It also adds some nice color.

 Extras: 2 go-kart tracks, extra charge. The large arcade is open from 8:00 A.M. to 2:00 A.M. daily. The Pavilion has an 1,800-seat auditorium that is regularly used as an alcohol-free teenage club. On occasion, name entertainment is booked in.

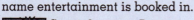

 Special events: Beginning of Year Appreciation Day, early April; Canadian–American Day, first day of the season; Sun Fest, held in conjunction with the city's chamber of commerce, first week of June.

 Season: March through October.

 Operating hours: Rides are open from 1:00 P.M. to midnight. Boardwalk shops and attractions are open from 8:00 A.M. to 2:00 A.M.

 Admission policy: Free gate, with rides on a pay-as-you-go basis. Pay-one-price available, under $20. Discount ride ticket books also available. Parking charge.

THE AMUSEMENT PARK GUIDE

 Top rides: Hydro Search, rapids ride; Log Flume, 2 drops and a tunnel; a circa-1915 Herschell–Spillman carousel with band organ; Haunted Inn, a dark ride; Super Skooter, bumper cars; Siberian Sleigh Ride, a Himalaya; Scrambler, set up inside with lights, fog, and sound; Caterpillar, with canvas top.

 Roller coasters: The Corkscrew (S); Galaxi, family (S).

 Plan to stay: 3½ hours.

 Best way to avoid crowds: Most people come here for the beaches and play at the park when they can't be on the beach. Therefore, daytime hours are the least crowded. Business picks up when the sun goes down or when the sky is overcast.

 Directions: Take Route 17 to Myrtle Beach. Turn east on 8th Avenue and go 4 blocks to Ocean Avenue. The park is located between 8th and 9th avenues, on Ocean Avenue.

Myrtle Waves Water Park
Highway 17 Bypass
at 10th Avenue North
Myrtle Beach, SC (803) 448–1026

The speed slides coming off the Turbo Twisters tower here are considered the three largest tubular slides in the world. They are 10 stories tall!

Although those slides stand out from the rest because of their height (and from the screams coming from them), the park has several other unique rides, including the Racing River. Located inside the Splash Zone area of the park, the river has a current of 10 mph, and riders hang on to floats as they speed around a figure-8 course.

The Night Flight is a black, fog-filled enclosed tube slide, and the Ocean in Motion is the wave pool. Tadpole is the children's activity area, and the Bubble Bay is a leisure pool, with bubbles and rain trees. In all, there are more than 30 rides and activities.

Open 10:00 A.M. to 7:00 P.M. during the summer peak hours, the park opens mid-May and runs through mid-September. An all-day waterplay pass is under $20, and for $5 more, you get an additional 6 days. That's quite a deal if you're going to be in the area for a week or less!

North Myrtle Beach Grand Prix
Highway 17
Windy Hill Section
North Myrtle Beach, SC (803) 272-7770

There's plenty of go-kart action here! With 7 different tracks, you'll find the right ride for you, whether it be on the slick track or in the mini-Ferraris.

In addition to the go-karts, there are 9 kiddie rides, bumper boats, a huge arcade with an indoor Q-Zar laser-tag arena, J.R.'s Slot Car Racing, and a NASCAR-themed restaurant.

Open March through October, 10:00 A.M. to midnight, everything is on a pay-as-you-go basis.

South of the Border
I-95 at U.S. 301/501
Hamer, SC (803) 774-2411

You'll see the billboards long before you arrive at this funky roadside attraction, located equidistant between New York and Florida. In addition to the gas and oil, and the clean bathrooms, you'll also find a motel, camp-grounds, restaurants, retail stores, a miniature golf course, and an amusement park.

There are 7 family rides here, including a carousel, a parachute drop, and a trolley ride. The complex is open year-round, the rides on a seasonal basis. Pay-as-you-go, hours vary.

Wild Water Waterpark & Family Fun Center
901 Highway 17 South
Surfside Beach, SC (803) 238-9453

On the Grand Strand, just south of Myrtle Beach, the park features a wide array of water and play activities for the entire family, ranging from water speed slides to a colorful carousel.

Among the waterpark offerings are an adult lounge pool with bubble jets; an interactive children's play area with slides, crawls, and pools; the Wipeout wave pool; 3 tube slides, 2 mat slides, and 4 speed slides.

The lazy river meanders through a shipwreck and offers riders an opportunity to divert off into a unique wave channel. Live concerts take place on the stage adjacent to the wave pool.

THE AMUSEMENT PARK GUIDE

In addition, there is a 3-ride kiddieland, 5 go-kart tracks, bumper boats, pirate-themed miniature golf, an arcade and food court. Open May through mid-September, daily, 10:00 A.M. to 7:00 P.M. Waterpark admission, under $17, with all other activities on a pay as you go basis.

SOUTH DAKOTA

Flags Of Fun
2802 Eglin
Rapid City, SD (605) 341–2186

Dubbed as the "cartbeat" of the Black Hills area, this facility features several drive-it-yourself rides, including go-karts, sprint-karts, and bumper boats. There are also mini-go-karts and mini-bumper boats for the kids, batting cages, and miniature golf.

Open daily 10:00 A.M. to 10:00 P.M., May through early-October, or as long as good weather holds out. Everything is priced on a per-activity basis.

Flintstones Bedrock City
West Highway 16 & Highway 385
Custer, SD (605) 673–4079

"Hey Wilma, look here—I've found a nifty amusement park named after me!" Yes, that's Fred Flintstone, whom you'll meet if you stop by this colorful little park. You'll also get a chance to meet Fred's neighbor, Barney Rubble.

Founded in 1966, the park replicates Bedrock, the Flintstones' hometown. Visitors can peek into the 20 Flintstone-style buildings or romp in the prehistoric playground, which features dinosaurs and huge birds made just for climbing.

A train ride takes guests around the park. Two old Volkswagens converted into Flintstone-style cars also give visitors a ride around the town. In the movie theater, you'll find a continuous showing of Flintstone cartoons; on the stage, an animated trio singing a happy song.

Food available at the Bedrock Drive-in—where Wilma and Betty work—includes Bronto Burgers, Dino Dogs, and Chick-a-Saurus sandwiches.

Open mid-May through Labor Day. Admission is pay-one-price, under $5. Hours vary; call first.

TENNESSEE

Dollywood
1020 Dollywood Lane
Pigeon Forge, TN (423) 428–9488

Co-owned by country singing superstar Dolly Parton, this 100-acre, heavily wooded Smoky Mountain theme park has a lively selection of the arts, crafts, food, music, and customs of the mountains. There's nothing like this park's Craftsmen Valley in any other park in the country.

Dolly grew up in this area, and she does whatever she can to promote and showcase the region. She has an apartment at the park and is here many times each year. Many of her family members work and perform at the park.

There are 21 rides, including 5 just for the little ones. Other attractions include a replica of Dolly's childhood home and the Dolly Parton Story museum.

Two distinctly themed areas, Jukebox Junction and Dollywood Boulevard, reflect Dolly's memories of growing up. Jukebox Junction is themed to the 1950s, and Dollywood Boulevard relives some of her earliest memories of the movies.

 Extras: Black-powder gun shooting and gold panning available for additional charge. U Pick Nick is an interactive family game show based on the programs of the Nickelodeon Network.

 Special events: National Crafts Festival, October; Smoky Mountain Christmas, featuring 300,000 lights, Thanksgiving through New Year's Day.

 Season: Late April through October. Reopens the day after Thanksgiving for its Christmas celebration.

 Operating hours: 9:00 A.M. to 6:00 or 9:00 P.M.

 Admission policy: Pay-one-price, under $28. All rides and shows, except in Celebrity Theatre, are included. Parking charge.

 Top rides: Thunder Road, motion-based simulator; Smoky Mountain Rampage, a raging-rapids ride; Mountain Slidewinder, a fast, downhill toboggan run in a rubber boat; Dollywood Express, a 5-mile excursion up the mountain on a 110-ton, coal-fired steam train; a circa-1924 Dentzel carousel in beautiful, original condition; Blazing Fury, a combination roller coaster, dark ride, and water ride that takes riders through a burning town.

 Roller coaster: Thunder Express, mine train (S).

 Plan to stay: 5 hours.

 Best way to avoid crowds: Come on Mondays, Thursdays, or Fridays. The park has an "in after 3:00 P.M., next day free" policy: Come for a few hours, go rest, and come back the next day free.

 Directions: Located 1 mile east of Highway 441 in Pigeon Forge, about 5 miles north of Gatlinburg. Turn at the Dollywood Information Center, located below the area's largest billboard and beside a 110-ton Dollywood Express locomotive.

 # TIM'S TRIVIA

Dolly Parton owns Dollywood, in Pigeon Forge, Tennessee, but her former singing buddy Kenny Rogers doesn't own Kennywood, in West Mifflin, Pennsylvania. That park is more than 50 years older than Parton's.

Fun Mountain
Parkway at Highway 321
Gatlinburg, TN (423) 436–4132

As its name implies, Fun Mountain is located on a mountain, and boy is it fun! What a great setting. Among the 15 rides are a chairlift up the mountainside, a Ferris wheel, a Himalaya, Sky Rocket reverse bungee, and go-karts. Additionally, there's an animated bear show, a laser tag game, a kids' play area, an arcade, and a well-stocked concessions stand.

Open year-round, with weekend operation during the fall, winter, and spring. Admission is free, with everything on a pay-as-you-go basis. Pay-one-price available, under $20, not including go-karts or Sky Rocket.

Libertyland
Mid-South Fairgrounds
940 Early Maxwell Boulevard
Memphis, TN (901) 274-1776
http://www.memphisnet.com/libertyland/

It is appropriate that this patriotic amusement park opened on July 4, 1976, the country's bicentennial. The 26-acre park has a colonial feel to it, and various colonial icons, including Independence Hall and the Liberty Bell, are replicated, as is the Statue of Liberty.

Nine of the park's 23 rides are located in Kiddie Korner and on Tom Sawyer's Island, where costumed characters, including D. J. Foxx and Hound Dog, perform daily.

 TIM'S TRIVIA

The Zippin' Pippin wooden roller coaster at Libertyland, in Memphis, Tennessee, was Elvis Presley's favorite. Elvis would rent out the entire park so that he and his family could enjoy the coaster, as well as the rest of the rides, without being bothered by fans.

 Special events: Libertyland Remembers Elvis, mid-August (Elvis Presley lived in Memphis and would rent the park out for his daughter and her friends); Christian Family Days, July; July 4 Birthday Party.

 Season: Mid-April through Labor Day.

 Operating hours: Opens at 10:00 A.M. or noon and closes at 9:00 P.M. Closed Mondays and Tuesdays.

 Admission policy: General admission, plus rides, or a pay-one-price ticket is available, under $17; some rides are included in the general admission ticket. A Twilight ticket purchased after 4:00 P.M. offers big savings.

 Top rides: Casey's Cannonball, a 15-minute ride around the park; Turnpike, antique cars; Kamikaze; Sea Dragon; the Old Hickory Log Flume; Surf City Slide, a double water slide on fiberglass sleds; Grand Carousel, a circa-1909 Dentzel carousel.

The Amusement Park Guide

Roller coasters: Zippin Pippin (W); Revolution, corkscrew/loop (S).

Plan to stay: 4 hours.

Best way to avoid crowds: Come Wednesday and plan your rides around the show schedule.

Directions: Located 7 miles from downtown Memphis, on the fairgrounds. Take the Airways exit off I–240 to East Parkway. The park entrance is 2 miles north, between Central and Southern.

Ober Gatlinburg All Seasons Resort
1001 Parkway
Gatlinburg, TN (423) 436–5423

As a true four-seasons resort, this wonderful mountainside facility has something for all members of the family, year-round. Visitors can enjoy indoor ice skating, midway games, a video arcade, batting cages, and other activities year-round, although skiing dominates the activities during the winter.

In summer there's plenty to do as well, including go-karts, alpine slide, bungee jumping, water slides, and a kiddieland with 4 rides and a play area. You'll also find a black bear habitat, an arts and crafts area, and various eateries.

A fun way to reach the park is via a tramway from downtown Gatlinburg. The tram carries 120 passengers more than 2 miles up the side of the mountain during the 10-minute journey.

All attractions, including the tram and bungee jump, are on a pay-as-you-go basis. Hours vary according to the time of year and the weather. It's best to call ahead.

Opryland
2802 Opryland Drive
Nashville, TN (615) 889-6600

It's music everywhere you go here at Opryland. The music show park, located adjacent to the historic Grand Ole Opry, also has 22 grand ole rides and a well-supervised, shaded kiddieland area. The wooded park is divided into various theme sections, including Do Wah Diddy City, Grizzly Country, New Orleans, and State Fair.

 Extras: Free petting zoo. Near Grizzly Country, there's a display showing country entertainer Roy Acuff's gun collection. Outside the gates, museums honoring the life and careers of Roy Acuff and Minnie Pearl are free to the public, as is the Grand Ole Opry Museum.

 Special events: Easter at Opryland, early April; Howl-O-Ween at Opryland, October weekends; Christmas in the Park, mid-November through December; Gospel Jubilee, Memorial Day weekend.

 Season: Late March through October.

Author's daughters on carousel, Opryland, Tennessee

The Amusement Park Guide

 Operating hours: 9:00 A.M. to 9:00 P.M.

 Admission policy: Pay-one-price, under $32. Parking charge.

 Top rides: Grizzly River Rampage, a raging-rapids ride; Old Mill Scream, shoot-the-chute; Opryland Railroad, with vintage locomotives, providing a trip through the park; Skycoaster.

 Roller coasters: Hangman, inverted (S); Chaos, indoor (S); Rock 'n' Roller Coaster, mine train (S); Screamin' Delta Demon, bobsled (S); Wabash Cannonball, corkscrew (S).

 Plan to stay: 6 hours.

 Best way to avoid crowds: Come midmorning during midweek and stay late. Big rush at opening time.

 Directions: 9 miles northeast of downtown Nashville. Take the Briley Parkway exit north from U.S. Route 40, or take the Briley Parkway exit east from I–65. Well-marked, separate exit off Briley Parkway for the park.

X-Site
4835 American Way
Memphis, TN (901) 795–3355

"Go for the Thrill Inside" is the slogan of the state's largest indoor fun center. And living up to its promise, the park has a lot of fun inside those doors!

There are 4 rides, including a Red Baron airplane and a Mini Himalaya; the X-Ploreland, loaded with ball crawls, tunnels, and slides; LaserPort laser tag; video batting cages; and a large arcade with video games and games of skill.

Hungry? There's a McDonald's inside! There is no admission charge, with all games, activities, and rides on a pay-as-you-play basis. There is a $5 cover charge on Friday nights from 7:00 P.M. to closing, but in exchange, you get $5 worth of tokens or tickets. Open Monday through Thursday, 10:00 A.M. to 10:00 P.M.; Friday and Saturday, 10:00 A.M. to midnight; and Sunday, 11:00 A.M. to 10:00 P.M.

TEXAS

Exhilarama
Memorial City Mall
Gessner at I-10
Houston, TX (713) 932-PLAY

Once you enter this popular family entertainment center, you'll realize why the owners named it what they did. It's full of exhilarating fun for the entire family. There are low-key activities such as kiddie rides soft-play units, and there's high-tech action, ranging from virtual reality to laser tag.

Among the 8 kiddie rides are bumper cars; a Mix Master; Cruise-A-Rama, cars; Ramaloons, balloon ride; and the Fly-A-Rama, high-flying Red Baron airplanes. The Romp-A-Rama is a participatory soft-play area. In addition there is the Virtual World Battle Tank Outpost that pits 8 players against each other in a special outpost facility.

Rides are on a pay-as-you-play basis, and there is a pay-one-price ticket available, under $10, with a special price of $5 before 2:00 P.M. Opens at 10:00 A.M. daily, closing at 10:00 P.M. weekdays, midnight on Fridays and Saturdays, and 9:00 P.M. Sundays.

 TIM'S TRIVIA

The word fun appears in more amusement park names than any other descriptive word

Funland Amusement Park
2006 Southwest Parkway
Wichita Falls, TX (817) 767-7911

Family fun at reasonable prices is what you'll find at this small, attractive, traditional park on the outskirts of town. Started in 1960 as a kiddieland, the well-maintained park now caters to young families with kids from ages 3 to 14. It has 14 rides, including 6 just for the wee ones.

 Extras: Miniature golf and a games-of-skill arcade. The city-operated park next door has a picnic pavilion and a child's playground.

The Amusement Park Guide

 Season: March through October.

 Operating hours: Opens Tuesday through Friday at 6:30 P.M. and Saturday and Sunday at 2:00 P.M.; closes nightly at 10:00 P.M.

 Admission policy: Free admission, with rides and attractions on a pay-as-you-go basis. Pay-one-price available, under $7.50. Free parking.

 Top rides: Tilt-A-Whirl; Paratrooper; a Ferris wheel; bumper cars; and a miniature train.

 Roller coasters: The Roller Coaster, family (S).

 Plan to stay: 2 hours.

 Best way to avoid crowds: This isn't a tourist park, so crowds aren't usually a problem. Weeknights are generally less crowded than weekends.

 Directions: Take the Southwest Parkway exit from Highway 281 and go west 2 miles to the park. Located about 5 miles from downtown.

Hurricane Harbor
1800 East Lamar Boulevard
Arlington, TX (817) 265-3356

There are 32 major water rides, slides, and attractions in five different areas of this 40-acre oasis, one of the largest and one of the first full-scale waterparks in the world. What a way to cool down! There are more than 3 million cool, fresh gallons of water flowing down the slides through three major pool areas and around the Lazy River.

Lagoona Beach, a new 7-acre themed area, opened in 1996, and offers 2 miniature golf courses, 4 sand volleyball courts, batting cages, laser tag, and a large arcade/restaurant.

Located across the interstate from Six Flags Over Texas, the waterpark was purchased by the Six Flags Corporation in 1995 to supplement the company's other offerings in the area. Picnics are allowed in the park, and there are a swim shop and a gift shop, just in case you forgot something.

Open daily mid-May through mid-September, from 9:00 or 10:00 A.M., to either 6:00 or 9:00 P.M. Admission is under $23, and there is a parking fee.

Joyland Amusement Park
McKenzie State Park
Lubbock, TX (806) 763–2719

Located in McKenzie State Park on its own 10-acre site, Joyland has been serving up entertainment to the area since the early 1940s. The midway is bright and clean, with a nice "local amusement park" feeling to it.

The entire park, including the rides, is well maintained by the Dean family, who have owned it since 1973. It has 23 rides, including 9 for kids.

 Special events: Weeknights at the park are sponsored by local businesses that offer special discounts.

 Season: Mid-March through mid-September.

 Operating hours: Opens at 7:00 P.M. during the week and 2:00 P.M. on weekends; closes nightly at 10:00 P.M.

 Admission policy: General admission, plus rides on a pay-as-you-go basis; pay-one-price also available, under $10. Free parking.

 Top rides: Vortex, a water coaster; bumper cars; Rock-O-Plane; Roll-O-Plane; Musik Express, a sky ride; Paratrooper.

 Roller coasters: Mad Mouse, family (S); Galaxy, family (S).

 Plan to stay: 3 hours.

 Best way to avoid crowds: Tuesday nights are the least crowded.

 Directions: Take 4th Street exit off I–27 and enter the state park. Follow the signs to Joyland.

The Amusement Park Guide

Jungle Jim's Playland
Bitters Road at Highway 281
San Antonio, TX (210) 490-9595

This is the Jungle Jim's that started them all—the original location. There are 5 mechanical kiddie rides, including a Ferris wheel, a mini-Himalaya ride, and flying jets. Also here are a games-of-skill arcade and Jungle Play, the company's trademarked participatory play area. Food service includes hot dogs and pizza, and activities encompass birthday parties and a Jungle Jim costumed character.

Admission is pay-one-price, under $7.50, or on a pay-as-you-play basis. Adults ride free at all times. Hours vary; call first.

Kiddie Park
3015 Broadway
San Antonio, TX (210) 824-4351

Well known throughout the area, this park is the oldest operating kiddieland in America and is now entertaining its fourth generation of kids. Established in 1925 adjacent to the sprawling Brackenridge City Park, Kiddie Park has 10 rides, including a circa-1918 Herschell–Spillman carousel.

Admission to the 1-acre park is free, with rides on a pay-as-you-go basis. A pay-one-price ticket is also available, under $5. Open Memorial Day through August, 10:00 A.M. to 10:00 P.M. The park is open the rest of the year, on a limited basis. Call for hours.

Note: If you're still eager for some action after you've done everything at Kiddie Park, cross the street to the city park, where you can enjoy pony rides, train rides, an aerial ride, and the San Antonio Zoo.

Neff's Amusement Park
Neff's Way, Riverpark Mall
San Angelo, TX (915) 653–3014

The action in this wonderful little city takes place down by the river. And this small family park is located downtown on 3 acres along the river. Situated next to the boardwalk, the park is divided by a walkway that runs from the street. The 7 kiddie rides are on one side, the 7 adult and family rides on the other.

The area around the amusement park is a riverside park, complete with a band shell, benches, walkways, and shopping areas, and the city's new art museum is slated to be built next to the rides' area.

 Extras: Arcade games.

 Special events: Fiesta Celebration, June; July 4 fireworks and celebration.

 Season: March through October.

 Operating hours: Opens at 6:00 P.M. during the week and 1:30 P.M. on weekends. Closes nightly at 10:30 P.M. Closed Mondays.

 Admission policy: Free admission to the park, with rides on a pay-as-you-go basis. Pay-one-price available on certain days, under $10. Free parking.

 Top rides: A train ride, taking you out of the park and along the river; bumper cars; a Ferris wheel; a circa-1906 Parker carousel.

 Plan to stay: 2 hours.

 Best way to avoid crowds: Tuesday nights are the least crowded.

 Directions: Located on the river between the Okes and Chadbourne bridges. Take Neff's Way off either of those avenues and follow it to the parking lot. Follow the path to the park.

The Amusement Park Guide

Sandy Lake Amusement Park
1800 Sandy Lake Road
Dallas, TX (214) 242-7449

"We don't cater to tourists or the rich people. We're here for the working families." Of course, both are welcome, but that's how the owner explains his family's park in the Dallas suburb of Carrollton. It's also the only outdoor amusement park in Dallas County.

Spread out over 96 acres, the park features 20 rides, clustered in groups under large pecan and oak trees. There are resting spots galore and a 2-acre lake. Probably the biggest draw here, though, is the "Texas-size" swimming pool: The largest in the area, it holds 1.5 million gallons of filtered water.

 Extras: Miniature golf, paddleboats, live pony rides, all available for extra charge.

 Special events: Easter Parade, when 40,000 candy eggs are dropped from a helicopter, Easter weekend; FunFest, when more than 1,200 school bands, choirs, and choral groups compete for trophies, April and May.

 Season: Easter through mid-September.

 Operating hours: Daily, 10:00 A.M. to 6:00 P.M. (The park has never been open after dark.)

 Admission policy: General admission, plus rides. Free parking.

 Top rides: Fun House, a classic Pretzel dark ride; a train ride around the park; Tilt-A-Whirl; Scrambler; a kiddie roller coaster; bumper cars.

 Plan to stay: 3 hours.

 Best way to avoid crowds: Come on Sunday afternoons, when crowds tend to be moderate—just enough people to make things interesting, but not so many as to slow you down.

 Directions: 15 miles north of Dallas at the Sandy Lake exit off I–35.

Schlitterbahn Waterpark & Resort
305 West Austin
New Braunfels, TX (210) 625–2351
http://www.schlitterbahn.com

The largest waterpark in Texas, this German-themed water wonderland is located on the banks of the spring-fed Comal River. The 65-acre park and resort features more than 30 rides and family activities in six themed areas, including 2 uphill water coasters, 9 tube chutes, and 17 water slides.

Also among the offerings are the Boogie Bahn surfing ride, a family wave pool; 5 swimming pools, 5 hot tubs, 5 children's water playgrounds; water and sand volleyball courts; 4 gift shops, 2 restaurants, and 20 refreshment stands.

You can buy an all-day ticket (under $23), a half-day pass, or a 2-day pass. The latter is the best deal and if you have the time. Stay around for 2 days, you'll be glad you did!

Open May through mid-September, from 10:00 A.M. to 8:00 P.M., you get a lot of free stuff with your admission ticket, including free parking, free inner tubes, free life vests, and free body boards. If you want to stay in the area, the park features cottages, motel rooms, condominiums, and duplex houses.

"Master Blaster," Schlitterbahn Waterpark, Texas

THE AMUSEMENT PARK GUIDE

Sea World of Texas
Lost Lagoon
10500 Sea World Drive
San Antonio, TX (210) 523–3630
http://www.4adventure.com

This is the largest and the newest of the Sea World parks. In fact, with 250 acres, it's the world's largest marine zoological park.

The 5-acre Lost Lagoon waterpark, included in park admission, has 4 slides, including the thrilling Sky Tubin', a 5-story-tall, 500-foot-long tube slide. Among other offerings are a wave pool and activity pools for the kids.

Also for the kids is Shamu's Happy Harbor, a 3-acre play area featuring both wet and dry interactive elements.

 Extras: Texas Walk, enabling you to walk through a state history in a garden containing statues of 16 famous Texans. A 90-minute behind-the-scenes tour is available, extra charge.

 Season: March through October.

"Texas Splashdown," Sea World of Texas

Operating hours: 10:00 A.M. to 11:00 P.M.

 Admission policy: Pay-one-price, under $30. Parking fee.

 Top rides: 2 water rides: Texas Splashdown, a flume; and the Rio Loco, a raging-rapids ride.

 Roller coaster: The Great White, inverted (S). ((This is the first Sea World park to add a roller coaster.)

 Plan to stay: 7 hours.

 Best way to avoid crowds: Come during the week, just before dinnertime.

 Directions: Located 16 miles northwest of downtown San Antonio, off State Highway 151 between Loop 410 and Loop 1604, on Sea World Drive.

Six Flags AstroWorld
9001 Kirby Drive
Houston, TX (713) 799–1234
http://www.sixflags.com

Talk about an oasis of plant life! This 75-acre park contains more than 600 varieties of plants and shrubs, and is home to the world's largest hanging basket, holding 5,000 flowering plants. The landscaping has been beautifully designed to fit into the park's twelve theme areas, each representing a classic culture and era of America's past. Also blended nicely into the surroundings are the park's 34 rides.

 Extras: The Southern Star Amphitheater books in top-name entertainers all season long; some shows carry an additional surcharge.

 Special events: Spring Break Out, March; Fright Fest, October weekends; Holiday in the Park, mid-November through January 1.

 Season: March through December.

THE AMUSEMENT PARK GUIDE

 Operating hours: Opens daily at 10:00 A.M. Closings vary.

 Admission policy: Pay-one-price, under $30. Parking charge. Special combination ticket available for AstroWorld's adjacent sister park, WaterWorld.

 Top rides: Dungeon Drop, a themed free-fall Thunder River, the world's first white-water raging-rapids ride; Bamboo Shoot, log flume; Antique Taxis, antique cars; a circa-1895 Dentzel carousel; Tidal Wave, shoot-the-chute; Astroway, a cable-car ride 100 feet above the park.

 Roller coasters: Batman The Escape, stand-up (S); Mayan Mindbender, indoor (S); Excalibur, mine train (S); Greezed Lightnin', shuttle loop (S); Serpent, mini–mine train (S); Texas Cyclone (W); Viper, looping (S); XLR-8, suspended (S); Ultra Twister (S).

 Plan to stay: 8 hours.

 Best way to avoid crowds: Come during the week. The park is easy to get around in: Though spread out, it has a circular pattern. Take your time, see things as you go, and you won't have to double back.

 Directions: Take the Kirby Drive exit off I–610; go north on Kirby to the park's parking lot.

Six Flags Fiesta Texas
The Ol' Waterin' Hole
I–10 and Loop 1604
San Antonio, TX (210) 697–5050
http://www.sixflags.com

Of all the theme parks in the country, this one probably was created in the most unique location. The 200-acre park is situated in an abandoned stone quarry, with dramatic 100-foot-tall limestone cliffs surrounding nearly three sides of the park.

The overall theme here is the music, culture, and history of this area of Texas. That theme is delivered through dramatic architecture, live stage productions, eateries, rides, and attractions. Rides and attractions fill the six beautifully themed areas: Los Festivales (Hispanic), Crackaxle Canyon (1920s Texas), Spassburg (German, featuring an 8-ride kinderland); Rockville (1950s), Fiesta Bay Boardwalk (seaside resort), and the Ol' Waterin' Hole (water activities and tubing).

The waterpark, a welcome relief from the hot summer afternoons, offers nearly 20 activities for the entire family, and is included in the price of park admission.

 Extras: Each night during peak season, The Lone Star Spectacular laser and fireworks show is projected onto the quarry walls in the back of the park. Great sound, great visuals. You've never seen anything like this. Skycoaster, extra fee.

 Season: April through October.

 Operating hours: Opens 10:00 A.M.; closes at varying times through the season.

 Admission policy: Pay-one-price, under $30. Parking charge.

 Top rides: The Gully Washer, raging rapids; Stop 39 Train, takes riders around park and through a tunnel in the cliffs; The Power Surge, shoot-the-chute; Motorama Turnpike, a ride in 1950s-era gas powered cars; Crows Nest Ferris Wheel; The Wipeout.

 Roller coasters: Roadrunner Express, mine train (S); The Rattler (W); Joker's Revenge, looping (S); Der Rollschuhcoaster, family (S).

 Plan to stay: 8 hours.

 Best way to avoid crowds: Crowds generally tend to head to roller coasters first and to the waterpark during the hot afternoon. To avoid the long lines, do the opposite.

 Directions: Located 15 miles northwest of downtown San Antonio, off Anderson Loop 1604. Take the La Cantera exit (555) off I–10, then follow signs to the park.

THE AMUSEMENT PARK GUIDE

TIM'S TRIVIA

There's enough lumber in Texas Giant, the roller coaster at Six Flags Over Texas in Arlington, to build thirty houses.

Six Flags Over Texas
2201 Road to Six Flags
Arlington, TX (817) 640-8900
http://www.sixflags.com

This 205-acre park is the mother ship of the Six Flags organization. In fact, it not only was the first Six Flags park to open (1961) but also the first major regional theme park in the country.

Beautiful at night because of the colorful lights, and beautiful in the day because of the colorful flowers and landscaping, the park has a total of 33 rides.

The mature, well-grown-in facility has 33 different areas reflecting the architecture fun and atmosphere of early Texas life: USA, Boomtown, Spain, Mexico, Good Times Square, Tower, France, Texas, Confederacy, and Looney Tunes Land.

 Extras: Two of the original attractions are still in operation: the Casa Magnetica (a tilt house) featuring gravity illusions, and the Six Flags Railroad, taking visitors on a trip around the park.

 Special events: Holiday in the Park, Thanksgiving through New Year's Day; Fright Fest, the last three weekends in October; Crafts Fair, September.

 Season: April through October. Reopens for Holiday in the Park.

 Operating hours: Opens daily at 10:00 A.M.; closes at varying times all season long, from 10:00 P.M. to midnight.

 Admission policy: Pay-one-price, under $31. Parking charge.

 Top rides: Yosemite Sam and the Gold River Adventure, a boat ride through a cartoon; Log Flume, the very first of its kind in the world; Air Racer, 90-foot-high airplanes; La Salle's River Rapids, raging rapids; Splash Water, shoot-the-chute; The Right Stuff Mach I Adventure, a simulated jet ride; Texas Chute Out, 200-foot-tall parachute ride; Oil Derrick, an observation tower; Silver Star Carousel, a circa-1926 Dentzel carousel.

 Roller coasters: Mr. Freeze, LIM Shuttle (S); Runaway Mountain, indoor (S); Texas Giant (W); Flashback, Boomerang (S); Shock Wave, 2-loop (S); Judge Roy Scream (W); Run-A-Way Mine Train (S); Mini Mine Train (S); La Vibora, bobsleds (S).

 Plan to stay: 8 hours.

 Best way to avoid crowds: Come on Sundays in fall or spring, or come early in the day during midweek in peak season. Avoid Saturdays any time of the year if you want to stay out of crowds.

Directions: In Arlington, halfway between Dallas and Ft. Worth, off I-30. Signs will give you fair warning that the exits to the park are approaching, and a huge electronic sign and the observation tower will mark the spot quite nicely.

Six Flags WaterWorld
9001 Kirby Drive
Houston, TX (713) 799-1234
http://www.sixflags.com

As part of the Six Flags Houston complex, WaterWorld offers a cooling alternative to the heat on the hot muggy days for which this part of Texas is known. There are more than a dozen rides, slides, and activities, including the Breaker Beach wave pool and the Lagoon Activity Center, where you'll find all kinds of slides, rings, and ropes.

A ride on The Edge takes you down the biggest slide in the complex. It's an 83-foot-high free-fall drop, and it is fast and thrilling! Mainstream is the lazy river, and Squirts Splash is a children's activity pool. There are a surf shop and 4 food outlets.

Adjacent to AstroWorld, there is an additional charge for the waterpark, and a combination two-park ticket may be purchased. You approach the park just as you would AstroWorld, but just after you cross over the bridge from the parking lot, turn right to the waterpark ticket booths. Once you pay, you can take a train to the park, or walk.

The Amusement Park Guide

Western Playland
6900 Delta
El Paso, TX (915) 772-3953

As you ride slowly across the tops of the trees and ride upon the Sky Ride, look out over the river and you'll see Mexico. That's how close this park is to the border. Located in Ascarate County Park, the facility has 31 rides, including 10 for kids, on 20 acres.

With its Spanish motif, the park features an abundance of colorful gardens, shade trees, benches, and adobe buildings.

 Extras: Go-karts, additional fee.

 Special events: July 4 fireworks and celebration.

 Season: March through mid-October.

 Operating hours: Opens at 6:30 P.M. during the week and at 2:00 P.M. weekends. Closes nightly at 10:00 P.M. Closed Mondays and Tuesdays.

 Admission policy: Pay-one-price, under $15. Also general admission, plus rides on a pay-as-you-go basis. Free parking.

 Top rides: Pharoah's Fury; Snake Mountain, a dry ride down a steep water slide; Splashdown, a log flume; a train ride, a 2½-mile trek around the park.

 Roller coasters: El Bandito, Zyklon family (S); Big Cheese Mad Mouse, family (S).

 Plan to stay: 4 hours.

 Best way to avoid crowds: Come on weekday nights or Sunday afternoons.

 Directions: Take the Trobridge exit off I-10. Go left and proceed through three traffic lights, turning right onto Delta. The park is located about 1 mile after you cross over an overpass.

Wet 'N' Wild Waterpark
Service Road, I–10 at Exit 0
Anthony (El Paso), TX (915) 886–2222
http://www.wetwild.com

It gets hot in El Paso, and the folks down here love their local waterpark. With nearly 20 attractions packed into 22 acres, there is virtually something for everyone. Centerpiece attractions include the Wild Island Wave Pool; Volcano River, an inner tube rapids ride; The Screamer, a 6-story-tall body slide; the Shotgun, a short slide with a long drop; Volcano Lake, an interactive play area for the kids; and Aquamaniac, an enclosed slide.

There's a Subway sandwich shop, and a wide selection of games in the Volcano Arcade. (This park is not affiliated with the Wet 'n' Wild waterpark chain.)

Open daily, late May through early September, at 10:00 or 11:00 A.M. and closes at either 6:00 or 7:00 P.M. Admission price is under $18. (They offer a special discount for Internet surfers, check it out!)

Wonderland Park
Highway 287 North
Amarillo, TX (806) 383–4712

This truly is a family park—the family that started it in 1951 still owns and operates it for the families of Amarillo. Located in the city's largest greenbelt, Thompson Park, Wonderland has 24 rides, including 7 for the little folks.

Founded as a kiddie park, the facility has grown and is now a popular place for the entire family. A flat, paved midway is lined with trees and flowers and contains lots of benches.

 Extras: Miniature golf, extra fee.

 Season: Mid-March through September.

 Operating hours: Open weekdays 7:00 to 10:30 P.M., and on weekends, 1:00 to 10:00 P.M.

 Admission policy: General admission, plus rides, or a pay-one-price ticket is available for weeknights, under $10, and on weekends, under $15 (the looping coaster and the dark ride are not included in the pay-one-price). Free parking.

THE AMUSEMENT PARK GUIDE

 Top rides: Pipeline Plunge, a dry ride down a water chute; Pirate Ship; Rattlesnake River, a raging-rapids ride; Fantastic Journey, a dark ride; Big Splash, a log flume.

 Roller coasters: Texas Tornado, 2-loop (S); Zyklon, family (S); Texas Express, family (S).

 Plan to stay: 3 hours.

 Best way to avoid crowds: Come during June. Thursday evenings are the slowest times.

 Directions: Located in the Texas Panhandle. Take the 24th Street or River Road exit off Highway 287; the park is located inside Thompson Park and is easily visible from the road.

UTAH

Lagoon Park
Lagoon A Beach
I-15 & Lagoon Drive
Farmington, UT (801) 451-8000

Summertime fun is both plentiful and varied in the state's largest amusement facility. From thrilling roller coasters to a charming pre-1900 pioneer village to a cool waterpark, there's enough here to keep the whole family busy.

There are 36 rides, including 12 for kids in Mother Gooseland. The 15-acre Pioneer Village features crafts, foods, and architecture from the pre-1900 Utah frontier, while Lagoon A Beach is a 6-acre waterpark offering a bevy of water activities, including 3 hot tubs, adult and children's slides, a lazy river, and activity pools for both adults and children.

Once located on the shores of the Great Salt Lake, this park moved inland to its own 9-acre lagoon and changed its name from Lake Park to Lagoon Park. The merry-go-round, skating rink, saloon, and cafe went along with the park. Today all that remains from that 1896 move is the wonderfully Victorian Lake Park Terrace, used as one of the picnic terraces for group outings.

Extras: Top Eliminator Dragster, extra charge; Skycoaster, extra fee; and an 18-hole miniature golf course called Putter Around the Park, extra charge, that features miniature versions of amusement park attractions, including a rollercoaster hole.

 Special events: Clogging Championships, several weekends in May; School Days, May; fireworks, July 4, and Utah's Pioneer Days, a state holiday, July 24; and Frightmares, weekends in October.

 Season: April through October.

 Operating hours: 11:00 A.M. to midnight.

 Admission policy: Pay-one-price, under $23; includes waterpark and "dry" rides. Parking charge. Park discount coupons are easily found at sponsoring retail stores.

 Top rides: A 153-foot-tall gondola Ferris wheel; River Rapids; Dracula's Castle, a dark ride; Flying Carpet, a 360-degree swinging platform; Tidal Wave, a pendulum pirate ship; a circa-1900 Herschell–Spillman carousel; a train ride around the lagoon and through a small zoo.

 Roller coasters: Fire Dragon, 2-loop (S); Roller Coaster (W); Jet Star II, family (S); Puff, kiddie (S).

 Plan to stay: 8 hours.

 Best way to avoid crowds: Sunday and Monday are the slowest days of the week. Saturday is the busiest.

 Directions: Located off I–15, 17 miles north of Salt Lake City and 17 miles south of Ogden. Take the Lagoon Drive exit.

The Amusement Park Guide

Raging Waters
1200 West 1700 South
Salt Lake City, UT (801) 977–8300

If you don't want to swim the Great Salt Lake, here's a crystal clear alternative! With 12 slides and a lot of water, this top-notch waterpark is the place for some great cool fun during the hot summer months.

The 2 children's play areas—Dinosaur Beach, with its "active volcano," and the Raging WaterWorks with slides, pools, and activities—provide some of the best water-based interactive fun for the little ones in this part of the country.

For the rest of the family, there's the H2O Roller Coaster (one of the world's first water roller coasters), the wave pool, games arcade, volleyball courts, a restaurant, and a beach shop. For the adults, there's a large, relaxing hot tub. Open daily, 10:30 A.M. to 7:30 P.M., Memorial Day through Labor Day. Admission, under $15.

VERMONT

Santa's Land
Route 5
Putney, VT (802) 387–5550

"Where the Spirit of Christmas is a Way of Life"—that's the slogan of this little park in the foothills of the Green Mountains. The alpine architecture throughout lends a fine touch to making this a fun outing for the entire family.

In addition to a train ride through a joyful Santa's Tunnel, the park offers a carousel, an iceberg-shaped giant slide, a petting zoo, a playground, and an animatronic show of animals preparing for Christmas.

Movies and cartoons are shown, and storytelling activities take place in the Little Red Schoolhouse. Santa and his elves are ready to greet visitors in his elegant home at the back of the park.

The Igloo Pancake House, housed in three white, igloo-shaped buildings, serves delicious pancakes and waffles; of course, real Vermont maple syrup is on every table. Several Christmas shops, too, provide top-notch shopping.

Open from May through Christmas; closed Thanksgiving and Christmas days. Pay-one-price, under $10.

VIRGINIA

Busch Gardens, The Old Country
Route 60
Williamsburg, VA (804) 253–3350
http://www.4adventure.com

With its 360 acres of heavily wooded, rolling hills, this is the most beautiful large theme park in the country. The architecture in each of the nine Old World European hamlets looks as though it has been there for years; hats off to the designers. It's not easy to build things that look 400 years old and at the same time make 40 modern rides look like they belong in the setting. But they did it here, quite nicely.

 Extras: The Royal Preserve Petting Zoo is free with admission. Self-guided brewery tours at the adjacent Anheuser–Busch Brewery offers free samples at the end. A special "Shopper's Pass" is available if you want to enter only to shop in the stores.

 Season: April through October.

 Operating hours: 10:00 A.M. to 10:00 P.M. or midnight.

 Admission policy: Pay-one-price, under $32. An after–5:00 P.M. twilight ticket discount is available, as is a second-day pass, for an additional $10. Parking charge.

 Top rides: King Arthur's Challenge, a 3-D ride simulator; Escape from Pompeii, a themed, indoor–outdoor shoot-the-chute; Haunts of the Old Country, a 4-D film experience; and The Land of the Dragons, an interactive children's play area with several kiddie rides and play elements; Roman Rapids, a raging-rapids ride; Le Scoot, a log flume; a scenic boat cruise down the Rhine River; a 1919 Allan Herschell carousel.

 Roller coasters: Alpengeist, inverted (S); Drachen Fire, multielement (S); Big Bad Wolf, suspended (S); Loch Ness Monster, 2-loop (S); Wild Izzy, Wild Mouse (S).

THE AMUSEMENT PARK GUIDE

 Plan to stay: 10 hours.

 Best way to avoid crowds: Come in spring or fall, when crowds are fewer. During the season, mid-week is best. Check the concert schedule; the park is generally much more crowded on big concert days.

 Directions: Take I–64 east into the Williamsburg area, follow the signs to get onto Route 60, and follow that route until you get to the park.

Ocean Breeze Fun Park
849 General Booth Boulevard
Virginia Beach, VA (804) 422–0718

There is a great deal of activity going on here in the park's four areas: MotorWorld, featuring 4 go-kart and Grand Prix tracks; Shipwreck Golf, a 36-hole miniature golf course whose holes represent a real shipwreck off the Virginia coast; WildWater Rapids, a waterpark; and Strike Zone, offering batting cages.

WaterWorld has 8 tube and body slides, a wave pool, an adult activity pool, and a children's activity pool.

The park is located 1 mile south of the Virginia Beach oceanfront and is open from April through September. Admission to WaterWorld is under $17, with all other activ-

"Drachen Fire," Bush Gardens, Virginia

ities on a pay-as-you-play basis. If you go to waterpark first, get your hand stamped, and you can enjoy all other activities at half-price.

Paramount's Kings Dominion Hurricane Reef
Route 30
Doswell, VA (804) 876–5000

The excitement of a visit to this park begins as you enter the front gate. Looming 330 feet into the air in front of you is a replica of the Eiffel Tower, and a good way to start your visit is to take a trip up to its observation deck to get a feel for what the park is all about.

The park is divided into seven areas: International Street, Old Virginia, The Congo, Wayne's World, Candy Apple Grove, and the Land of Hanna–Barbera, a great little kiddie-ride area. All 55 rides, including the 20 for kids, are divided among the different sections.

Hurricane Reef has all the elements of a major waterpark except a wave pool. There are several body and tube slides, as well as a lazy river and a children's play area.

 Extras: Splat City is a 3-acre, wet-and-messy children's activity area themed to the fun and attitude of cable television's Nickelodeon network for kids. The 6,500-seat Showplace Amphitheatre offers top-name entertainers on a regular basis throughout the season. There's a charge to these concerts in addition to park admission. The most wooden roller coasters of any park in North America.

 Season: End of March through mid-October.

 Operating hours: 10:00 A.M. to 9:00 or 10:00 P.M.

 Admission policy: Pay-one-price, under $30. Parking charge.

 Top rides: White Water Canyon, a raging-rapids ride; Shenandoah, a log flume; a 1917 Philadelphia Toboggan Company carousel.

 Roller coasters: Rebel Yell, twin racing (W); Scooby Doo, junior (W); The Grizzly (W); Shockwave, stand-up (S); Anaconda, looping (S);

THE AMUSEMENT PARK GUIDE

Hurler (W); Outer Limits: Flight of Fear, indoor (S); Avalanche Bobsled (S).

 Plan to stay: 10 hours.

 Best way to avoid crowds: Tuesday is the least busy day. Get there early and head to the major rides first.

 Directions: Located 20 miles north of Richmond. Take Exit 40 (Doswell) off I–95; the park is right there.

 # TIM'S TRIVIA

The Eiffel Tower exists, albeit one-third scale, in two American parks: Kings Island amusement park, near Cincinnati, Ohio, and Kings Dominion, in Doswell, Virginia.

Water Country USA
Route 199 & I–64
Williamsburg, VA (804) 229–9300/
(800) 343–SWIM
http://www.4adventure.com

If you enjoyed the 1950s and 1960s surf scene, or think you might, you'll love this place. The theming is based on those two decades, from music to food. Surfer music and a surfer attitude prevail as thousands hang ten each summer at the mid-Atlantic's largest themed waterpark.

There are more than a dozen slides among the total of 30 rides and water activities. Among the slides you'll find the Wild Thang, the Malibu Pipeline, and Big Daddy Falls, the park's largest attraction. The Rambling River is the lazy river; Surfer's Bay is the wave pool. The H2O UFO is a fun children's interactive play area.

Owned by the Busch Entertainment Corporation, the park is adjacent to Busch Gardens. Open May through early September at 10:00 A.M., closing times vary. A 1-day admission to the waterpark is under $23, and a 3-day combination pass with Busch Gardens sells for under $50.

WASHINGTON

Enchanted Village
Wild Waves
36201 Enchanted Parkway South
Federal Way, WA (206) 661–8001

Combined, these two parks are known as the Enchanted Parks, and you certainly can double your pleasure during a day full of fun here!

Enchanted Village is the amusement park, featuring 30 acres of rides and attractions. Among its 23 rides are a Ring of Fire, the Red Robin Railway, a circa-1905 antique carousel, and 8 kiddie rides. There are animal exhibits, live shows, games of skill, eateries, and a gift shop.

Wild Waves is the Northwest's largest waterpark, offering 6 water slides, the Raging River lazy river, a wave pool, and a cooling interactive play area for the little ones. There are also a games arcade, eateries, and a gift shop at the waterpark.

Both parks are open daily from late-May through Labor Day at 11:00 A.M. In addition, the amusement park is open on weekends from mid-April through May and in September. Closing times vary with season. Pay-one-price for Enchanted Village is under $15, and a pay-one-price for both parks is available for under $20.

THE AMUSEMENT PARK GUIDE

Fun Forest
Seattle Center
370 Thomas Street
Seattle, WA (206) 728-1585

What a festive place this is! On the site of the 1962 World's Fair, the amusement park is only a part of the entire Seattle Center, which also features the famous Space Needle.

A colorful flag pavilion and the festive architecture make this entire center a treat to visit. The ride park itself contains 19 rides, including 8 for kids in a separate kiddieland. It was built as part of the entertainment package for the fair and has been in operation ever since.

 Extras: Miniature golf and a large games arcade. The monorail runs from the center to the Westlake Mall in the downtown area of the city.

 Special events: Bite of Seattle, a food fair, mid-July; Bumbershoot, a music festival with lots of arts and crafts, Labor Day weekend.

 Season: March through October.

 Operating hours: Opens daily at noon; closes at midnight.

 Admission policy: Free gate, with rides and attractions on a pay-as-you-play basis. Pay-one-price available during the week only, under $16. Parking charge.

 Top rides: Gondola Ferris wheel; Jet Spin; Wild River, a log flume; Galleon, a swinging pirate ship; bumper boats; a carousel.

 Roller coaster: Windstorm, family (S).

 Plan to stay: 4 hours.

 Best way to avoid crowds: The park gets very crowded during festivals and special events but is less crowded during the early part of the week and during fall.

Directions: Take Exit 167 (Mercer Street) west off I-5, and continue for 1 mile. The park is located adjacent to the highly visible Space Needle.

Riverfront Park
North 507 Howard Street
Spokane, WA (509) 625–6600

Located downtown along the Spokane River, this 100-acre park was the site of the 1974 World's Fair. Beautifully landscaped, the park offers an IMAX theater, miniature golf, and 12 rides, including a gondola ride over the spectacular Spokane Falls. (A rainbow consistently lies on the mist around the falls, so this may be the only ride in the world that goes over a rainbow.) Additional attractions include a 1909 Looff carousel, completely restored in 1990, that lets you grab for the brass ring; Dragon, a family roller coaster; and an SR-2 ride simulator.

Admission to the grounds is free, and all attractions are on a pay-as-you-go basis. A pay-one-price ticket is available, which includes all attractions, including the IMAX theater and golf, under $10. Most attractions are open from March 1 through mid-October. Various attractions in the park have different hours; call first.

WEST VIRGINIA

Camden Park
Route 60 West
Huntington, WV (304) 429–4321

A walk down the tree-lined midway here takes a person back to the 1950s. The architecture, the selection of rides and games, and the wonderful neon lighting make this a not-to-be-missed traditional park.

There are 26 rides, including 10 for kids, and a steamboat that offers rides on the Ohio River. This may also be the only park in the country that has an Indian burial mound within its gates. It was created 2,000 years ago by the Athena Indians.

 Extras: Pizza Hut franchise.

 Special events: Cartoon Day, when costumed cartoon characters visit the park, early August; Fireworks and Country Music, held every holiday weekend.

THE AMUSEMENT PARK GUIDE

 Season: May through September.

 Operating hours: Weekdays, noon to 10:00 P.M.; weekends, 11:00 A.M. to 10:00 P.M. Closed Mondays.

 Admission policy: Small gate fee, with rides and attractions on a pay-as-you-go basis. Pay-one-price also available, under $13.

 Top rides: Whip; Kiddie Whip; bumper cars; West Virginia Logging Company, a log flume; Haunted Mansion.

 Roller coasters: Big Dipper (W); Lil' Dipper, junior (W); Thunderbolt Express, shuttle loop (S).

 Plan to stay: 6 hours.

 Best way to avoid crowds: Come on Tuesdays.

 Directions: Take Exit 6 off I–64, go 300 yards, and turn left on Madison. The road dead-ends into the park in 3 miles.

WISCONSIN

Bay Beach Amusement Park
1313 Bay Beach Road
Green Bay, WI (414) 448–3365

A favorite with locals since 1920, this park has 13 rides, including 5 for children. You'll find lots of shade around, and usually a cool breeze is blowing in off Green Bay.

This may be the only park in the world that still charges 10 cents a ticket. Three rides in the park cost 30 cents each, 9 cost 20 cents, and 1 costs a dime.

In addition to the rides, the park offers a wading pool for the little ones, softball diamonds, volleyball courts, and a horseshoe pit for adults. Staff will even lend you the athletic equipment to play.

 Extras: A wildlife sanctuary, with nature center, year-round hiking trails, and educational programs. Food and grills may be brought into park.

Season: May through September.

 Operating hours: 10:00 A.M. to 6:00 or 9:00 P.M.

 Admission policy: Free admission, with rides on a per-ride basis. Free parking.

 Top rides: A train ride through the park and along Green Bay; a giant slide; bumper cars; a merry-go-round; a Ferris wheel; Yo-Yo.

 Plan to stay: 2 hours.

 Best way to avoid crowds: There is rarely a large crowd here, but come early morning or early evening and you'll find the least competition for the fun.

 Directions: Located on Green Bay. Take the Irwin Avenue exit off Highway 43 and follow the signs.

Big Chief Kart & Coaster World
Highway 12
Wisconsin Dells, WI (608) 254-2490

A most remarkable park if you're looking for thrills! There are 3 adult go-kart tracks, a kiddie go-kart track, and 3 world-class wooden roller coasters, one for adults, one for the entire family. There is also a video arcade.

 Roller coasters: Cyclops (W); Pegasus, junior (W); Zeus (W).

Admission is free and all rides are on a pay-as-you-go basis, with each ride taking one token. Open May through October. Hours and days of operation vary, depending on season and weather.

Circle M Corral Family Fun Park
10295 Highway 70 West
Minocqua, WI (715) 356-4441

Sheriff Parker, the mascot, is the one you have to deal
with at this western family park. Family-owned and -oper-
ated, the place is clean, safe, and fun for all members of the
family.

Attractions include a train ride through the scenic pines
and a dark tunnel, go-karts, bumper boats, miniature golf,
horseback riding, pony rides, a water slide, and a kiddieland with a variety of rides and attractions.

The park has a unique, pay-one-price admission system,
whereby you can mix and match the attractions you want.
Hours vary; call first.

Little A-Merrick-A
Highway 19
Marshall, WI (608) 655-3181

Named for its owner and founder, Lee Merrick, this fun
park was built in 1991 to house and show off Merrick's collection of one-third-scale trains, one of the largest such col-
lections in the world.

It has grown into a full-scale amusement park, featuring
14 rides, including a Mad Mouse roller coaster, a Toboggan
ride, and a monorail. The miniature train ride is a 2½-mile
journey around the park and through the countryside.

There are also a go-kart track, a railroad-themed miniature golf course, and the Haunted Shack attraction. The
train collection consists of 5 steam engines, 4 diesel locomotives, and 25 cars.

Open daily Memorial Day through Labor Day, noon to 8:00
P.M. Admission is free, with the option to buy individual ride
tickets, or the 5-hour, pay-one-price unlimited pass for
approximately $11, which does not include go-karts or
miniature golf.

Noah's Ark
1410 Wisconsin Dells Parkway/
Highway 12
Wisconsin Dells, WI (608) 254-6351
http://www.wisdells.com/noahs

You should expect a great deal from a facility that claims
to be "America's Largest Waterpark." You won't be disap-
pointed here; the owners have made sure of that.

Located in the popular summer resort area of the Wisconsin Dells, there are 65 acres of water-related activities in the park, including 12 restaurants, 5 gift shops, go-karts, a kiddie roller coaster, bumper boats, miniature golf, and 20 picnic pavilions containing 600 picnic tables. There is also a candy store, where fudge and candy apples are made fresh daily.

Among the 60 different family water attractions are 2 wavepools, 2 lazy rivers, 31 waterslides, and 4 kiddie activity pools. The Black Thunder waterslide, featuring 4 dark, enclosed black slides, is one of the most popular rides in the park.

Open daily, Memorial Day through Labor Day weekend, 9:00 A.M. to 8:00 P.M. A pay-one-price admission, good for all rides, slides, and activities, is available, under $27.

Riverview Park
Highway 12
Wisconsin Dells, WI (608) 254-2608

Keeping busy is no problem in the Wisconsin Dells. There are literally hundreds of attractions, but this park stands out from the rest. It truly has something for everyone and is considered the state's largest "U-Drive 'Em" park.

In all, the park has 11 mechanical rides, 22 water activi-

Noah's Ark Waterpark, Wisconsin

The Amusement Park Guide

ties, and 10 U-Drive 'Ems—all this on 35 acres. And you'll find plenty of shade and benches throughout, as well as a walk-through haunted house.

 Season: May through October.

 Operating hours: 9:00 A.M. to 11:00 P.M. WaterWorld closes at 8:00 P.M.

 Admission policy: Free admission, plus attractions, or a pay-one-price ticket to "slide, ride, and drive" all day is available, under $16. An all-day waterpark ticket available, under $11. Free parking.

 Top rides: A Himalaya ride; a skyride; Grand Prix cars; Ultimate Rush, reverse rush; Wild Island activity pool; Tilt-A-Whirl.

 Roller coaster: The Galaxi (S).

 Plan to stay: 4 hours.

 Best way to avoid crowds: Come early during the week or on weekends in spring and fall.

 Directions: Located near the boat docks on Highway 12, just south of Highway 13. Take Exit 87 (Highway 13) off I–90/94 to Highway 12.

Thumb Fun Park
Highway 42
Fish Creek, WI (414) 868–3418

Nestled in the lovely countryside, this family entertainment center has a variety of rides and slides as well as a magnificent haunted mansion. Among the offerings are 4 kiddie rides (including a carousel); go-karts; bumper boats; kiddie bumper boats; miniature golf; 5 waterslides; and the Polliwog Pond children's play pool.

There's a small general admission charge, and there are several ticket deals from which to choose. The most popular ticket sells for under $16, and includes unlimited use of the slides and your choice of five other attractions.

Slides are open daily from Memorial Day to Labor Day,

238

opening at 10:30 A.M. The other attractions are open daily from Memorial Day to mid-October, opening at 10:00 A.M. The park closes early evening.

TIM'S TRIVIA

Three major amusement parks opened during our nation's 1976 bicentennial: Liberty-land, Memphis, Tennessee; Paramount's Great America, Santa Clara, California; and Six Flags Great America, Gurnee, Illinois.

CANADA

Canada, like the United States, has a varied selection of amusement parks. Some are big corporate parks, others are smaller family operations, but each has its own personality and its own following.

Operation- and attractionwise, Canadian parks don't differ much from U.S. parks. The goal is the same: to create an environment in which kids of all ages can have fun.

Following is a sampling of Canadian parks, by province, that will give you a good idea of what the country has to offer.

ALBERTA

Calaway Park
Trans-Canada Highway at
Springbank Road
Calgary, AB (403) 240–3822

Wide-open, green spaces and a breathtaking view of the Rocky Mountains are what you'll first notice at this 60-acre park, just 6 miles west of the city. In addition to Mother Nature's attractions, you'll also find 23 rides, miniature golf, and a host of games, shows, shops, and other offerings.

Calaway Park—founded in 1982 as western Canada's first major entertainment park—abounds with brightly hued flowers throughout the summer season. Signature attractions here include the Shoot-the-Chute, a flume ride; Ocean Motion, pirate ship; and the Hardly Horribles Haunted House.

 **Roller coasters:** Corkscrew (S); Superjet, kiddie (S).

Musical revues are presented daily, and street entertainment is common and plentiful.

Among the 20 eateries in the park is the Terrace Garden Restaurant, the best bet for a tasty, sit-down meal in a cafe setting.

Guests have a choice of two admission plans: one provides admission and shows, with no rides included; and the other is a pay-one-price arrangement that includes admission, shows, and rides, under $20.

Galaxyland Amusement Park
8770 170th Street
Indoors at West Edmonton Mall
Edmonton, AB (403) 444–5300
http://www.westedmall.com/parks/galaxy.htm

 Advertised as the "Eighth Wonder of the World," the entire $1 billion West Edmonton Mall itself could almost be classified as an amusement park. Nevertheless, inside the mall is Fantasyland—an incredible 9-acre amusement complex that is considered the largest indoor park in North America.

 Included in the park's 23 rides is Mindbender, a 12-story-tall, triple-looping roller coaster. Nearby in the mall are other attractions, such as a full-scale waterpark; a miniature golf course; Deep Sea Adventure, featuring 4 full-size submarines; a regulation-size ice-skating rink; a dolphin show; and an authentic Spanish galleon.

 Other major rides include the Drop of Doom free-fall ride and the Perilous Pendulum Swing Ship.

 Food is available on a limited basis within the park itself, but the 812-store mall offers literally hundreds of eateries. Games, souvenirs, and child-care areas are plentiful.

 Roller coaster: Mindbender, 3-loop (S).

 Admission to the park is free, with rides on a pay-as-you-go basis or a pay-one-price ticket is available, under $32. The hours are basically the same as those in the mall. Free parking.

 # TIM'S TRIVIA

There are more submarines in the "Deep Sea Adventure" attraction at Fantasyland in the West Edmonton Mall (Alberta, Canada) than in the entire Canadian navy.

The Amusement Park Guide

Heritage Park
1900 Heritage Drive SW
Calgary, AB (403) 259-1900

The past unfolds here at Canada's largest historical village. The 66-acre park features more than 150 exhibits, including homes and buildings representing western Canada prior to 1914.

The "antique midway" has 9 classic amusement rides, including a Ferris wheel; Whip; Caterpillar, a swing ride; boat swing; and a circa-1905 carousel. In addition there is a full-size steam train and a sternwheeler boat.

Open daily mid-May through early September, 9:00 A.M. to 5:00 P.M., and on weekends during spring and fall. Admission, including the amusement and historical attractions, is under $17.

World Water Park
8770 170th Street
Indoors at West Edmonton Mall
Edmonton, AB (403) 444-5310
http://www.westedmall.com/parks/wpark.htm

You must see this water wonderland to believe it! Inside this huge shopping mall, you'll find a tropical-themed waterpark with more than 20 different water attractions with something for every member of the family. Spread out over an area equivalent to five professional football fields, the park offers a huge wave pool, a lazy river, hot tubs, and speed, tube, and body slides.

The Little Caribbean area is a children's activity pool area where parents can play along with their kids. There is a kiddie pool, a small water playground with slides and interactive activities. For sun worshipers, the large glass dome over the wave pool allows sunbathing along the beach, without the outdoor heat and humidity.

Park hours range from 10:00 A.M. to noon, and closing is at 7:00 or 8:00 P.M., depending on the day of the week. Admission is under $32 for unlimited use.

BRITISH COLUMBIA

DinoTown
53480 Trans-Canada Highway
Rosedale, BC (604) 794-7410

You'll think you've walked back 2,000 years when you enter the front gates of this wonderful little children's park, just north of Vancouver.

The 11-acre park specializes in "people-powered" rides, including paddleboats, pedal cars, and hand-powered bumper cars. Other features include a children's playground, complete with treehouse; a dinosaur park, where little ones can climb on big statues; miniature golf; a "liquid playground"; and a cartoon train ride around the prehistoric city.

A live music and dance show, featuring Dexter and Dusty Bones, takes place several times each day. And when they aren't performing, the characters roam the park.

There are several walk-up food stands, and management encourages families to bring their own lunches and make a day of it. The park has a number of nice picnic areas where barbecue grills are permitted.

Open from Mother's Day through Labor Day, 10:00 A.M. to 8:00 P.M. Admission is pay-one-price, under $10, and parking is free.

Playland Family Fun Park
East Hastings Street
In Exhibition Park
Vancouver, BC (604) 255-5161

http://www.pne.bc.ca/playland

Nearby mountains provide a picturesque backdrop to this 10-acre, well-kept, traditional park. Located 6 miles from downtown Vancouver, the park becomes the cornerstone for Canada's largest fair, the Pacific National Exhibition, in late August each year.

If you can arrange your trip here to coincide with the fair, do so, for you'll find a truly amazing lineup of rides, shows, and other attractions. Be aware, though, that such timing also means you'll find the park at its busiest and most crowded.

In addition to go-karts, there are 2 miniature golf courses and a good selection of standard park rides, including the

THE AMUSEMENT PARK GUIDE

Wild Wasser log flume, and Space Monster, a dark ride. Games of skill, 7 food outlets, strolling entertainers, and a separate, well-supervised kiddieland round out the attractions.

 Roller coasters: Roller Coaster (S); Corkscrew (S).

The park is open from Easter Sunday through September. Hours vary; call first.

NEW BRUNSWICK

Crystal Palace
499 Paul Street
Dieppe, NB (506) 856–8324

Located just a few blocks from the city limits of Moncton, this free-standing indoor entertainment center is situated in the parking lot of a large regional mall.

The 1.3-acre ride area lies under a high glass dome and includes 8 mechanical rides and a large, ship-themed participatory play area. Among the rides are a carousel, a wave swinger, bumper cars, and a Red Baron. Also here are an SR-2 simulator, a large video-game and games-of-skill arcade, and a miniature golf course with a pirate theme. During summer, 5 additional rides are in operation outside.

 Roller coaster: Bullet, family (S).

Adjacent to the ride area is a food court; McGinnis Landing, a restaurant; an 8-screen movie theater; and a 120-room hotel with fantasy suites.

Open daily, year-round. Admission is free, with rides on a pay-as-you-go basis. Free parking in mall lot; a shuttle bus operates between Crystal Palace and the main entrance of the mall.

NOVA SCOTIA

Upper Clements Amusement Park
Old #1 Highway
Upper Clements, NS (902) 532-7557

The early twentieth century is the theme of this 26-acre park, located between Annapolis and Digby in a heavily wooded, rural area of the province.

Although the park opened only in 1989, it looks like its been here for years. The buildings were either built to resemble early structures or are actual historical buildings that were moved in, such as the rare, round Dutch barn. The crafts village features an assortment of local artisans, including several carousel carvers, who created all the horses on the park's carousel.

And in addition to that carousel are 9 rides, including the Sississiboo Sizzler, a flume ride; antique cars; The Tree Topper, a wooden roller coaster; and a train excursion. There are several kiddie rides as well. The miniature golf course is on a Nova Scotia–shaped island in the park's lake, giving a person a chance to putt around the province! In addition, there are paddle boats, pony rides, and go-karts, all for extra fee.

 Roller coaster: The Tree Topper (W).

The park offers 3 restaurants: Call of the Wild, Jake's Landing, and Kedge Lodge. All are rustic-looking facilities that serve a full menu, from salmon and steak to corn dogs. And the bakery's aroma is enough to stop you in your tracks.

Admission is pay-one-price, under $17, which includes rides and an all-you-can-eat buffet lunch or dinner. Next-day admission is included but does not include food. The park closes at dusk every night during its peak summer period.

ONTARIO

Centreville
Centre Island
Toronto, ONT (416) 203-0405

You'll need to take a ferry to Centre Island, a nicely landscaped and wooded 640-acre city park, to find this neat little park.

The 14-acre amusement park was designed to resemble a turn-of-the-century Ontario village and contains 19 family rides, including antique cars, white swan boats, a flume, and the Haunted Barrel Works. There is also a miniature golf course.

Roller coaster: Toronto Island Monster, family (S).

The 7 food stands in the park serve a variety of foods, from steaks to fried chicken to hot dogs. Make sure, too, to stop by the fabulous O. Bumble ice-cream parlor for a wonderful ice-cream treat.

There are many other activities on the island that you may wish to partake of while visiting. Among them are a swimming pool, bike trails, boating, and fishing.

The entire complex here is low-key and offers a good way to spend a quiet, relaxing afternoon with your family.

Open May through September, 10:30 A.M. to dusk. Rides are pay-as-you-play; a pay-one-price available, under $17. An all-day, unlimited use pass for a family of four, under $50.

Chippewa Park
Highway 61B
Thunder Bay, ONT (807) 622-9777

Overlooking Lake Superior, this 260-acre municipal park has all the fun stuff any municipal park is supposed to have, with a zoo, playing fields, and picnic areas, plus a tidy little amusement area.

There are 8 rides, including a family roller coaster, a circa-1930 carousel with wooden horses, bumper cars, and 4 rides just for the kids.

The park is open year-round, while the amusement area is open daily from late-May through Labor Day. Rides are on a pay-as-you-go basis, with each charging between $1.50 and $2 per ride.

Marineland of Canada
7657 Portage Road
Niagara Falls, ONT (905) 356-8250

Originally a marine park, this facility has added rides over the years, making it a great place to visit.

Along with the killer-whale, dolphin, and sea-lion shows, there are now 10 rides, including 4 for kids. A castlelike structure in the middle of the 300-acre grounds houses a deer-petting park, and a huge, man-made mountain in the back of the amusement park contains the Dragon Mountain, a roller coaster that has one of the most interesting ride entrances in North America, complete with cave.

Roller coaster: Dragon Mountain, looping (S).

Walter Ostanek, Canada's polka king, entertains guests daily during the peak season.

Among the many eateries are the Hungry Lion Restaurant and Beer Garden, featuring a wide assortment of fast-food items, including breakfast, and the Hungry Bear Restaurant and Beer Garden, a full-menu, sit-down establishment. Food may be brought into the park, and there are at least 100 places where a nice, relaxing picnic can be enjoyed.

Pay-one-price admission, under $23, and parking is free. *Note:* The rides and attractions are spread out, with a great deal of space in between, so you should plan to do a lot of walking.

Ontario Place
955 Lakeshore Boulevard West
Toronto, ONT (416) 314-9811

It's hard to believe you're in anything but a city park as you stroll the beautiful 96 acres of this facility. Located along the shores of Lake Ontario, the park is quiet, relaxing, green, and well kept. It's also one of the largest entertainment complexes in the city. There's an IMAX theater here, as well as 2 other, smaller film houses. Live-action shows take place on numerous stages throughout, and street performers are everywhere.

There is an additional charge for most rides and attractions, which include the Wilderness Adventure Ride, a log flume; several water slides and rides; bumper boats; pedal boats; and miniature golf.

During the day, the emphasis is on children and the young family: A Lego Creative Play Center features more than 1 million Lego pieces to play with; a children's village offers a large participatory play area; and a children's theater provides entertainment for the little ones.

At night, the park turns into an adult entertainment center, one with a nightclub atmosphere. The 6 sit-down, table-service restaurant offerings range from fine dining at Atlantis to casual dining at Breakers or Jam'z. In addition there are numerous walk-up eateries and a 6-restaurant food court.

Admission is pay-one-price, under $6, with most rides and attractions costing extra. Free admission daily after 6:00 P.M. Parking fee.

Paramount Canada's Wonderland Splash Works
9580 Jane Street
Maple, ONT (905) 832-7000
http://www.canada.ibm.net:80/wonderland

Bring your walking shoes, and make sure you get a guidebook and map at the front gate, because this is a large park. With 300 beautifully landscaped acres, 50 rides, including 9 roller coasters; and eight areas with elaborate themes, there's enough here to please every member of your family.

Whitewater Bay, the country's largest outdoor wave pool, is the focal point of the park's Splash Works. All water in the 20-acre waterpark is heated, and admission is included in park entrance fees.

This is coaster heaven. There are more roller coasters here—9 in all—than in any other Canadian park, and the stand-up coaster, SkyRider, is the only one of its kind in the country.

One of the first things you'll see as you enter is the spectacular International Fountain, especially dazzling after dark, when the computerized light show begins. Just beyond the fountain is the 150-foot-high Wonder Mountain, a $5 million man-made mountain that contains the Thunder Run coaster. And Kid's Kingdom offers a large lineup of pint-sized rides and activities. The Drop Zone, free fall, themed after the movie of the same name, provides a great, stomach-wrenching ride.

Roller coasters: Roller coasters: Dragon Fyre, corkscrew loop (S); Mighty Canadian Minebuster (W); Wilde Beast (W); Ghoster Coaster, junior (W); SkyRider, stand-up (S); Thunder Run Mine Train (S); The Bat, looping (S); Vortex, suspended (S); Top Gun, inverted (S).

For the kids, Hanna–Barbera Land. And don't miss the excellent lineup of shows, including musical revues, comedy acts, and marine-life presentations.

Plan to spend the entire day if you want to see and do everything. Admission is pay-one-price, under $35. The major season runs from early May through early September.

SportsWorld
100 SportsWorld Drive
Kitchener, ONT (519) 653–4442

They've got all the entertainment bases covered here at SportsWorld. Water activities, sports games, thrill rides, and children's play areas are all on the agenda.

The rides include a Ferris wheel, carousel, Tilt-A-Whirl, train, and numerous kiddie rides. Other activities include a petting zoo, go-karts, batting cages, indoor driving range, miniature golf, and Canada's tallest rock-climbing wall. A video arcade features more than 100 games.

The Jammin' Jungle is an indoor participatory play area for the kids. Built to resemble a huge hunting lodge, Moose Winooski's is a large, sit-down restaurant that offers "a Northern adventure in dining." The 4.5-acre waterpark has a wave pool, 5 slides, a children's play area, and a hot rock spa.

Some of the activities are open year-round, with most of the outdoor action open during the late spring through early fall months. Everything is in operation between Memorial Day and Labor Day. Admission to the facility is free, with everything on a pay-as-you-play basis. There are several ticket options for unlimited-use activities, and a pass that covers unlimited use of virtually everything is available, under $25. Located adjacent to Highway 401, at the Highway 8 exit.

PRINCE EDWARD ISLAND

Rainbow Valley
Route 6
Cavindish, PEI (902) 963-2221

The countryside comes alive here in one of eastern Canada's largest amusement parks. Founded in 1967, the park has a fun combination of traditional rides and water activities.

Among its 12 rides are a motion-based dark ride, a monorail trip around the lake, a kiddie roller coaster, a trail ride, and 6 different types of boat rides. The waterpark side has five different waterslides and an additional flume ride, where you slide down a water chute in a small raft. There are 4 live shows, a petting area and live animal show, games, a maze, and a shooting gallery.

Open daily, June through Labor Day at 9:00 A.M. (11:00 A.M. on Sundays), with closing at various times, depending on the weather and crowds. Pay-one-price admission, under $11.

QUEBEC

La Ronde
Ile Saint-Helene
Montreal, PQ (514) 872-6222

The skyline of this island park is exciting. The towering, dual-track, wooden roller coaster, Le Monstre, and the 150-foot-tall Ferris wheel beckon as the visitor approaches.

The park is located in the center of the St. Lawrence River on St. Helen's Island, the site of the 1967 World's Fair. And it's every bit as immaculate and colorful today as it was then, offering a distinct international flavor and a festive atmosphere.

Roller coasters: Le Monstre, racing (W); La Boomerang (S); Le Dragon, enclosed (S); Le Super Manege, corkscrew (S); Le Petites Montagnes Russes, junior (S); Cobra, stand-up (S).

Make sure you ride the Ferris wheel; it provides a breath-taking view of the surrounding area, including the adjacent 21-slide Aqua Parc and the Montreal Aquarium.

There's some great food here, and you'll find just about anything you might have a craving for, even a Big Mac—a McDonald's franchise is right in the park.

Unlike most parks in North America, this one does not permit guests, once they enter, to leave and reenter. So don't leave anything in the car, expecting to get it later. Instead, use the coin lockers near the front gate, and make sure you bring a sweater or jacket, since the island gets quite chilly after dark, even in midsummer.

Rides and attractions don't open until 11:00 A.M., but they do stay open until midnight during peak season. The major season runs from late May through early September. Admission is pay-one-price, under $25.

AMUSEMENT PARKS BY STATE AND PROVINCE

United States

Alabama
Waterville USA, Gulf
Shores, 2

Alaska
Alaskaland, Fairbanks, 2

Arizona
Castles & Coasters,
Phoenix, 3

Enchanted Island, Phoenix,
3

Old Tucson Studios,
Tucson, 4

Arkansas
Burns Park Funland, North
Little Rock, 5

War Memorial Amusement
Park, Little Rock, 6

California
Adventure City, Stanton, 7

Balboa Fun Zone, Newport
Beach, 7

Belmont Park, San Diego, 8

Castle Amusement Park,
Riverside, 9

Disneyland, Anaheim, 10

Escondido Family Fun
Center, Escondido, 12

Frasier's Frontier, El Cajon,
12

Funderland, Sacramento,
13

Funderwoods, Lodi, 13

Golf N' Stuff, Norwalk, 14

Knott's Berry Farm, Buena
Park, 14

Oasis Water Park, Palm
Springs, 15

Pacific Park, Santa Monica,
16

Paramount's Great
America, Santa Clara,
17

Pharaoh's Lost Kingdom,
Redlands, 18

Pixieland Park, Concord, 19

Raging Waters In Lake
Cunningham Regional
Park, San Jose, 19

Raging Waters, San Dimas,
20

Rotary Kids Country,
Fresno, 20

Santa Cruz Beach
Boardwalk, Santa Cruz,
21

Santa's Village, Skyforest,
22

Parks by State and Province

White Water, Marietta, 60

Idaho

Silverwood Theme Park, Athol, 61

Illinois

Blackberry Historical Farm, Aurora, 62

Kiddieland, Melrose Park, 62

Knight's Action Park, Springfield, 63

Six Flags Great America, Gurnee, 64

Three Worlds of Santa's Village, Dundee, 66

Indiana

Adventureland, North Webster, 67

Bear Creek Farms, Bryant, 68

Columbian Park, Lafayette, 69

Fort Wayne Children's Zoo, Fort Wayne, 69

Fun Spot Amusement Park, Angola, 70

Holiday World, Santa Claus, 71

Indiana Beach, Monticello, 72

Indianapolis Zoo, Indianapolis, 73

River Fair Family Fun Park Indoors at the River Falls Mall, Clarksville, 74

Splashin' Safari, Santa Claus, 71

Iowa

Adventureland, Des Moines, 75

Arnolds Park, Arnolds Park, 76

Kansas

Carousel Park, Overland, 77

Joyland, Wichita, 78

Theel Kiddieland, Leavenworth, 79

Kentucky

Guntown Mountain, Cave City, 79

Hurricane Bay Waterpark, Louisville, 80

Kentucky Kingdom, Louisville, 80

Louisiana

Blue Bayou, Baton Rouge, 82

Carousel Gardens, New Orleans, 82

Fun Fair Park, Baton Rouge, 83

Hamel's Park, Shreveport, 84

PARKS BY STATE AND PROVINCE

The Amusement Park Guide

The Amusement Park Guide

THE AMUSEMENT PARK GUIDE

The Amusement Park Guide

ABOUT THE AUTHOR

As Southeast editor for *Amusement Business Newsweekly*, an international trade publication for the outdoor mass entertainment industry, Tim O'Brien travels the world's highways and byways for a living.

His interest in parks began early, having grown up across from Buckeye Lake Amusement Park, near Columbus, Ohio, and the love affair continued as he grew. For his Master's thesis in film production at Ohio State University, he produced a film documentary on the rides at Sandusky, Ohio's Cedar Point.

He calls his job a "great marriage," as it combines his previous experience as a news reporter and editor with his love of parks. As Tim says, "There's something special in writing about people whose main business is to make people happy."

Tim is also an accomplished photographer and a roller-coaster "freak," having ridden many of the world's greatest coasters.